# PYTHO

## PROGRAMS
### *for*
## ASTRONOMICAL
## SOLUTIONS

*Planetary Positions, Lunar and Solar Eclipses,*
*Pictures, Videos and Maps*

MANOHAR NARAYAN PUROHIT

INDIA • SINGAPORE • MALAYSIA

# Notion Press

No.8, 3rd Cross Street
CIT Colony, Mylapore
Chennai, Tamil Nadu – 600004

First Published by Notion Press 2020
Copyright © Manohar Narayan Purohit 2020
All Rights Reserved.

ISBN 978-1-63633-595-7

# CONTENTS

# PREFACE

Astronomy is one of the oldest sciences and has been pursued, all over the world, by Mathematicians and scientists since time immemorial. In today's modern age the scientists have attained utmost perfection in Astronomical calculations. This has been possible only because of computers and advancement in various fields of science and Technology. Today we are able to calculate the positions of celestial objects and the timings of lunar and solar eclipses with utmost accuracy. The methods to be adopted have been fully explained in detail in the book **'A Guide to Astronomical Calculations with illustrative solved examples'** which has been popular and appreciated worldwide.

However it is felt that only knowing the methods is not sufficient. The calculations are so lengthy and tedious that the manual calculation become impracticable. Hence computer programing becomes necessary.

The advantage of Computer programs is that they can give us not only the mere mathematical solutions within a very short time but also can give us visual results such as pictures, videos, graphs and maps etc., but that is possible only with ingenious computer programs.

Today, computer has become a part of everyone's life and is available in almost every home. Few people know Computer programming. This book is meant for those who are interested in computer programming and in Astronomy. It will be really a fun preparing astronomical projects and get the joy of creation after seeing the wonderful outcomes of the same. One can predict the planetary positions, predict the lunar and solar eclipses, calculate their exact timings and produce visual simulations like pictures, videos and maps of the eclipses. So it will all be a fun along with lots of information and knowledge.

Python is chosen as the programming language as it is found to be most popular and also produces best results. There may be alternative ways to write the programs but method adopted here is one that can be said to be the most suitable for the situations and also easy for learners.

It is presumed that the reader knows something of computer programming and is conversant with one or the other programming language as, nowadays, computer programming is taught to the students at High-School-level itself.

The purpose of this book is not to teach Python programming but to teach how to use python programming for Astronomical solutions. If the reader is a beginner and interested in knowing more about python programming, much information, tutorials and books are freely available in social media like internet and U-Tube etc., starting from '*how to install Python*' to '*advanced python programming*'. However, to start with, some basic information is provided in this book. Also Python's most noteworthy features have been incorporated in the programs given in this book which can give the reader a very good idea of the language's flavor and style.

In this book methods, theory and formulae have not been explained in full detail as the same can be very well traced within the programs. However, if one is interested in understanding the theory and methods in more detail it is advisable to read the book **'A Guide to Astronomical Calculations with illustrative solved examples'.**

If one is more comfortable with programming language other than Python, even then, the logic and algorithms used in this book can be very much helpful in writing these programs in that language.

It is also possible that the reader can download Python package in his computer, open the Python editor and just write down the programs as directed in this book and get the results. At the same time, get the feel of Python programming and the knowledge of Astronomical calculations and enjoy the satisfaction of creation!

Manohar Purohit

# FOREWORD

Interests of astronomy enthusiasts, almost universally, remain limited to star gazing and factual information about astronomical events - like eclipses, their timings and stages, maps of shadow path, etc. Hardly does one wonder about 'how do you know it', or 'can I do it myself and enjoy the thrill of comparing my results with reality'. If tried, it will certainly be a great satisfying pleasure of creativity and achievement.

It's truly heartening to note that not merely arousing such interest and urge amongst the enthusiasts, but to offer a guiding and helping hand is the real prime focus of this book. Prof. Manohar Purohit has taken every care to see that the scare of calculations, complex astronomical calculations in special, of the desiring reader will not prove a barrier in such a pleasure. The author himself has taken all the pains and hard work to put it in Python- a relatively simpler and easy programming language. All that a beginner needs is the availability of a computer, introductory familiarity with programming and downloaded Python-package on your computer. In other words, 'Get set and go' situation!

After his first book - 'A Guide to Astronomical Calculations with illustrative solved examples' - this is a step ahead by the author. Hopefully it will inspire many to make a beginning, and enjoy the pleasure of their creativity and achievements.

Prof. Purohit, a self-made achiever in very diverse arenas like engineering, astronomy, music, Sanskrit, etc., certainly deserves special thanks and appreciation for his desire and urge to motivate and to help readers in expanding the horizon of astronomy enthusiasts. I wish him, and this book, every success.

Prof. V. G. Gambhir
President
*Marathi Vidnyan Parishad*
*(Solapur Vibhag)*

# SUMMARY OF CHAPTERS AND APPENDICES

**Chapter 1**. Introduction to Python Programing language and **how to use this book.**

**Chapter 2.** This chapter defines various functions specifically designed for Astronomical calculations.

**Chapter 3.** In this chapter a program of calculating the planetary positions is given.

**Chapter 4.** This chapter describes a program which generates list and catalogue of lunar eclipses.

**Chapter 5.** In this chapter the program of complete solution to lunar eclipses will be given. This program produces pictures and videos of lunar eclipses.

**Chapter 6.** The program given in this chapter generates a list of solar eclipses during the years chosen by the user.

**Chapter 7.** In this chapter the program of complete solution to solar eclipses is given. This program produces pictures and videos of solar eclipses.

**Chapter 8.** This chapter describes a program which generates a detailed catalogue of solar eclipses.

**Appendix-1** Table of DeltaT    (1600 to 2400)

**Appendix-2** List of Lunar Eclipses (1901 to 2100)

**Appendix-3** List of Solar Eclipses (1901 to 2100)

**Appendix-4** Names of variables and constants with their description

**Appendix-5** List of User-made functions

**Appendix-6** Catalogue of Lunar Eclipses (2001 to 2100)

**Appendix-7** Catalogue of Solar Eclipses (2001 to 2100)

# 1. INTRODUCTION

## 1.1 What is Computer Program?

*Computer program* is a series of statements or commands asking the computer to do the desired operations in a logical sequence. The programs are written in a specific language termed as *programming language*. There are many programming languages and *Python* is one of them.

## 1.2 Python

Python is a general purpose programming language started by Guido van Rossum, which became very popular in short time mainly because of its simplicity and code readability. It enables the programmer to express his ideas in fewer lines of code without reducing any readability.

Python's elegant syntax and dynamic typing, together with its interpreted nature, make it an ideal language for scripting and application development.

The Python interpreter and the extensive standard library are freely available from Python Web site https://www.python.org/, and may be freely distributed. Many third party Python modules and tools are also freely available.

In this book Python 3.7 (64 bit) in windows 10 has been used along with few third party modules like Numpy and OpenCV (cv2). In addition, few self-made modules containing several self-made functions also have been introduced.

### OpenCV

*OpenCV* (Open Source Computer Vision) is a cross-platform library using which we can develop real-time computer vision applications. It mainly focuses on image processing, video capture and analysis including features like face detection and object detection.

### NumPy

**NumPy** is a **Python** package which stands for 'Numerical Python'. It is a library for the Python programming language, adding support for large, multi-dimensional arrays and matrices, along with a large collection of high-level mathematical functions to operate on these arrays.

## 1.3 Basic Requirement

Before starting your programming projects 'Python' should have been installed in your computer along with cv2 and numpy.

After installing the required files it is advisable to create shortcuts to the following applications by bringing their icons to the desktop for operational convenience.

IDLE (Python 3.7
64-bit)

python

Python37 -
Shortcut

## 1.4 IDLE

IDLE is Python's Integrated Development and Learning Environment.

IDLE has two main window types, the **Shell** window and the **Editor** window. These two types of windows can be approached from one to another. It is also possible to have multiple windows simultaneously.

## 1.5 Python Shell

It is an interactive window and the commands written in here are instantly responded to. To start with, please observe the commands and responses in the following figure.

```
Python 3.7.3 Shell                                    —    □    ×
File  Edit  Shell  Debug  Options  Window  Help
Python 3.7.3 (v3.7.3:ef4ec6ed12, Mar 25 2019, 22:22
:05) [MSC v.1916 64 bit (AMD64)] on win32
Type "help", "copyright", "credits" or "license()"
for more information.
>>> Name = "India"
>>> x = 18
>>> y = 4
>>> print("Hello " + Name)
Hello India
>>> x + y
22
>>> x - y
14
>>> x / y
4.5
>>> x // y
4
>>> x % y
2
>>> x**y
104976
>>> print(Name + " is a great Country)
India is a great Country
>>>
```

The first three statements are ***assignment statements***, assigning values to the variables. They also serve the purpose of declaring what type of variables they are. The interpreter recognizes the type of variable from the value assigned to each of them and preserves them in the memory.

Name = "India" indicates that Name is a *string* variable.

x = 18 and y = 4 indicate that x and y are integer variables.

It can be seen that there is not any response to these three statements because the computer is not informed about what to do with these variables.

Next some statements are mathematical expressions. On pressing 'enter-key' the interpreter promptly returns the values of your mathematical expressions. When a print command is entered, it prints what you have asked to print. Note that if these statements were written without the first three you would have got error-messages to all other commands like,

"name 'Name' is not defined", 'name x is not defined' etc.

*Rule: All variables and constants should be defined before they are used in any statement in the program.*

## 1.6 IDLE Editor

A typical IDLE Editor window is shown below.

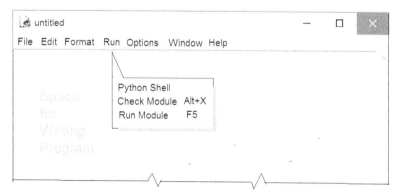

This is where the computer programs are scripted.

Here several commands can be written at a time. Write all the statements in a logical sequence. Save the file by some name with extension '.py'. Then using the Menu 'Run => Run Module=>' run the program. If there are no errors, the results of your program will be seen on a newly appearing Python Shell and may be also in other forms like pictures, videos or output-files. But, if there are any errors, the program fails to execute and the errors are notified on the shell.

One basic difference between the *Shell* and the *Editor* may be noted here. In the python shell if you write just '6+4' and enter => you get the result as 10. In a python program it will be wrong. If you want to print the result, the statement should be 'print (6 + 4)'

## 1.7 Python Console

This is a command prompt window with black background and works similar to IDLE Shell.

```
C:\Users\MR. PUROHIT\Desktop\python.exe                              —    □    ×

Python 3.7.3 (v3.7.3:ef4ec6ed12, Mar 25 2019, 22;22:2019)
[MSC  v.1916 64 bit (AMD64] on win32
Type "help", "copyright", "credits" or "licence" for more information
>>> Name = "India"
>>> x = 18
>>> y = 4
>>> print("Hello " + Name)
Hello India
>>> x + y
22
>>> x - y
14
>>> x / y
4.5
>>> x // y
4
>>> x % y
2
>>> x**y
104976
>>> print(Name + " is a great Country")
India is a great Country
>>>
```

## 1.8 Are You Ready for Programming?

To see if all the requisite *modules* have been installed in your computer to be in readiness for programming, following checks can be applied.

Open the Python shell and write the following commands.

import math =>        (Note that it is not 'Import' but 'import')

import cv2 =>

import numpy =>

If you do not get any error notification you can presume that you are now ready for the python programming for Astronomical Solutions. Because if any of the modules is not properly installed in your computer you get the error message. Generally these modules are placed in a sub-folder of Python folder **Python\Python37\Lib\site-packages.**

## 1.9 Rules of the Language

**Syntax**

**Syntax** refers to the spelling and grammar of a programming language. **Computers** are inflexible machines that understand what you type only if you type it in the exact form that the **computer** expects. The expected form is called the **syntax**.

Every character, brackets, commas, single quote, double quote, colon, slash, back slash, asterisk, hash, has a special meaning and should be used strictly according to the rules of syntax.

**Statement**

Generally one statement should be written in one line.

If required, more than one statement may be written in one line separated by semi-colon (;)

If the statement is too long to be accommodated in a single line, it can be extended to the next line by putting a back-slash. In Python, a **backslash** ( \ ) is a **continuation** character, and if it is placed at the end of a **line**, it is considered that the **line** is continued, ignoring subsequent newlines. Only string literals (string surrounded quotes) are concatenated if they are written consecutively.

### Indent

Indent is the space between the left margin and the start of a line. The default indent is of four spaces. All the statements within a *function* or within a *for* or *while* loops and *if* statements must be indented. If there are indented blocks within an indented block the margin goes on increasing.

Indent is a necessary part of syntax and must be followed carefully.

## 1.10 Functions

A **function** is a set of one or more statements for some specific computation. The idea is to put some commonly or repeatedly required tasks together in a **function**, so that instead of writing the same code again and again in different situations, we can *call* the **function**.

A function may take one or more *arguments* as inputs or may not take any.

A function runs only when it is called. One or more different functions can be called within another function.

A function may *return* some calculated single value or multiple values and it can also be made to produce outputs in the form of pictures, files or videos. Some functions may not return any value but keep the computed values of *global variables* in memory for use elsewhere.

A function is defined using the key word **def** followed by *FunctionName* and ends with a colon (:). As per the rules of syntax the block of statements within a function must be written with *indent*.

There are several inbuilt functions in Python. But some functions are available in different *Modules* which are required to be *imported*. Some new functions specific to the project can be created by the programmer.

If several functions are required to be used in different programs they can be put together in a *module* which can be imported into different programs. However if one or more functions are required to be used in a single program they can be included in the program itself.

## 1.11 Module

Module is a file containing a set of functions. We may also include definitions of variables and constants in the module. Module is a Python file with extension '**.py**'. If we want to use the functions in any module it has to be *imported*. By importing a module we will be able to use the functions contained therein in our program.

There are many Modules included in the Python Library. However some third party modules such as **numpy** and **cv2** are required to be installed additionally.

Some functions specific to Astronomy have been created by the Author and included in this book. A list of these functions is given in Appendix-5.

Module, being a Python file, can be *run* through the IDLE interpreter. As it generally contains only the functions, when it is run, no output is produced on the *Shell*. Because functions do not work unless they are called for. However all the functions in the module are stored in the interpreter's memory so that after running the module we can use the shell to call any function from that module and get the desired outputs. We are going to take advantage of this property of the interpreter to check the correctness and validity of the *functions* in the *Modules* created by us.

## 1.12 Variables and Constants

Variables, constants and functions must always be defined prior to using them in the program. *Names* of variables and constants must start with a letter or the underscore character and cannot start with a number. It can only contain alpha-numeric characters and underscores (A - z, 0 - 9, and _). *Names* are case-sensitive (age, Age and AGE are three different names). They should form a *continuous string.* Spaces are not allowed.

Preferably the *names* should be suggestive of what they are meant for. However, when single letters or very short names are used it becomes difficult for a stranger to understand what they are meant for. Therefore, for the convienience of readers a list of names of variables and constants used in this book, along with their description, is given in Appendix-4.

## 1.13 How to Use This Book

All the programs in this book have been successfully tried. So if you just write down these programs in the python IDLE of your computer *as they are* and run them they should run perfectly, even if you may not know the theory behind all the calculations. If you study the programs carefully you can definitely find out the logic and the formulae used in the calculations, though the theory behind them is not explained in detail in this book. However those who are interested in knowing the theory in detail are requested to read my book **'A Guide to Astronomical Calculations with illustrative solved examples'** published by Notion Press in which everything is explained step by step in detail.

After installing Python and other required supplementary packages as already told, you can start to build the projects. First thing you have to do is start scripting the module named **AstroMODULE.** (Please see Chapter 2).

All the matter to be scripted in the programs (termed as *Source Code*) are printed in **'Consolas'** fonts and *'framed'* so that you can differentiate it with other explanatory matter which is printed in 'Times New Roman' fonts. Therefore you have to script only the program-part which is given in the $\boxed{\text{frames}}$. *Serial numbers of the lines are printed for the convenience of the reader. They are not to be included in your coding.*

**A special feature in this book is that some *additional* functions have also been included which are not necessarily required for the projects as such but are helpful in checking the correctness of our own functions.**

To begin with, open a blank file, script the program AstroMODULE and save it by name 'AstroMODULE.py'. In this file you have to do the scripting of the functions one by one in the same order as given in Chapter 2. The explanation regarding the purpose of each function and the arguments needed are given at the start of the function. How to apply checks, what commands are to be given and what should be the standard output of these commands are given at the end of each function.

After typing the code of each function in a file 'AstroMODULE.py'. Save and run it. If there are no errors python Shell will appear without any remarks. Then you type the suggested commands in the shell as instructed and press the enter-key to get the results. Then compare the output results on the shell with the suggested *standard outputs*. If your outputs tally with the standard outputs, your program is successful and you can proceed to script the next function, and so on. Symbol (=>) is used to suggest *'enter key'*.

If your output do not tally with the standard output you will have to make necessary corrections and repeat the process.

## 1.14 User Inputs

In the programs user inputs are designed to be taken through GUI. Console inputs have been intentionally avoided so that the programs can further be transformed in to ***Stand-alone executable applications***. Some of the *GUI*s may be omitted in the beginning and can be bypassed by directly defining and initializing the required data.

## 1.15 Stand-Alone Applications

After satisfactory completion of the projects, they can be converted into *Stand-alone executable applications* using '**Auto-Py-to Exe**', so that they can be run on any computer without the presence of Python in it. '**Auto-Py-to Exe**' is an amazing application for converting python file into .exe file. It can be installed in your computer using pyintaller.

## 2. ASTRO MODULE

This chapter defines various functions specially designed for Astronomical calculations. All these functions will be included in one module named 'AstroMODULE'. This module will have to be invariably imported into all the programs given in this book.

## 2.1 Initializing Constants

This is not a function but a set of statements assigning values to some constants useful in Astronomy.

```
 |#Constants and importing modules
1|earthrad = 6378.137
2|sunrad = 696000.0
3|moonrad = 1737.1
4|AU = 1.49597870691e8
5|K = 0.27235227 #Moon/Earth ratio
6|R = 109.12278047 #SUN/Earth ratio
7|ff = 0.99664718 #flattening effect
8|ff2 = ff*ff
```

**Ckeck:**

earthrad => 6378.137

sunrad =>   696000.0

moonrad => 1737.1

## 2.2 Trigonometric Functions

Generally trigonometric functions in all the programming languages deal with radians whereas practically we use the angles in degrees. So new trigonometric functions have been introduced which deal with **angles in degrees** directly. Key words 'sn()', 'cs()' and 'tn()' have been used in place of 'sin()', 'cos()' and 'tan()'. 'asn()', 'acs()', 'atn()', 'atn2()' have been used in place of asin(), acos(), atan() and atan2() respectively.

```
1|import math
2|pi = math.pi
```

```
1|def degs(x):
2|    return x*180.0/math.pi
```

```
1|def rads(x):
2|    return x*math.pi/180.0
```

```
1|def rev(x):
2|    return x -(x//360)*360
```

```
1|def sqrt(x):
2|    return(math.sqrt(x))
```

```
1|def sn(x):
2|    return math.sin(math.radians(x))
```

```
1|def cs(x):
2|    return math.cos(math.radians(x))
```

```
1|def tn(x):
2|    return math.tan(math.radians(x))
```

```
1|def asn(x):
2|    return math.degrees(math.asin(x))
```

```
1|def acs(x):
2|    return math.degrees(math.acos(x))
```

```
1|def atn(x):
2|    return math.degrees(math.atan(x))
```

```
1|def atn2(y,x):
2|    return math.degrees(math.atan2(y,x))
```

**Check:**

sn(30) => 0.5,  cs(30) => 0.8660,  tn(30) => 0.5773, sn(0.5) => 30.0,

atn(0.5) => 26.565, atn(1.0) => 45.0,  atn2(1,3) => 18.4349 and so on.

## 2.3  Function for Number of Days from Epoch J2000 (Ndays)

This function calculates the number of terrestrial days elapsed since the Epoch J2000, that is 1st January 2000 12:00 Noon.

This function takes three arguments (date, month, year) and returns number of complete days elapsed since J2000.

```
1|def caldays(d,m,y):
2|    md = [0,0,31,59,90,120,151,\
3|            181,212,243,273,304,334]
4|    leap = 0
5|    if y%4==0 and y%100 != 0:
6|        leap = 1
7|    N = md[m]
8|    if leap == 1 and m <=2:
```

```
 9|          N = N-1
10|      days = y*365 + y//4 - y//100 \
11|              + y//400 + N + d - 730485.5
12|      return days
```

**Check:** caldays(1,1,2025) = 9131.5

## 2.4 Function for Calculating Obliquity, Nutation and GST

This Function takes *numbar of days* as argument and returns

1) obliquity  2) Nutation in longitude  and , 3) Greenwich Sidereal Time (GST), all in degrees.

```
 1|def Obl_Nut_GST(x):
 2|    global Obl,dpsi,GST
 3|    T = x/36525.0
 4|    Om = rev((450160.398036 \
 5|             - 6962890.5431*T \
 6|             +7.4722*T**2  \
 7|             + 0.007702*T**3 \
 8|             - 0.00005939*T**4)/3600)
 9|    D = rev((1072260.703690 \
10|            + 1602961601.2090*T\
11|            - 6.3706* T**2 \
12|            + 0.006593*T**3 \
13|            - 0.00003169*T**4)/3600)
14|    F = rev((335779.526232 \
15|            + 1739527262.8478*T \
16|            - 12.7512*T**2 \
17|            - 0.001037*T**3 \
18|            + 0.00000417*T**4)/3600)
19|    L0 = rev(Om + F)
```

```
20|     Ls = rev(L0 - D)
21|     dpsi = (-17.2*sn(Om) \
22|             - 1.32*sn(2*Ls) \
23|             - 0.23*sn(2*L0) \
24|             + 0.21*sn(2*Om))/3600.0
25|     Obl0 = 23.43927944 - 3.562E-7*x
26|     dObl = (9.20*cs(Om) \
27|             + 0.57*cs(2*Ls) \
28|             + 0.10*cs(2*L0)\
29|             - 0.09*cs(2*Om))/3600.0
30|     Obl = Obl0 + dObl
31|     GMST0 = rev(280.46061837\
32|                 + 360.98564736*x)
33|     dST = dpsi*cs(Obl)
34|     GST = GMST0 + dST
35|     return Obl,dpsi,GST
```

**Ckeck:**

Obl_Nut_GST(8000) => returns a list

(23.437575123939936, -0.004365982540864939, 245.63549260709235)

## 2.5 Function for Calculation of DeltaT

This function takes (date, month, year) as arguments and returns DeltaT in seconds.

```
1|def calDeltaT(date,month,year):
2|    dt = 0.0
3|    DelT = 0.0
4|    md = [0,0,31,59,90,120,151,\
5|          181,212,243,273,304,334]
6|    #y = year + (month + 0.5)/12.0
```

```
 7|     y = year + (md[month] + date)/365.25
 8|     #y = year + 0.5
 9|
10|     if year<=-500:
11|         u = (y-1820)/100
12|         dt = -20 + 32*u*u
13|     elif 500 <= year < 1600:
14|         u = (y-1000)/100
15|         dt = 1574.2 -556.01*u\
16|             + 71.23472*u**2 \
17|             + 0.310781*u**3\
18|             - 0.8503463*u**4 \
19|             - 0.005050998*u**5 \
20|             + 0.0083572073*u**6
21|     elif(1600 <= year <1700):
22|         u = (y-1600)
23|         dt =120 - 0.9808*u\
24|             -0.01532*u**2 \
25|             + u**3/7129
26|     elif 1700 <= year <1800:
27|         t= y-1700
28|         dt= 8.83 +0.1603*t \
29|         -0.0059285*t**2\
30|         + 0.00013336*t**3\
31|         - t**4/1174000
32|     elif 1800 <= year<1860:
33|         t= y-1800
34|         dt = 13.72 -0.332447*t\
35|             + 0.0068612*t*t\
36|             + 0.0041116*t**3\
37|             - 0.00037436*t**4\
38|             + 0.0000121272*t**5 \
39|             - 0.0000001699*t**6 \
```

```
40|                    + 0.000000000875*t**7
41|     elif 1860 <= year <1900:
42|         t= y-1860
43|         dt = 7.62  + 0.5737*t\
44|             - 0.251754*t*t \
45|             + 0.01680668*t**3 \
46|             - 0.0004473624*t**4\
47|             + t**5/233174
48|     elif 1900 <= year < 1920:
49|         t=y-1900
50|         dt = -2.79 + 1.494119*t \
51|             - 0.0598939*t*t\
52|             + 0.0061966*t**3 \
53|             - 0.000197*t**4
54|     elif 1920 <= year<1941:
55|         t = y-1920
56|         dt = 21.20 + 0.84493*t \
57|             - 0.076100*t*t \
58|             + 0.0020936*t*t*t
59|     elif 1941 <= year<1961:
60|         t = y - 1950
61|         dt = 29.07 + 0.407*t \
62|             - t*t/233 \
63|             + t*t*t/2547
64|     elif 1961 <= year< 1986:
65|         t = y - 1975
66|         dt = 45.45 + 1.067*- t*t/260 \
67|                - t*t*t/718
68|     elif 1986 <= year < 2005:
69|         t=y-2000
70|         dt = 63.86 + 0.3345*t\
71|                - 0.060374*t*t \
72|                + 0.0017275*t**3 \
```

```
73|                    + 0.000651814*t**4 \
74|                    + 0.00002373599*t**5
75|    elif 2005 <= year < 2050:
76|        t = y - 2000
77|        dt = 62.92 + 0.32217*t\
78|                 + 0.005589 *t*t
79|    elif 2050 <= year < 2150:
80|        t = (y-1820)/100
81|        dt = -20 +32*t*t \
82|             - 0.5628*(2150 - y)
83|    elif year>=2150:
84|        t = (y - 1820)/100
85|        dt = -20 +32*t*t
86|    #correction for luner acceleration
87|    if year<1955 or year>2005:
88|        c = -0.000012932*(y-1955)**2
89|        DelT = dt + c
90|    return DelT
```

**Check:**

calDeltaT(1,1,2025) => 74.40565043076367 seconds

calDeltaT(1,1,2400) => 1053.9292721147722 seconds

To check the correctness of this function for the complete range from year 1600 to 2400, the following function is used.

## 2.6 Function for Tabulating DelataT Values

This function does not take any argument and generates a table of DeltaT for the years 1600 to 2400. The tables are printed to the output shell as well to a file named 'DeltaT.txt'.

```
 1|def TableDeltaT():
 2|    y1,y2 = 1600,2401
 3|    sp = "          "
 4|    table = "Year"+sp[:4]+"1"+sp+"2"\
 5|            +sp+"3"+sp+"4"+sp+"5" \
 6|            +sp+"6"+sp+"7"+sp+"8"+sp+"9"
 7|    print("Values of DeltaT for the year\
 8|          {:d} to {:d}".format(y1,y2-1))
 9|    print('-'*76)
10|    print(table)
11|    print('-'*76)
12|    for year in range(y1,y2):
13|        deltat = calDeltaT(1,1,year)
14|        if year%10==0:
15|            print("\n{:5d}"\
16|                  .format(year),end="   ")
17|        print("{:6.1f}".\
18|              format(deltat),end="   ")
19|    print("\n"+'-'*76)
20|    #FILE WRITING
21|    y1,y2 = 1600,2401
22|    f = open("DeltaT.txt","w")
23|    f.write("\nValues of DeltaT for years\
24|          {:d} to {:d}".format(y1,y2))
25|    f.write("\n"+'-'*76)
26|    f.write("\n"+table)
27|    f.write("\n"+'-'*76)
28|    for year in range(y1,y2):
29|        deltat = calDeltaT(1,1,year)
30|        if year%10==0:
31|            f.write("\n{:5d}".format(year))
```

```
32|            f.write("{:6.1f}".format(deltat))
33|      f.write("\n"+"-"*76)
34|      f.close()
```

**How to check the correctness of function 'calDeltaT(Ndays)' ?**

Call this function. **TableDeltaT()** => . It will generate a table on the IDLE. It also generates a text file 'DelataT.txt' containing the same table. Compare the table so generated with the Standard Table given in Appendix-1. If your table differs from the Standard table make necessary corrections in the function calDeltaT(date,month,year).

## 2.7 Function for Calculating Ndays

*Ndays* is the number of days elapsed since J2000 including deltaT.

**Ndays** generally forms the basis of all astronomical calculations.

This function takes (date, month, year) as arguments and returns Ndays and *delatad* (deltaT in terms of days)

```
1|def cal_d(date,month,year):
2|    du0 = caldays(date,month,year)
3|    deltaT = calDeltaT(date,month,year)
4|    deltad = deltaT/86400.0
5|    d = du0 + deltad
6|    return d,deltad
```

## 2.8 Function for Calculating Ecliptic Longitude of Sun

This function takes Ndays as argument and returns the celestial longitude of Sun in degrees.

```
1|def LonSun(d):
2|    Obl,dpsi,GST = Obl_Nut_GST(d)
3|    l = rev(280.461 + 0.9856474*d)
4|    m = rev(357.528 + 0.9856003*d)
5|    dl =  rev(1.915*sn(m)\
6|              + 0.020*sn(2*m))
7|    lon0 = rev(l + dl)
8|    lon = lon0 + dpsi
9|    return lon
```

**Check:**

LonSun(8000) => 244.4462150087858

## 2.9 Function for Calculating Geocentric Distance and Parallax of Sun

This function takes Ndays as argument and returns Two values, geocentric distance and in km and Parallax of Sun.

```
 1|def rpSun(x):
 2|    Obl,dpsi,GST = Obl_Nut_GST(x)
 3|    l = rev(280.461 + 0.9856474*x)
 4|    m = rev(357.528 + 0.9856003*x)
 5|    dl =  rev(1.915*sn(m)\
 6|              + 0.020*sn(2*m))
 7|    lon0 = rev(l + dl)
 8|    lon = lon0 + dpsi
 9|    lat = 0.0
10|    r = 1.00014 - 0.01671*cs(m)\
11|              - 0.00014*cs(2*m)
12|    r = r*149597870.691
13|    ps = asn(6378.14/r)
14|    return r,ps
```

**Check:**

rpSun(8000) => (147634817.717949, 0.0024753002638944538)

That is, Distance of Sun = 147634817.71794 km

And Parallax of Sun = , 0.0024753002638944538

## 2.10 Function for Calculating Coordinates of Sun

This function takes Ndays as argument and returns geocentric coordinates xsun, ysun, zsun of Sun and the distance of Sun respectively in the form of a *List*. All the values returned will be in Astronomical Units. These are used in calculating the coordinates of all other planets.

```
 1|def Sunxyzr(d):
 2|    global xsun,ysun,zsun,res
 3|    l = rev(280.461 + 0.9856474*d)
 4|    m = rev(357.528 + 0.9856003*d)
 5|    dl =  rev(1.915*sn(m) + 0.020*sn(2*m))
 6|    lon0 = rev(l + dl)
 7|    pLong[0] = lon0 + dpsi
 8|    pLat[0] = 0.0
 9|    r = 1.00014 - 0.01671*cs(m)\
10|             - 0.00014*cs(2*m)
11|    xsun = r*cs(lon0)
12|    ysun = r*sn(lon0)
13|    zsun = 0.0
14|    res = r
15|    return xsun,ysun,zsun,res
```

Example: Sunxyzr(8000) =>

(-0.42562997274094244, -0.8903745959716834, 0.0, 0.986877801375223)

That means

Xsun = -0.42562997274094244 AU

Ysun = -0.8903745959716834 AU

Zsun =  0.0 AU

Distance = 0.986877801375223 AU

## 2.11 Function for Calculating Lunisolar Arguments

LuniSolar Arguments are the important parameters required for calculating the positional coordinates of Moon.

This function takes Ndays as argument and returns twelve items viz., Om, Ms, Mm, D, F, L0, Ls, E, E2, A1, A2, A3 all in degrees, respectively in the form of an array.

```
 1|def LuniSolar(x):
 2|    global Om,Ms,Mm,D,F,L0,Ls
 3|    global E,E2,A1,A2,A3
 4|
 5|    T = x/36525.0
 6|    Om = rev((450160.398036 \
 7|            - 6962890.5431*T\
 8|            +7.4722*T**2 \
 9|            + 0.007702*T**3\
10|            - 0.00005939*T**4)/3600)
11|    Ms = rev((1287104.79305 \
12|            +129596581.0481*T\
13|            -0.5532*T**2 \
14|            + 0.000136*T**3 \
15|            - 0.00001149*T**4)/3600)
16|    Mm = rev((485868.249036 \
17|            +1717915923.2178*T\
```

```
18|                    + 31.8792 *T**2 \
19|                    + 0.051635*T**3 \
20|                    - 0.00024470*T**4)/3600)
21|    D = rev((1072260.70369 \
22|                 + 1602961601.2090*T \
23|                 - 6.3706* T**2 \
24|                 + 0.006593*T**3 \
25|                 - 0.00003169*T**4)/3600)
26|    F = rev((335779.526232 \
27|                 + 1739527262.8478*T\
28|                 - 12.7512*T**2 \
29|                 - 0.001037*T**3 \
30|                 + 0.00000417*T**4)/3600)
31|    L0 = rev(Om + F)
32|    Ls = rev(L0 - D)
33|    E = 1 - 0.002516*T - 0.0000074*T**2
34|    E2 = E*E
35|    A1 = rev(119.75 + 131.849*T)
36|    A2 = rev(53.09  + 479264.29*T)
37|    A3 = rev(313.45 + 481266.484*T)
38|    return Om,Ms,Mm,D,F,L0,Ls,E,E2,A1,A2,A3
```

**Check:**

LuniSolar(8000) => should return

(61.414535625429835, 322.3313558572645, 254.90744100502343, 263.8430353189178, 88.07382793110446, 149.4883635565343, 245.64532823761647, 0.9994485703912025, 0.9988974448570185, 148.62863107460643, 265.41908966460323, 244.31576317589497)

## 2.12 Function for Calculating Ecliptic Longitude of Moon

This function takes Ndays as argument and returns the celestial longitude of Moon in in degrees (0 to 360).

```
 1|def LonMoon(x):
 2|    global dl_array
 3|    global Om,Ms,Mm,D,F,L0,Ls
 4|    global E,E2,A1,A2,A3
 5|    global Lm,dl,dl1,dphi,dl_array
 6|    Om,Ms,Mm,D,F,L0,Ls, \
 7|        E,E2,A1,A2,A3 = LuniSolar(x)
 8|    dl00 = 0.0
 9|    dl01 =   6.288774*sn(Mm)
10|    dl02 = + 1.274027*sn(2*D - Mm)
11|    dl03 = + 0.658314*sn(2*D)
12|    dl04 = + 0.213618*sn(2*Mm)
13|    dl05 = - E*0.185116*sn(Ms)
14|    dl06 = - 0.114332*sn(2*F)
15|    dl07 = + 0.058793*sn(2*D - 2*Mm)
16|    dl08 = + E*0.057066*sn(2*D - Ms - Mm)
17|    dl09 = + 0.053322*sn(2*D + Mm)
18|    dl10 = + E*0.045758*sn(2*D - Ms)
19|    dl11 = + E*0.040923*sn(Mm - Ms)
20|    dl12 = - 0.034720*sn(D)
21|    dl13 = - E*0.030383*sn(Ms + Mm)
22|    dl14 = + 0.015327*sn(2*D - 2*F)
23|    dl15 = - 0.012528*sn(2*F + Mm)
24|    dl16 = - 0.010980*sn(2*F - Mm)
25|    dl17 = + 0.010675*sn(4*D - Mm)
26|    dl18 = + 0.010034*sn(3*Mm)
27|    dl19 = + 0.008548*sn(4*D - 2*Mm)
28|    dl20 = - E*0.007888*sn(Ms - Mm + 2*D)
```

```
29|      d121 = - E*0.006766*sn(2*D + Ms)
30|      d122 = + 0.005163*sn(Mm - D)
31|      d123 = + E*0.004987*sn(Ms + D)
32|      d124 = + E*0.004036*sn(Mm - Ms + 2*D)
33|      d125 = + 0.003994*sn(2*Mm + 2*D)
34|      d126 = + 0.003861*sn(4*D)
35|      d127 = + 0.003665*sn(2*D - 3*Mm)
36|      d128 = + E*0.002689*sn(2*Mm - Ms)
37|      d129 = + 0.002602*sn(Mm - 2*F - 2*D)
38|      d130 = + E*0.002390*sn(2*D - Ms - 2*Mm)
39|      d131 = - 0.002348*sn(Mm + D)
40|      d132 = + E2*0.002236*sn(2*D - 2*Ms)
41|      d133 = - E *0.002120*sn(2*Mm + Ms)
42|      d134 = - E2*0.002069*sn(2*Ms)
43|      d135 = + E2*0.002048*sn(2*D - Mm - 2*Ms)
44|      d136 = - 0.001773*sn(Mm + 2*D - 2*F)
45|      d137 = - 0.001595*sn(2*F + 2*D)
46|      d138 = + E*0.001215*sn(4*D - Ms - Mm)
47|      d139 = - 0.001110*sn(2*Mm + 2*F)
48|      d140 = + 0.000892*sn(Mm - 3*D)
49|      d141 = - E*0.000810*sn(Ms + Mm + 2*D)
50|      d142 = + E*0.000759*sn(4*D - Ms - 2*Mm)
51|      d143 = + E2*0.000713*sn(Mm - 2*Ms)
52|      d144 = + E2*0.000700*sn(Mm - 2*Ms - 2*D)
53|      d145 = + E*0.000691*sn(Ms - 2*Mm + 2*D)
54|      d146 = + E*0.000596*sn(2*D - Ms - 2*F)
55|      d147 = + 0.000549*sn(Mm + 4*D)
56|      d148 = + 0.000537*sn(4*Mm)
57|      d149 = + E*0.000520*sn(4*D - Ms)
58|      d150 = + 0.000487*sn(2*Mm - D)
59|      d151 = - E*0.000399*sn(2*D + Ms - 2*F)
60|      d152 = - 0.000381*sn(2*Mm - 2*F)
61|      d153 = + E*0.000351*sn(D + Ms + Mm)
```

```
62|     dl54 = - 0.000340*sn(3*D - 2*Mm)
63|     dl55 = + 0.000330*sn(4*D - 3*Mm)
64|     dl56 = + E*0.000327*sn(2*D - Ms + 2*Mm)
65|     dl57 = - E2* 0.000323*sn(2*Ms + Mm)
66|     dl58 = + E*0.000299*sn(D + Ms - Mm)
67|     dl59 = + 0.000294*sn(2*D + 3*Mm)
68|     dl_array = [dl00,dl01,dl02,dl03,dl04,\
69|                 dl05,dl06,dl07,dl08,dl09,\
70|                 dl10,dl11,dl12,dl13,dl14,\
71|                 dl15,dl16,dl17,dl18,dl19,\
72|                 dl20,dl21,dl22,dl23,dl24,\
73|                 dl25,dl26,dl27,dl28,dl29,\
74|                 dl30,dl31,dl32,dl33,dl34,\
75|                 dl35,dl36,dl37,dl38,dl39,\
76|                 dl40,dl41,dl42,dl43,dl44,\
77|                 dl45,dl46,dl47,dl48,dl49,\
78|                 dl50,dl51,dl52,dl53,dl54,\
79|                 dl55,dl56,dl57,dl58,dl59]
80|     dphi = (-17.2*sn(Om) \
81|             - 1.32*sn(2*Ls))/ 3600.0
82|     dphi = dphi + (-0.23*sn(2*L0)\
83|             + 0.21*sn(2*Om))/3600.0
84|     dl1 = 0.003958* sn(A1) \
85|            + 0.001962*sn(Om)\
86|              + 0.000318*sn(A2)
87|     dl = 0.0
88|     for i in range(60):
89|         dl = dl + dl_array[i]
90|     Lm = L0 + dl + dl1 + dphi
91|     return Lm
```

**Check:**

LonMoon(8000) = > 142.52462584144263 degrees

## 2.13 Function for Listing the dl_array

This also takes Ndays as argument and prints out list of dl_array. If the LonMoon(Ndays) fails to return the correct answer, this function can be used to check where the coding has gone wrong.

```
 1|def pr_dl_array(x):
 2|    print("Check LonMoon Calculations")
 3|    print("List of dl_array on d =",x)
 4|
 5|    Lm = LonMoon(x)
 6|    dl = 0
 7|    for i in range(60):
 8|        print("{:3d} {:13.8f}"\
 9|              .format(i+1,dl_array[i]))
10|        dl = dl + dl_array[i]
11|    Lm = L0 + dl + dl1 + dphi
12|    print("L0    =",L0)
13|    print("dl    =",dl)
14|    print("dl1   =",dl1)
15|    print("dphi  =",dphi)
16|    print("          -------------")
17|    print("Lm    =",Lm)
```

To check the dl_array for Ndays = 8000...

Call the function **pr_dl_array(8000)=>** and to get the following listing.

Check LonMoon Calculations
List of dl_array for Ndays = 8000
1   0.00000000
2  -6.07185189
3  -1.27252911
4   0.14039725
5   0.10740616

| | |
|----|--------------|
| 6 | 0.11306089 |
| 7 | -0.00768145 |
| 8 | 0.01804228 |
| 9 | -0.04340347 |
| 10 | 0.04733731 |
| 11 | -0.01958373 |
| 12 | -0.03776626 |
| 13 | 0.03451973 |
| 14 | 0.01837578 |
| 15 | -0.00225531 |
| 16 | -0.01184937 |
| 17 | 0.01076939 |
| 18 | 0.01052751 |
| 19 | 0.00706064 |
| 20 | -0.00082779 |
| 21 | 0.00646658 |
| 22 | -0.00517888 |
| 23 | -0.00080194 |
| 24 | -0.00359589 |
| 25 | 0.00396925 |
| 26 | -0.00269826 |
| 27 | -0.00160897 |
| 28 | 0.00307499 |
| 29 | -0.00035003 |
| 30 | -0.00260154 |
| 31 | 0.00196952 |
| 32 | -0.00085099 |
| 33 | -0.00199051 |
| 34 | -0.00196251 |
| 35 | 0.00199941 |
| 36 | -0.00042128 |
| 37 | 0.00162528 |
| 38 | 0.00044409 |

```
39   0.00107086
40   0.00062131
41  -0.00005256
42  -0.00034117
43  -0.00051953
44  -0.00035347
45   0.00020958
46  -0.00023391
47   0.00029067
48  -0.00042228
49  -0.00046678
50   0.00011727
51  -0.00044480
52   0.00028749
53   0.00016901
54   0.00030044
55   0.00033292
56  -0.00030880
57  -0.00002752
58  -0.00000242
59  -0.00014366
60  -0.00015757
L0   = 149.4883635565343
dl   = -6.962838056878421
dl1  = 0.0034663243275921897
dphi = -0.004365982540864939
Lm   = 142.52462584144263
```

## 2.14 Function for Calculating Ecliptic Latitude of Moon

This function takes Ndays as argument and returns the celestial latitude of Moon in in degrees (-90 to +90).

```
 1|def LatMoon(x):
 2|    global Om,Ms,Mm,D,F,L0,Ls
 3|    global E,E2,A1,A2,A3
 4|    global b,db,b_array
 5|    Om,Ms,Mm,D,F,L0,Ls,\
 6|           E,E2,A1,A2,A3 = LuniSolar(x)
 7|    b01 = + 5.128122*sn(F)
 8|    b02 = + 0.280602*sn(Mm + F)
 9|    b03 = + 0.277693*sn(Mm - F)
10|    b04 = + 0.173237*sn(2*D - F)
11|    b05 = + 0.055413*sn(2*D + F - Mm)
12|    b06 = + 0.046271*sn(2*D - F - Mm)
13|    b07 = + 0.032573*sn(2*D + F)
14|    b08 = + 0.017198*sn(2*Mm + F)
15|    b09 = + 0.009266*sn(2*D + Mm - F)
16|    b10 = + 0.008822*sn(2*Mm - F)
17|    b11 = + E*0.008216*sn(2*D - Ms - F)
18|    b12 = + 0.004324*sn(2*D - F - 2*Mm)
19|    b13 = + 0.004200*sn(2*D + F + Mm)
20|    b14 = + E*0.003359*sn(F - Ms - 2*D)
21|    b15 = + E*0.002463*sn(2*D + F - Ms - Mm)
22|    b16 = + E*0.002211*sn(2*D + F - Ms)
23|    b17 = + E*0.002065*sn(2*D - F - Ms - Mm)
24|    b18 = + E*0.001870*sn(F - Ms + Mm)
25|    b19 = + 0.001828*sn(4*D - F - Mm)
26|    b20 = - E*0.001794*sn(F + Ms)
27|    b21 = - 0.001749*sn(3*F)
28|    b22 = + E*0.001565*sn(Mm - Ms - F)
29|    b23 = - 0.001491*sn(F + D)
30|    b24 = - E*0.001475*sn(F + Ms + Mm)
31|    b25 = + E*0.001410*sn(F - Ms - Mm)
32|    b26 = + E*0.001344*sn(F - Ms)
33|    b27 = + 0.001335*sn(F - D)
```

```
34|      b28 = + 0.001107*sn(F + 3*Mm)
35|      b29 = + 0.001021*sn(4*D - F)
36|      b30 = + 0.000833*sn(F + 4*D - Mm)
37|      b31 = + 0.000777*sn(Mm  - 3*F)
38|      b32 = + 0.000671*sn(F + 4*D - 2*Mm)
39|      b33 = + 0.000607*sn(2*D - 3*F)
40|      b34 = + 0.000596*sn(2*D + 2*Mm - F)
41|      b35 = + E*0.000491*sn(2*D + Mm - Ms -F)
42|      b36 = + 0.000451*sn(2*Mm - F - 2*D)
43|      b37 = + 0.000439*sn(3*Mm - F)
44|      b38 = + 0.000422*sn(F + 2*D + 2*Mm)
45|      b39 = + 0.000421*sn(2*D - F - 3*Mm)
46|      b40 = - E*0.000366*sn(Ms + F + 2*D - Mm)
47|      b41 = - E*0.000351*sn(Ms + F + 2*D)
48|      b42 = + 0.000331*sn(F + 4*D)
49|      b43 = + E*0.000315*sn(2*D + F - Ms + Mm)
50|      b44 = + E2*0.000302*sn(2*D - 2*Ms - F)
51|      b45 = - 0.000283*sn(Mm + 3*F)
52|      b46 = - E*0.000229*sn(2*D+Ms+Mm-F)
53|      b47 = + E*0.000223*sn(D+Ms-F)
54|      b48 = + E*0.000223*sn(D+Ms+F)
55|      b49 = - E*0.000220*sn(Ms-2*Mm-F)
56|      b50 = - E*0.000220*sn(2*D+Ms-Mm-F)
57|      b51 = - 0.000185*sn(D+Mm -F)
58|      b52 = + E*0.000181*sn(2*D-Ms-2*Mm-F)
59|      b53 = - E*0.000177*sn(Ms+2*Mm+F)
60|      b54 = + 0.000176*sn(4*D-2*Mm-F)
61|      b55 = + E*0.000166*sn(4*D-Ms-Mm-F)
62|      b56 = - 0.000164*sn(D+Mm-F)
63|      b57 = + 0.000132*sn(4*D +Mm-F)
64|      b58 = - 0.000119*sn(D-Mm-F)
65|      b59 = + E*0.000115*sn(4*D-Ms-F)
66|      b60 = + E2*0.000107*sn(2*D-2*Ms+F)
```

```
67|
68|    b_array = [b01,b02,b03,b04,b05,b06,b07,\
69|               b08,b09,b10,b11,b12,b13,b14,\
70|               b15,b16,b17,b18,b19,b20,b21,\
71|               b22,b23,b24,b25,b26,b27,b28,\
72|               b29,b30,b31,b32,b33,b34,b35,\
73|               b36,b37,b38,b39,b40,b41,b42,\
74|               b43,b44,b45,b46,b47,b48,b49,\
75|               b50,b51,b52,b53,b54,b55,b56,\
76|               b57,b58,b59,b60]
77|    db = -0.002235*sn(L0) \
78|        + 0.000382*sn(A3)\
79|          + 0.000175*sn(A1-F)\
80|            + 0.000175*sn(A1+F)\
81|              + 0.000127*sn(L0-Mm)\
82|                - 0.000115*sn(L0+Mm)
83|    b = 0.0
84|    for i in range(60):
85|        b = b + b_array[i]
86|    Bm = b + db
87|    return Bm
```

**Check:**

LatMoon(8000) => 5.230932685205794

## 2.15 Function for Listing the b_array.

This also takes Ndays as argument and prints out list of b_array. If the LatMoon(Ndays) fails to return the correct answer, this function can be used to check where the coding has gone wrong.

```
 1|def pr_b_array(x):
 2|    print("Check LatMoon Calculations")
 3|    print("List of b_array on d =",x)
 4|    Lm = LatMoon(x)
 5|    b = 0
 6|    for i in range(60):
 7|        print("{:3d} {:13.8f}"\
 8|              .format(i+1,b_array[i]))
 9|        b = b + b_array[i]
10|    Bm = b + db
11|    print("Sum b  =",b)
12|    print("db     =",db)
13|    print("Bm     =",Bm)
```

To check the b_array for Ndays = 8000.

Operate the function **pr_b_array(8000)=>** and you will get the following listing.

```
Check LatMoon Calculations
List of b_array on d = 8000
 1   5.12522444
 2  -0.08212781
 3   0.06325282
 4   0.17039765
 5   0.00082441
 6  -0.00379524
 7  -0.03157214
 8  -0.01456700
 9  -0.00398624
10   0.00777057
11   0.00729811
12  -0.00406844
13   0.00205749
```

| | |
|---|---|
| 14 | -0.00224391 |
| 15 | 0.00153312 |
| 16 | -0.00202760 |
| 17 | -0.00139096 |
| 18 | 0.00065910 |
| 19 | -0.00024205 |
| 20 | -0.00138164 |
| 21 | 0.00174011 |
| 22 | -0.00064869 |
| 23 | 0.00020965 |
| 24 | 0.00120295 |
| 25 | -0.00109261 |
| 26 | 0.00109026 |
| 27 | -0.00009849 |
| 28 | 0.00081229 |
| 29 | -0.00094190 |
| 30 | 0.00016552 |
| 31 | -0.00012575 |
| 32 | -0.00066965 |
| 33 | -0.00060306 |
| 34 | -0.00045271 |
| 35 | 0.00010361 |
| 36 | -0.00043365 |
| 37 | -0.00030136 |
| 38 | 0.00030138 |
| 39 | 0.00024081 |
| 40 | 0.00021920 |
| 41 | 0.00021642 |
| 42 | 0.00029608 |
| 43 | -0.00004564 |
| 44 | 0.00012773 |
| 45 | -0.00010082 |
| 46 | 0.00020420 |

| | |
|---|---|
| 47 | 0.00014884 |
| 48 | -0.00015965 |
| 49 | -0.00021885 |
| 50 | -0.00011964 |
| 51 | -0.00017458 |
| 52 | -0.00009729 |
| 53 | 0.00006114 |
| 54 | 0.00017450 |
| 55 | 0.00008310 |
| 56 | -0.00015476 |
| 57 | 0.00008089 |
| 58 | 0.00011687 |
| 59 | -0.00011104 |
| 60 | -0.00005166 |

```
Sum b = 5.232608441472344
db    = -0.0016757562665500548
Bm    = 5.230932685205794
```

Every term in the array can be tallied and corrections can be made in the function accordingly.

## 2.16 Function for Geocentric Distance of Moon

This function takes Ndays as argument and returns the geocentric distance of Moon in km.

```
1|def DistMoon(x):
2|    global Om,Ms,Mm,D,F,L0,Ls
3|    global E,E2,A1,A2,A3
4|    global rm,r0,dr,dr_array
5|    Om,Ms,Mm,D,F,L0,Ls,\
6|        E,E2,A1,A2,A3 = LuniSolar(x)
7|    r0 = 385000.56
8|    dr01 = - 20905.355*cs(Mm)
```

```
 9|     dr02 = - 3699.111*cs(2*D - Mm)
10|     dr03 = - 2955.968*cs(2*D)
11|     dr04 = -  569.925*cs(2*Mm)
12|     dr05 = + E*48.888*cs(Ms)
13|     dr06 = - 3.149*cs(2*F)
14|     dr07 = + 246.158*cs(2*D - 2*Mm)
15|     dr08 = - E*152.138*cs(2*D - Ms - Mm)
16|     dr09 = - 170.733*cs(2*D + Mm)
17|     dr10 = - E*204.586*cs(2*D - Ms)
18|     dr11 = - E*129.620*cs(Ms - Mm)
19|     dr12 = + 108.743*cs(D)
20|     dr13 = + E*104.755*cs(Ms + Mm)
21|     dr14 = + 10.321*cs(2*D - 2*F)
22|     dr15 = 0
23|     dr16 = + 79.661*cs(Mm - 2*F)
24|     dr17 = - 34.782*cs(4*D -Mm)
25|     dr18 = - 23.210*cs(3*Mm)
26|     dr19 = - 21.636*cs(4*D - 2*Mm)
27|     dr20 = + E*24.208*cs(Ms - Mm + 2*D)
28|     dr21 = + E*30.824*cs(2*D + Ms)
29|     dr22 = - 8.379*cs(D - Mm)
30|     dr23 = - E*16.675*cs(Ms + D)
31|     dr24 = - E*12.831*cs(Mm - Ms + 2*D)
32|     dr25 = - 10.445*cs(2*Mm + 2*D)
33|     dr26 = - 11.650*cs(4*D)
34|     dr27 = + 14.403*cs(2*D - 3*Mm)
35|     dr28 = - E*7.003*cs(Ms - 2*Mm)
36|     dr29 = 0
37|     dr30 = + E*10.056*cs(2*D - Ms - 2*Mm)
38|     dr31 = + 6.322*cs(Mm + D)
39|     dr32 = - E2*9.884*cs(2*D - 2*Ms)
40|     dr33 = + E*5.751*cs(2*Mm + Ms)
```

```
41|     dr34 = 0
42|     dr35 = - E2*4.950*cs(2*D - Mm - 2*Ms)
43|     dr36 = + 4.130*cs(Mm + 2*D - 2*F)
44|     dr37 = 0
45|     dr38 = - E*3.958*cs(4*D - Ms - Mm)
46|     dr39 = 0
47|     dr40 = + 3.258*cs(3*D - Mm)
48|     dr41 = + E*2.616*cs(Ms + Mm + 2*D)
49|     dr42 = - E*1.897*cs(4*D - Ms - 2*Mm)
50|     dr43 = - E2*2.117*cs(2*Ms - Mm)
51|     dr44 = + E2*2.354*cs(2*D + 2*Ms - Mm)
52|     dr45 = 0
53|     dr46 = 0
54|     dr47 = - 1.423*cs(Mm + 4*D)
55|     dr48 = - 1.117*cs(4*Mm)
56|     dr49 = - E*1.571*cs(4*D - Ms)
57|     dr50 = - 1.739*cs(D - 2*Mm)
58|     dr51 = 0
59|     dr52 = - 4.421*cs(2*Mm - 2*F)
60|     dr53 = 0
61|     dr54 = 0
62|     dr55 = 0
63|     dr56 = 0
64|     dr57 = + E2* 1.165*cs(2*Ms + Mm)
65|     dr58 = 0
66|     dr59 = 0
67|     dr60 = + 8.752*cs(2*D - Mm - 2*F)
68|     dr_array = [dr01,dr02,dr03,dr04,dr05,\
69|                 dr06,dr07,dr08,dr09,dr10,\
70|                 dr11,dr12,dr13,dr14,dr15,\
71|                 dr16,dr17,dr18,dr19,dr20,\
72|                 dr21,dr22,dr23,dr24,dr25,\
73|                 dr26,dr27,dr28,dr29,dr30,\
```

```
74|                            dr31,dr32,dr33,dr34,dr35,\
75|                         dr36,dr37,dr38,dr39,dr40,\
76|                         dr41,dr42,dr43,dr44,dr45,\
77|                         dr46,dr47,dr48,dr49,dr50,\
78|                         dr51,dr52,dr53,dr54,dr55,\
79|                         dr56,dr57,dr58,dr59,dr60 ]
80|     dr = 0
81|     for i in range(60):
82|         dr = dr + dr_array[i]
83|     rm = r0 + dr
84|     return rm
```

**Check:**

DistMoon(8000) = 393749.0879545906 km

## 2.17 Function for Listing the dr_array

This function takes Ndays as argument and prints out list of dr_array. If the DistMoon(Ndays) fails to return the correct answer, this function can be used to check where the coding has gone wrong.

```
 1|def pr_dr_array(x):
 2|    print("Check Moon Distance
 3| Calculations")
 4|    print("List of dr_array on d =",x)
 5|    Lm = DistMoon(x)
 6|    dr = 0
 7|    for i in range(60):
 8|        print("{:3d} {:13.8f}"\
 9|                .format(i+1,dr_array[i]))
10|        dr = dr + dr_array[i]
11|
```

```
12|      rm = r0 + dr
13|      print("r0 =",r0)
14|      print("dr =",dr)
15|      print("rm =",rm)
```

For example if you want to check the dr_array for Ndays = 8000.

Operate the function **pr_dr_array(8000)=>** and you should get the following listing.

```
Check Moon Distance Calculations
List of dr_array on d = 8000
 1 5443.31794821
 2 -179.32264893
 3 2887.96227615
 4  492.64626312
 5   38.67635239
 6    3.14188485
 7  234.28059067
 8 -98.64479948
 9 -78.58845469
10  184.77710748
11 -49.73496697
12 -11.66297063
13 -83.35159847
14   10.20865325
15    0.00000000
16   15.52774659
17  -5.76181992
18 -16.49129384
19  21.53430900
20 -13.83941123
21 -19.80953652
22   -8.27730880
```

| | |
|---|---|
| 23 | 11.54049829 |
| 24 | 2.28461184 |
| 25 | -7.70097911 |
| 26 | -10.59024138 |
| 27 | -7.83679155 |
| 28 | 6.93952213 |
| 29 | 0.00000000 |
| 30 | 5.68688058 |
| 31 | -5.89217280 |
| 32 | 4.47870785 |
| 33 | -2.16676964 |
| 34 | 0.00000000 |
| 35 | -4.83856219 |
| 36 | -1.65041205 |
| 37 | 0.00000000 |
| 38 | 1.86526750 |
| 39 | 0.00000000 |
| 40 | -3.25233819 |
| 41 | 2.37104069 |
| 42 | 1.38150403 |
| 43 | -1.83585388 |
| 44 | -2.24329714 |
| 45 | 0.00000000 |
| 46 | 0.00000000 |
| 47 | 0.90935671 |
| 48 | -0.55223752 |
| 49 | -1.52963947 |
| 50 | 0.70809555 |
| 51 | 0.00000000 |
| 52 | -3.96224539 |
| 53 | 0.00000000 |
| 54 | 0.00000000 |
| 55 | 0.00000000 |

| | |
|---|---|
| 56 | 0.00000000 |
| 57 | -1.16368277 |
| 58 | 0.00000000 |
| 59 | 0.00000000 |
| 60 | -1.01062972 |
| r0 = | 385000.56 |
| dr = | 8748.527954590603 |
| rm = | 393749.0879545906 |

Every term in the array can be verified and corrections can be made ln the function if required.

## 2.18 Function for Calculating RA and Declination from Ecliptic Latitude and Longitude

This function takes ecliptic longitude and latitude as arguments and returns RA and declination.

```
1|def radc(lon,lat):
2|    global Obl
3|    ra = rev(atn2(sn(lon)*cs(Obl) \
4|                  -tn(lat)*sn(Obl),cs(lon)))
5|    dc = asn(sn(lat)*cs(Obl) \
6|                  + cs(lat)*sn(Obl)*sn(lon))
7|    return ra, dc
```

## 2.19 Function for Calculating Right Assension and Declination of Moon

This function takes *Ndays* as argument and returns RA and Declination of moon in degrees in the form of *List*.

```
1|def radcMoon(x):
2|    Obl,dpsi,GST = Obl_Nut_GST(x)
3|    ra,dc = radc(LonMoon(x),LatMoon(x))
4|    return ra,dc
```

**Check:**

radcMoon(8000) => (146.67479530816425, 18.94372322235627)

That means RA of Moon is 146.67479530816425 degrees and

Declination of Moon is 18.94372322235627degrees.

## 2.20 Function for Calculating RA, Declination and Distance of Sun

This function takes Ndays as argument and returns RA and Declination of Moon in degrees and geocentric distance of Moon in Astronomical Units.

```
 1|def SunValues(x):
 2|    Obl,dpsi,GST = Obl_Nut_GST(x)
 3|    l = rev(280.461 + 0.9856474*x)
 4|    m = rev(357.528 + 0.9856003*x)
 5|    dl =  rev(1.915*sn(m) + 0.020*sn(2*m))
 6|    lon0 = rev(l + dl)
 7|    lon = rev(lon0 + dpsi)
 8|    lat = 0.0
 9|    r = 1.00014 - 0.01671*cs(m)\
10|        - 0.00014*cs(2*m)
11|    r = r*149597870.691/6378.137
12|                    #convert ER Units
13|    rasun, dcsun = radc(lon,lat)
14|    return rasun,dcsun,r
```

**Check:**

SunValues(8000) = >

(242.47488835640758, -21.029102711838494, 23147.012633618408)

## 2.21 Function for Calculating RA and declination of Moon's shadow

This function takes Ndays as argument and returns RA and declination of Moon's shadow (always opposite to Sun) in degrees.

```
 1|def radcShadow(x):# Opposite of Sun
 2|    Obl,dpsi,GST = Obl_Nut_GST(x)
 3|    l = rev(280.461 + 0.9856474*x)
 4|    m = rev(357.528 + 0.9856003*x)
 5|    dl =  rev(1.915*sn(m) + 0.020*sn(2*m))
 6|    lon0 = rev(l + dl)
 7|    lon = lon0 + dpsi
 8|    lat = 0.0
 9|    r = 1.00014 - 0.01671*cs(m)\
10|              - 0.00014*cs(2*m)
11|    rasun, dcsun = radc(lon,lat)
12|    return rev(rasun+180),(-dcsun)
```

**Check:**

radcShadow(8000) =>

(62.474888356407575, 21.029102711838494)

## 2.22 Function for Calculating RA, Declination and Distance of Moon

This function takes Ndays as argument and returns RA and Declination of Moon in degrees and geocentric distance of Moon in Astronomical Units.

```
1|def MoonValues(x):
2|    Obl,dpsi,GST = Obl_Nut_GST(x)
3|    Lm = LonMoon(x)
4|    Bm = LatMoon(x)
5|    Rm = DistMoon(x)/6378.137
6|    ramoon, dcmoon = radc(Lm,Bm)
7|    return ramoon, dcmoon,Rm
```

**Check:**

MoonValues(8000) = >

(146.67479530816425, 18.94372322235627, 61.73418475560977)

## 2.23 Function for Distance and Parallax of Moon

This function takes Ndays as argument and returns geocentric distance of Sun in km and Parallax of Sun.

```
1|def rpMoon(x):
2|    rm = DistMoon(x)
3|    pm = asn(6378.14/(rm))
4|    return rm,pm
```

**Check:**

rpMoon(8000) = > (393749.0879545906, 0.9281456074322332)

## 2.24 Function for Converting Hours to String with Hour:min format

This takes Hours as argument asnd returns a string in hour:min format

```
1|def htohm(hr):
2|    if hr < 0.0:
3|        hr +=24.0
```

```
4|      h = int(hr)
5|      m = int((hr - h)*60+0.5)
6|      hm = "%02d:"%h + "%02d"%m
7|      return hm
```

**Check:**

htohm(12.75) => '12:45'

## 2.25 Function for Converting Hours to Hour:Minute:Second format

This function takes hours as arguments and returns a sting in h:m:s format.

```
 1|def hms(hr):
 2|     if hr >= 24.0:
 3|         hr -=24.0
 4|     if hr < 0.0:
 5|         hr +=24.0
 6|     h = int(hr)
 7|     m = (hr - h)*60
 8|     s = (m - int(m))*60
 9|     m = int(m)
10|     s = int(s+.5)
11|     hms = "%02dh"%h + "%02dm"%m + "%02ds"%s
12|     return hms
```

**Check:**

hms(8.125) => '08:07:30'

## 2.26 Function to Convert Month Number to Month Name

This function takes Month Name (Jan, Feb.. etc.) as argument and returns the Month's number (1 to 12)

```
1|def MonthNum(MonthName):
2|    MonthList = ('','Jan','Feb','Mar',\
3|                     'Apr','May','Jun',\
4|                     'Jul','Aug','Sep',\
5|                     'Oct','Nov','Dec' )
6|    mn = MonthList.index(MonthName)
7|    return mn
```

**Check:**

MonthNum(Aug) => 8

## 2.27 Function to Convert Month Number to Month Name

This function take Month Number as argument and returns Month name

```
1|def MonthName(x):
2|    MonthName = ['','Jan','Feb','Mar',\
3|                    'Apr','May','Jun',\
4|                    'Jul','Aug','Sep',\
5|                    'Oct','Nov','Dec' ]
6|    return MonthName[x]
```

**Check:**

MonthName(9) => 'Sep'

## 2.28 List of Number of Days in Each of 12 Months of a Year

This function takes year as the argument and returns a list of 13 numbers representing the number of days in Month[0] to Month[12] in the given year.

Month[0] being a dummy number which is always zero.

```
1|def dim(y):#Days in Months
2|    global dm
3|    dm = [0,31,28,31,30,31,30,\
4|          31,31,30,31,30,31]
5|    if y%4== 0 and y%100!=0 or y%400 == 0:
6|        dm[2] = 29
7|    return dm
```

**Check:** dim(2020)=>  [0, 31, 29, 31, 30, 31, 30, 31, 31, 30, 31, 30, 31]

## 2.29 Function Strdat(y,m,d)

This function takes date, month and year as arguments and returns a string of day and date in the required format.

```
1|import datetime as dt
2|def strdat(d,m,y):
3|    dat =dt.date(y,m,d)
4|    mydat = dat.strftime("%A, %B %d, %Y")
5|    return mydat
```

**Check:** strdat(15,8,1947 )=> returns    'Friday, August 15, 1947'

## 2.30 Function chkfile(filename)

This function checks for the presence of any given file in the given path. If it is not found, gives a warning message.

```
 1|def chkfile(filename):
 2|    global fileYes
 3|    warning = "File \'" + filename \
 4|               + "\' Missing"
 5|    try:
 6|        f = open(filename,"r")
 7|    except IOError:
 8|        fileYes = 0
 9|        win3 = tk.Tk()
10|        win3.geometry("250x150+550+300")
11|        win3.resizable(width=False,\
12|                       height=False)
13|        win3.title("WARNING!")
14|        messagebox.showwarning\
15|               ("WARNING!", warning)
16|        win3.destroy()
17|        sys.exit()
```

## 2.31 Function for Swapping the Values of Two Variables

This function takes two values as arguments and returns the swapped values.

```
 1|def swap(var1,var2):
 2|    return num1,num2
```

**Check:**

swap(10.35, 40.80) => returns  (40.8, 10.35)

swap('Sun','Moon') => returns  ('Moon', 'Sun')

# 3. PLANETARY POSITIONS

In this chapter a program of calculating the planetary positions is given. It calculates positions of all planets, Sun and Moon at a given instant of time on a given date and tabulates the results. The tables are saved in a file 'PLNT.TXT'.

## 3.1 Importing Modules and Definitions

```
 1|from AstroMODULE import *
 2|import tkinter as tk
 3|from tkinter import ttk
 4|from tkinter import *
 5|from tkinter import messagebox
 6|pLong =[0.0]*10
 7|pLat= [0.0]*10
 8|pRA = [0.0]*10
 9|pDecl = [0.0]*10
10|ep = [0.0]*10
11|sp = [0.0]*10
12|ph = [0.0]*10
13|plnt = ["SUN","MOON","MERCURY","VENUS",\
14|            "MARS","JUPITER","SATURN",\
15|            "URANUS","NEPTUNE","PLUTO"]
16|dpsi = 0.0;Obl = 0.0;GST = 0.0; Ayan = 0.0
17|d = 0.0
```

## 3.2 Function ProcessPlanets( )

This function displays a GUI (Graphic User Interface) to allow the user to fill in the required data, and then does all the necessary calculations using the various other functions.

```
 1|def ProcessPlanets():
 2|    win = tk.Tk()
 3|    win.geometry("600x250+400+250")
 4|    win.resizable(width=False, height=False)
 5|    win.title("PLANETARY POSITIONS")
 6|    #Labels
 7|    label0 = ttk.Label(win,\
 8|            text = 'FINDING'\
 9|                 +'PLANETARY POSITIONS',
10|           font = "Times 18")
11|    label0.place(x='120',y = '30')
12|    label1 = ttk.Label(win,\
13|        text = 'Enter Date and Time :',\
14|        font = "Times 14")
15|    label1.place(x='100',y = '80')
16|    label2 = ttk.Label(win,\
17|        text = 'Date   Month   Year'
18|        +      'Hour   Mins',
19|           font ='Times 12')
20|    label2.place(x='255',y = '60')
21|    #Entry boxes
22|    dat_var =tk.StringVar()
23|    dat_entrybox = ttk.Entry(win,\
24|            width = 3, \
25|            textvariable = dat_var)
26|    dat_entrybox.place(x = '260',y = '80')
27|    dat_entrybox.focus()
28|    mon_var = tk.StringVar()
```

```
29|    mon_entrybox = ttk.Entry(win,\
30|         width = 3,\
31|         textvariable = mon_var)
32|    mon_entrybox.place(x = '305', y = '80')
33|    yer_var =tk.StringVar()
34|    yer_entrybox = ttk.Entry(win,\
35|         width = 6,\
36|         textvariable = yer_var)
37|    yer_entrybox.place(x = '345', y = '80')
38|    hour_var =tk.StringVar()
39|    hour_entrybox = ttk.Entry(win,\
40|         width = 3,\
41|         textvariable = hour_var)
42|    hour_entrybox.place(x = '405', y = '80')
43|    mins_var =tk.StringVar()
44|    mins_entrybox = ttk.Entry(win,\
45|         width = 3,\
46|         textvariable = mins_var)
47|    mins_entrybox.place(x = '445', y = '80')
48|    def action():
49|         global date,month,year,hour,mins
50|         label3 = ttk.Label(win, text = \
51|            "SEE FILE 'PLNT.TXT'\
52|                   FOR RESULTS",\
53|            font = "times 14 bold")
54|         label3.place(x='70',y = '170')
55|         win.destroy()
56|         date = int(dat_var.get())
57|         month = int(mon_var.get())
58|         year = int(yer_var.get())
59|         hour = int(hour_var.get())
60|         mins = int(mins_var.get())
61|         print('h = ',hour)
```

```
62|            prPlanets(date,month,year,hour,mins)
63|            PlntMsg()
64|      def ChkEntry():
65|          warning = 'INVALID ENTRIES !'\
66|                      + '\nENTER VALID DATA'\
67|                      + 'AND CLICK SUBMIT'
68|          x1 = dat_var.get()
69|          x2 = mon_var.get()
70|          x3 = yer_var.get()
71|          x4 = hour_var.get()
72|          x5 = mins_var.get()
73|          if x1.isdigit() \
74|              and x2.isdigit()\
75|              and x3.isdigit()\
76|              and x4.isdigit()\
77|              and x5.isdigit()\
78|              and 13>int(x2)>0\
79|              and dim(int(x3))[int(x2)]\
80|                            >int(x1)>0:
81|              action()
82|          else:
83|              messagebox.showwarning\
84|                  ("WARNING!", warning)
85|              dat_var.set("")
86|              mon_var.set("")
87|              yer_var.set("")
88|              hour_var.set("")
89|              mins_var.set("")
90|              dat_entrybox.focus()
91|      submit_button = tk.Button(win,\
92|                  text = 'Submit',\
93|                  font = 'Times 14',\
```

```
94|                    command=ChkEntry)
95|      submit_button.place(x='275', y='120')
96|      win.mainloop()
```

This function displays a Graphic User Interface as shown below to allow the user to fill in the required data, namely, Date, Month, Year and time in Hours and Minutes at which it is desired to calculate the planetary positions. The curser is initially focused in the Date-entry box and can be moved forward by pressing tab key or with the mouse.

After filling the data user has to click on Submit-button.

If the data filled is not valid the program will display warning and resets the GUI and executes the program only after the valid data is entered and submitted.

## 3.3 Function Sunxyzr(Ndays )

This takes Number of days (*Ndays*) as argument and computes the geocentric coordinates of Sun and returns xsun, ysun, zsun, being the geocentric Cartesian coordinates of Sun and **res** , the distance of Sun, all in Astronomical Units.

```
 1|def Sunxyzr(d):
 2|    global xsun,ysun,zsun,res
 3|    l = rev(280.461 + 0.9856474 * d)
 4|    m = rev(357.528 + 0.9856003 * d)
 5|    dl =  rev(1.915 * sn(m)\
 6|                + 0.020 * sn(2*m))
 7|    lon0 = rev(l + dl)
 8|    pLong[0] = lon0 + dpsi
 9|    pLat[0] = 0.0
10|    r = 1.00014 - 0.01671 * cs(m)\
11|                - 0.00014 * cs(2*m)
12|    xsun = r * cs(lon0)
13|    ysun = r * sn(lon0)
14|    zsun = 0.0
15|    res = r
16|    return xsun,ysun,zsun,res
```

## 3.4 Function Perturb( )

This function takes Ndays as argument and calculates the perturbation-corrections for Jupiter, Saturn and Uranus. It does not return anything but stores the values in memory.

```
 1|def Perturb(x):
 2|    global Mj,Ms,Mu,prPerturb
 3|    global j_array,s_array,u_array
 4|    global pcLatSat,pcLonSat
 5|    global pcLonJup,pcLonUrn
 6|    #Jupiter's Heliocentric longitude
 7|    Mj = rev( 20.01962795 + 0.0830853001*x)
 8|    Ms = rev(317.01716634 + 0.0334442282*x)
 9|    Mu = rev(142.60808871 + 0.0117258060*x)
10|    j1 = -0.332 * sn(2*Mj - 5*Ms - 67.6)
```

```
11|     j2 = -0.056 * sn(2*Mj - 2*Ms + 21.0)
12|     j3 =  0.042 * sn(3*Mj - 5*Ms + 21.0)
13|     j4 = -0.036 * sn( Mj  - 2*Ms)
14|     j5 =  0.022 * cs( Mj  -  Ms )
15|     j6 =  0.023 * sn(2*Mj - 3*Ms + 52.0)
16|     j7 = -0.016 * sn( Mj  - 5*Ms - 69.0)
17|     pcLonJup = j1+j2+j3+j4+j5+j6+j7
18|     #Saturn's Heliocentric longitude
19|     s1 =  0.812 * sn(2*Mj - 5*Ms - 67.6)
20|     s2 = -0.229 * cs(2*Mj - 4*Ms -  2.0)
21|     s3 =  0.119 * sn( Mj  - 2*Ms -  3.0)
22|     s4 =  0.046 * sn(2*Mj - 6*Ms - 69.0)
23|     s5 =  0.014 * sn( Mj  - 3*Ms + 32.0)
24|     pcLonSat = s1+s2+s3+s4+s5
25|     s6 =  0.018 * sn(2*Mj - 6*Ms - 49.0)
26|     s7 = -0.020 * cs(2*Mj - 4*Ms -  2.0)
27|     pcLatSat = s6+s7
28|     #Corrections for Uranus(Harshal)
29|     u1 =  0.040 * sn( Ms  - 2*Mu + 6.0 )
30|     u2 =  0.035 * sn( Ms  - 3*Mu + 33.0)
31|     u3 = -0.015 * sn( Mj  -  Mu  + 20.0)
32|     pcLonUrn = u1+u2+u3
33|     j_array = [j1,j2,j3,j4,j5,j6,j7]
34|     s_array = [s1,s2,s3,s4,s5,s6,s7]
35|     u_array = [u1,u2,u3,0,0,0,0]
```

## 3.4 Function prPerturb( )

This function prints  the perturbation corrections computed by the previous function. This can be used for checking the correctness of the function Perturb()

```
 1|def prPerturb():
 2|
 3|    print("Perturbations ckeck values")
 4|    print("Mj = " + "%13.8f"%Mj)
 5|    print("Ms = " + "%13.8f"%Ms)
 6|    print("Mu = " + "%13.8f"%Mu)
 7|    for i in range(7):
 8|        print("j"+"%d ="%(i+1)\
 9|         +"%11.8f"%j_array[i]\
10|          +"  s"+"%d ="%(i+1)\
11|           +"%11.8f"%s_array[i]\
12|            +" u"+"%d ="%(i+1)\
13|             +"%11.8f"%u_array[i])
14|    print("pcLonJup = " + "%13.8f"%pcLonJup)
15|    print("pcLonSat = " + "%13.8f"%pcLonSat)
16|    print("pcLatSat = " + "%13.8f"%pcLatSat)
17|    print("pcLonUrn = " + "%13.8f"%pcLonUrn)
```

**Check:** Call the function Perturb(8000) => there will be no output.

Then call prPurturb() => you should get the following output.

```
Perturbations ckeck values
Mj = 324.70202875
Ms = 224.57099194
Mu = 236.41453671
j1 =-0.00608910   s1 = 0.01489263   u1 = 0.03540213
j2 = 0.03693224   s2 = 0.07500877   u2 =-0.03498509
j3 =-0.03320947   s3 =-0.09448491   u3 =-0.01424241
j4 = 0.02968990   s4 =-0.03365426   u4 = 0.00000000
j5 =-0.00386980   s5 = 0.00954602   u5 = 0.00000000
j6 = 0.01068820   s6 =-0.00817796   u6 = 0.00000000
j7 = 0.00867838   s7 = 0.00655098   u7 = 0.00000000
pcLonJup =   0.04282033
```

pcLonSat = -0.02869175
pcLatSat = -0.00162697
pcLonUrn = -0.01382537

## 3.4 Function calPlanets( )

This function takes Ndays as arguments and evaluates the planetary orbital elements and calculates positional coordinates of the planets and their distances from the Sun and Earth. This function does not return anything but stores the calculated values in the memory for further use.

```
1|def calPlanets(d):
2|    global pLat,pLong,ep,sp
3|    global xsun,ysun,zsun,dpsi
4|    N0 = [0,0,48.33134869, 76.67993699 , \
5|            49.55743166, 100.45424153, \
6|            113.66343585,  74.00052097, \
7|            131.78064526]
8|    dN = [0,0, 3.24587E-5 , 2.46590E-5 , \
9|            2.11081E-5 , 2.76854E-5 , \
10|            2.38980E-5 , 1.39780E-5 , \
11|            3.0173E-5  ]
12|    i0 = [0,0, 7.00470007 , 3.39460004 , \
13|            1.84969997 , 1.30299977 , \
14|            2.48859984 , 0.77330003 , \
15|            1.76999962 ]
16|    di = [0,0, 5.00E-8, 2.75E-8,\
17|            -1.78E-8, -2.557E-7,\
18|            -1.081E-7,1.9E-8,-2.55E-7]
19|    w0 = [0,0,29.12411522, 54.89102076,\
20|            286.50164394, 273.87772468,\
21|            339.39394465, 96.66124585, \
22|            272.84609096]
```

```
23|     dw = [0,0,1.0144E-5,  1.38374E-5,\
24|               2.92961E-5, 1.64505E-5,\
25|               2.97661E-5, 3.0565E-5, \
26|                          - 6.027E-6]
27|     a0 = [0, 0, 0.387098, 0.723330,\
28|               1.523688, 5.202560,\
29|             9.554750, 19.18170998, \
30|                    30.05826005 ]
31|     da = [0, 0, 0.00, 0.00, 0.00, 0.00, \
32|             0.00, -1.55E-8, 3.313E-8]
33|     e0 = [0 ,0, 0.205635, 0.006773,\
34|               0.093405, 0.04849801,\
35|               0.05554599, 0.04731801,\
36|                          0.008606   ]
37|     de = [0, 0, 5.93E-10, -1.302E-9,\
38|             2.516E-9, 4.469E-9,\
39|             -9.499E-9, 7.45E-9, 2.15E-9]
40|     M0 = [0, 0, 174.79470166, 50.40839534, \
41|             19.38813116, 20.01962795, \
42|             317.01716634,142.60808871,\
43|             260.25609272]
44|     dM = [0, 0 ,4.0923344368, 1.6021302244,\
45|             0.5240207766, 0.0830853001, \
46|             0.0334442282, 0.011725806, \
47|             0.005995147]
48|     xsun,ysun,zsun,res = Sunxyzr(d)
49|     for k in range(2,9):
50|         N = rev(N0[k] + dN[k]*d)
51|         i = i0[k] + di[k]*d
52|         w = rev(w0[k] + dw[k]*d)
53|         a = a0[k] + da[k]*d
54|         e = e0[k] + de[k]*d
```

```
55|         M = rev(M0[k] + dM[k]*d)
56|         E0 = M + degs(e)*sn(M)
57|
58|         for j in range(5):
59|             E1 = E0 - (E0 - degs(e)*sn(E0) \
60|                     - M)/(1 - e*cs(E0))
61|             if abs(E0 - E1) < 0.00000001:
62|                 break
63|             E0 = E1
64|         x = a*(cs(E0)- e)
65|         y = a*sn(E0)*sqrt(1-e*e)
66|         r = sqrt(x*x + y*y)
67|         v = rev(atn2(y,x))
68|         xh = r * (cs(N) * cs(v + w)\
69|                 - sn(N)*sn(v + w)*cs(i))
70|         yh = r * (sn(N) * cs(v + w)\
71|                 + cs(N)*sn(v + w)*cs(i))
72|         zh = r * (sn(v + w) * sn(i))
73|         rh = sqrt(xh*xh + yh*yh \
74|                         + zh*zh)
75|         Lh = atn2(yh,xh)
76|         Bh = atn2(zh,sqrt(xh * xh \
77|                         + yh * yh))
78|         #Perturbation Corrections
79|         if k==5 or k==6 or k==7:
80|             Perturb(d)
81|             if k==5:
82|                 pclon = pcLonJup
83|                 pclat = 0
84|             if k==6:
85|                 pclon = pcLonSat
86|                 pclat = pcLatSat
87|             if k==7:
```

```
 88|                    pclon = pcLonUrn
 89|                    pclat = 0
 90|               lon1 = Lh + pclon
 91|               lat1 = Bh + pclat
 92|               xh = r * cs(lon1) * cs(lat1)
 93|               yh = r * sn(lon1) * cs(lat1)
 94|               zh = r * sn(lat1)
 95|           xe = xsun + xh
 96|           ye = ysun + yh
 97|           ze = zsun + zh
 98|           re = sqrt(xe*xe+ye*ye+ze*ze)
 99|           lon0 = rev(atn2(ye, xe))
100|           lat = atn(ze/sqrt(xe*xe + ye*ye))
101|           pLong[k] = lon0 + dpsi
102|           pLat[k] = lat
103|           ep[k] = re
104|           sp[k] = r
```

## 3.5 Function calPluto( )

This function takes Ndays as argument and calculates positional coordinates of the Pluto and its distances from the Sun and Earth. This function does not return anything but stores the calculated values in the memory for further use.

The method used for calculating the position of Pluto differs from that used for other planets.

```
1|def CalPluto(x):
2|    s = rev( 50.08018875 +  0.033459652*x)
3|    p = rev(238.95594788 +  0.003968789*x)
4|    xsun,ysun,zsun,res = Sunxyzr(x)
5|    a1  = 238.95081054 + 0.00400703*x
6|    a2  = - 19.799 * sn (p)
```

```
 7|     a3  =    19.848 * cs (p)
 8|     a4  =     0.897 * sn (2*p)
 9|     a5  = -   4.956 * cs (2*p)
10|     a6  =     0.610 * sn (3*p)
11|     a7  =     1.211 * cs (3*p)
12|     a8  = -   0.341 * sn (4*p)
13|     a9  = -   0.190 * cs (4*p)
14|     a10 =     0.128 * sn (5*p)
15|     a11 = -   0.034 * cs (5*p)
16|     a12 = -   0.038 * sn (6*p)
17|     a13 =     0.031 * cs (6*p)
18|     a14 =     0.020 * sn ((s-p))
19|     a15 = -   0.010 * cs ((s-p))
20|     lon = a1+a2+a3+a4+a5+a6+a7+a8+a9+a10\
21|              +a11+a12+a13+a14+a15
22|     b1  = -   3.9082
23|     b2  = -   5.453 * sn (p)
24|     b3  = -  14.975 * cs (p)
25|     b4  =     3.527 * sn (2*p)
26|     b5  =     1.673 * cs (2*p)
27|     b6  = -   1.051 * sn (3*p)
28|     b7  =     0.328 * cs (3*p)
29|     b8  =     0.179 * sn (4*p)
30|     b9  = -   0.292 * cs (4*p)
31|     b10 =     0.019 * sn (5*p)
32|     b11 =     0.100 * cs (5*p)
33|     b12 = -   0.031 * sn (6*p)
34|     b13 = -   0.026 * cs (6*p)
35|     b14 =     0.011 * cs ((s-p))
36|     lat = b1+b2+b3+b4+b5+b6+b7+b8+b9 \
37|              +b10+b11+b12+b13+b14
38|     c1  =    40.72
```

```
39|      c2  =    6.68*sn (p)
40|      c3  =    6.90*cs (p)
41|      c4  = - 1.18*sn (2*p)
42|      c5  = - 0.03*cs (2*p)
43|      c6  =    0.15*sn (3*p)
44|      c7  = - 0.14*cs (3*p)
45|      r   =    c1+c2+c3+c4+c5+c6+c7
46|      xe = r * cs(lat) * cs(lon)
47|      ye = r * sn(lon) * cs(lat)
48|      ze =       r * sn(lat)
49|      xg = xsun + xe
50|      yg = ysun + ye
51|      zg = zsun + ze
52|      rg = sqrt(xg*xg+yg*yg+zg*zg)
53|      lon0 = rev(atn2(yg,xg))
54|      pLat[9] = asn(zg/rg)
55|      pLong[9] = lon0 + dpsi
56|      ep[9] = rg
57|      sp[9] = r
```

## 3.6 Function PlntPos( )

This function takes (date, month, year, hour, mins) as arguments and generates two arrays, array of ecliptic longitudes and array of latitudes of sun, Moon and the planets and returns the two arrays in the form of *lists*, namely pLong and pLat .

```
1|def PlntPos(date,month,year,hours,mins):
2|    global d,Ayan,deltaT
3|    du0 = caldays(date,month,year)
4|    deltaT = calDeltaT(date,month,year)
5|    deltaD = deltaT/86400
6|    d = du0 + deltaD\
```

```
 7|              + hour/24.0 + mins/1440.0
 8|     Obl,dpsi,GST = Obl_Nut_GST(d)
 9|     Ayan = 23.853 + 3.82447045e-5*d
10|     calPlanets(d)
11|     pLong[1] = LonMoon(d)
12|     pLat[1]= LatMoon(d)
13|     ep[1] = DistMoon(d)
14|     CalPluto(d)
15|     return pLong, pLat
```

## 3.7 Function prPlanets( )

This function takes (date, month, year,hour, mins) as arguments and prints out two tables on to the console as well as to a file named 'PLNT. TXT'.

```
 1|def prPlanets(date,month,year,hours,mins):
 2|     PlntPos(date,month,year,hours,mins)
 3|     f = open('PLNT.TXT','w')
 4|     def spc(x):
 5|         return " "*x
 6|     print("\nPLANETARY POSITIONS ON,"\
 7|         + "%02d-"%date + "%02d-"%month\
 8|         + "%d"%year + " at %02d:"%hour \
 9|         + "%02d UT"%mins)
10|     print("DeltaT = " + "%4.2f s"%deltaT\
11|            + " Ndays = " + "%13.8f;"%d \
12|            + " Ayanamsha =" +\
13|               "%12.8f"%Ayan )
14|     print("-"*68)
15|     print("Planets"+ spc(9) + "Longitude"\
16|         + spc(6) + "Latitude" +spc(4)\
```

```
17|            + "Right Ascen" + spc(3)\
18|            + "Declination")
19|     print("-"*68)
20|     for k in range(0,10):
21|         pRA[k],pDecl[k] = radc\
22|                     (pLong[k],pLat[k])
23|         print("%-12s"%plnt[k]\
24|             + " %13.8f"%pLong[k]\
25|             + " %13.8f"%pLat[k]\
26|             + " %13.8f"%pRA[k] \
27|             + " %13.8f"%pDecl[k])
28|     print("-"*68)
29|     print("\nTable of Distances"\
30|             + "(in AU) and % Phase Factors")
31|     print("Distance of Earth from Sun ="\
32|                         + "%10.8f AU"%res)
33|     print("-"*56)
34|     print("Planets"+spc(7)+"DistFromEarth" \
35|             + spc(2) +"DistFromSun"+spc(3)\
36|             +"phase factor")
37|     print("-"*56)
38|     for k in range(2,10):
39|         ph[k] = 100*((sp[k]+ep[k])**2 \
40|             - res**2)/(4*sp[k]*ep[k])
41|         print("%-12s"%plnt[k] \
42|             + " %13.8f"%ep[k] \
43|             + " %13.8f"%sp[k] \
44|             + " %13.8f"%ph[k])
45|     print("-"*56)
46|
47|     # File writing
48|     f.write("\nPLANETARY POSITIONS ON"\
```

```
49|              + "%02d-"%date + "%02d-"%month\
50|              + "%d"%year + " at %02d:"%hour\
51|              + "%02d UT"%mins)
52|    f.write("\nDeltaT = " \
53|              + "%4.2f sec;"%deltaT \
54|              + " Ndays = " + "%13.8f;"%d \
55|              + " Ayanamsha =" \
56|              + "%12.8f"%Ayan )
57|    f.write("\n" + "-"*68)
58|    f.write("\nPlanets"+ spc(9)\
59|              + "Longitude"\
60|              + spc(6) + "Latitude" +spc(4)\
61|              + "Right Ascen" + spc(3)\
62|              + "Declination")
63|    f.write("\n" +"-"*68)
64|    for k in range(0,10):
65|        pRA[k],pDecl[k] = \
66|              radc(pLong[k],pLat[k])
67|        f.write("\n%-12s"%plnt[k] \
68|              + " %13.8f"%pLong[k]\
69|              + " %13.8f"%pLat[k]\
70|              + " %13.8f"%pRA[k]\
71|              + " %13.8f"%pDecl[k])
72|    f.write("\n" + "-"*68)
73|    f.write("\n\nTable of Distances"\
74|              + "(in AU) and % Phase Factors")
75|    f.write("\nDistance of"\
76|              + "Earth from Sun ="\
77|              + "%10.8f AU"%res)
78|    f.write("\n" +"-"*56)
79|    f.write("\nPlanets"+spc(7) \
80|              +"DistFromEarth"+spc(2)\
```

```
81|                    +"DistFromSun"+spc(3)\
82|                    +"phase factor")
83|      f.write("\n" + "-"*56)
84|      for k in range(2,10):
85|          ph[k] = 100*((sp[k]+ep[k])**2 \
86|                  - res**2)/(4*sp[k]*ep[k])
87|          f.write("\n%-12s"%plnt[k]\
88|                  + "%13.8f"%ep[k]\
89|                  + "%13.8f"%sp[k]\
90|                  + "%13.8f"%ph[k])
91|      f.write("\n" + "-"*56)
92|      f.close()
93|      print("See file 'PLNT.TXT for results")
```

If data is entered through GUI giving date and time and submit-button is clicked this function is automatically called and prints out planets at on the given date at the given time.

This function can also be called with the required arguments directly. If the values are not assigned to the variables *hour* and *mins* before calling this function, it assumes zero time and prints the results at zero UT on the given date.

**Check:**

By calling prPlanets(1,1,2025,0,0) => we should get the following output on the shell as well in the output file 'PLNT.TXT'.

```
POSITIONS OF SUN, MOON AND PLANETS ON 01-01-2025 at 00:00 UT
DeltaT = 74.41 sec; Ndays = 9131.50086118; Ayanamsha = 24.20223155
--------------------------------------------------------------
Planets         Longitude     Latitude    Right Ascen   Declination
--------------------------------------------------------------
SUN             280.81710259   0.00000000  281.76387099  -22.99775496
MOON            293.91480768  -4.60982793  296.68160279  -25.86019527
MERCURY         259.87582458   1.11270139  259.07786075  -21.94266914
VENUS           327.71563293  -1.40489699  330.39810840  -13.58481509
```

```
MARS          121.93308278    3.91489425  125.14188228   23.54201368
JUPITER        73.22194518   -0.60004561   71.88897310   21.78968871
SATURN        344.53023922   -1.97743742  346.52209025   -7.91424436
URANUS         53.65215069   -0.25244620   51.33532156   18.44087899
NEPTUNE       357.29588260   -1.28530731  358.02984031   -2.25466487
PLUTO         301.05795329   -3.27320914  304.05724671  -23.11463271
-----------------------------------------------------------------
Table of Distances (in AU) and % Phase Factors
Distance of Earth from Sun = 0.98330594 AU
-----------------------------------------------------------------
Planets       DistFromEarth  DistFromSun   phase factor
-----------------------------------------------------------------
MERCURY          1.14802640   0.42030854   77.34226126
VENUS            0.75081200   0.72249084   55.47608276
MARS             0.65684915   1.61262478   98.74006475
JUPITER          4.18884092   5.08070766   99.79858325
SATURN          10.04807527   9.65321706   99.79097709
URANUS          18.85224503  19.53409183   99.96592262
NEPTUNE         30.09089717  29.87635404   99.97439223
PLUTO           36.03635451  35.11696348   99.99759755
-----------------------------------------------------------------
```

## 3.8 Function PlntMsg( )

This function sends a message on screen indicating where to see the results of the computations.

```
 1|def PlntMsg():
 2|    global top
 3|    top = Tk()
 4|    top.geometry("450x100")
 5|    msg = "See file 'PLNT.TXT' for results"
 6|    def stop():
 7|        print("ok")
 8|        #top.destroy()
 9|    B1 = Button(top, text = msg,\
10|                    font = 'Consolas 16',\
```

```
11|                    bg = 'yellow',fg = 'red')
12|     B1.place(x = 40,y = 20)
13|     top.bind("<Key>", stop)
14|     top.mainloop()
```

## 3.9 Main Program of Planetary Positions

Using the functions in the modules already explained, the program of finding the planetary positions becomes most simplified. The function *ProcessPlanets()* includes everything from taking data from the user till the end.

```
# ---Main Program----
1|ProcessPlanets()
```

In the file 'PLNT.TXT' you will find the table showing the values of Longitude, Latitude, Right Ascension and Declination of Sun, Moon and all the planets. Also in another table you will find the distances of all the planets from Earth and Sun and their phase factors.

You may note that the values of NDays, DeltaT, and *Ayanmsha\** are also printed at the top of the tables for tallying purpose. *Ayanamsha* is the difference between the tropical (*Sayan*) longitude and sidereal (*Nirayan*) longitude. *Nirayan* longitudes are used by Indian astrologers.

In the above programs Sayan longitudes are given. *Nirayan* longitudes can be found by deducting *Ayanamsha* from *Sayan* longitudes.

> Nirayan longitude = Sayan longitude – Ayanamsha

# 4. LIST OF LUNAR ECLIPSES

This is a program which generates list and catalogue of lunar eclipses. Though it possible to prepare the lists for any number of years, here they are prepared for the years from 1901 to 2100.

## 4.1 Importing Modules

All functions from **AstroMODULE,** tkinter and other modules are imported.

```
1|from AstroMODULE import *
2|import tkinter as tk
3|from tkinter import *
4|from tkinter import messagebox
5|import numpy as np
6|import cv24
```

## 4.2 Function GetYears( )

This function displays a GUI for the user to enter the years (*from* and *to)* required to prepare a list of lunar eclipses.

```
1|def GetYears():
2|    global Entry
3|    Entry = 0
4|    year1, year2 = 0,0
5|    Title = "SELECT PERIOD FOR"\
6|            + "LISTING OF LUNAR ECLIPSES"
```

```
 7|      win = tk.Tk()
 8|      win.geometry("700x250+400+250")
 9|      win.resizable(width = False,\
10|                      height = False)
11|      win.title(Title)
12|      #Labels
13|      label1 = tk.Label(win,\
14|            text = Title,font = 'times 20')
15|      label1.place(x='30',y = '20')
16|      label2 = tk.Label(win,\
17|          text = 'From Year'\
18|          +' '*14 + 'To Year',\
19|            font = 'times 18')
20|      label2.place(x='200',y = '60')
21|      #Entry boxes
22|      Year1_var = tk.StringVar()
23|      Year1_entrybox = tk.Entry(win,\
24|          width = 15, \
25|          textvariable = Year1_var)
26|      Year1_entrybox.place(x='200',y='100')
27|      Year1_entrybox.focus()
28|      Year2_var = tk.StringVar()
29|      Year2_entrybox = tk.Entry(win,\
30|          width = 15, \
31|          textvariable = Year2_var)
32|      Year2_entrybox.place(x='390',y='100')
33|      def Process():
34|          global yr1,yr2,Entry
35|          yr1 = Year1_var.get()
36|          yr2 = Year2_var.get()
37|          Entry = 1
38|          win.destroy()
39|      def ChkEntry():
```

```
40|              warning = "BAD ENTRIES !"\
41|                 +" \nENTER VALID DATA"\
42|                 +"AND CLICK SUBMIT"
43|            x1 = Year1_var.get()
44|            x2 = Year2_var.get()
45|            if x1.isdigit()\
46|                and x2.isdigit()\
47|                and int(x1) < int(x2):\
48|                Process()
49|            else:
50|                messagebox.showwarning\
51|                    ("WARNING!", warning)
52|                Year1_var.set("")
53|                Year2_var.set("")
54|                Year1_entrybox.focus()
55|        submit_button = tk.Button(win,\
56|                text = 'Process',\
57|                font = 'Times 14',\
58|                command = ChkEntry)
59|        submit_button.place(x='300',y='150')
60|        win.mainloop()
61|        win.quit
62|        if Entry == 0:
63|            sys.exit()
64|        else:
65|            return int(yr1),int(yr2)
```

This function, if a user so desires, can be omitted by just initializing year1 = 1901 and year2 = 2100 for simplifying the program.

The appearance of GUI displayed by the above function is shown below.

## 4.3 Function LE_Components( )

This function does not take any argument and calculates the various components of lunar eclipses on a pre-calculated opposition time and date. This function does not return anything. The values of the global variables within this function are retained in memory and will be useful for further processing.

```
 1│def LE_Components():
 2│    global oppo,letype,N_Penumbral
 3│    global magn,magn2,strCT
 4│    global N_Total,N_Partial,N_All
 5│    du1 = 0; du2 = 0
 6│    dt1 = 0; dt2 = 0
 7│    contact = [0,0,0,0,1,0,0,0,0]
 8│    T1 = int(oppo)
 9│    T2 = T1+1
10│    d1 = d+T1/24.0
11│    d2 = d+T2/24.0
12│    ram1,dcm1 = radcMoon(d1)
13│    ram2,dcm2 = radcMoon(d2)
14│    ras1,dcs1 = radcShadow(d1)
15│    ras2,dcs2 = radcShadow(d2)
```

```
16|     dra1 = (ram1 - ras1)
17|     dra2 = (ram2 - ras2)
18|     ddc1 = dcm1 - dcs1
19|     ddc2 = dcm2 - dcs2
20|     x1= (dra1)* cs(dcm1)
21|     y1 = ddc1
22|     x2 = (dra2)* cs(dcm2)
23|     y2 = ddc2
24|     xdash = x2-x1
25|     ydash = y2-y1
26|     M = atn2(x1,y1)
27|     N = atn2(xdash,ydash)
28|     m = x1/sn(M)
29|     n = xdash/sn(N)
30|     dTmid = (-m/n) * cs(M - N)
31|     Tmid = T1+dTmid
32|     msm = m*sn(M-N)
33|     gma = abs(msm)
34|     #fresh calculations at MidEclipse
35|     dmid = d1+dTmid/24.0
36|     rm,pm = rpMoon(dmid)
37|     rs,ps = rpSun(dmid)
38|     sdsun  = asn(sunrad /rs)
39|     sdmoon = asn(moonrad /rm)
40|     rp = 1.01*(ps+pm+sdsun) # Danjon's Method
41|     ru = 1.01*(ps+pm-sdsun)
42|     n1 = ru + sdmoon
43|     n2 = ru - sdmoon
44|     n3 = rp + sdmoon
45|     n4 = rp - sdmoon
46|     magn = (n1 - abs(msm))/(2*sdmoon)
47|     magn2 = (n3 - abs(msm))/(2*sdmoon)
```

```
48|     if magn >= 1.0:
49|         letype = "Total"
50|         N_Total += 1
51|         N_All +=1
52|     elif magn <1.0 and magn >=0.0:
53|         letype = "Partial"
54|         N_Partial += 1
55|         N_All +=1
56|     elif magn < 0.0 and magn2 > 0.0:
57|         letype = "Penumbral"
58|         N_Penumbral += 1
59|         N_All +=1
60|     if n1 > gma:
61|         dt1 = sqrt( n1*n1 - msm*msm)/n
62|         contact[2] = contact[6] = 1
63|     if n2 > gma:
64|         dt2 = sqrt( n2*n2 - msm*msm)/n
65|         contact[3] = contact[5] = 1
66|     if n3 > gma:
67|         du1 = sqrt( n3*n3 - msm*msm)/n
68|         contact[0] = contact[8] = 1
69|     if n4 > gma:
70|         du2 = sqrt( n4*n4 - msm*msm)/n
71|         contact[1] = contact[7] = 1
72|     tx[0] = Tmid-du1
73|     tx[1] = Tmid-du2
74|     tx[2] = Tmid-dt1
75|     tx[3] = Tmid-dt2
76|     tx[4] = Tmid
77|     tx[5] = Tmid+dt2
78|     tx[6] = Tmid+dt1;
79|     tx[7] = Tmid+du2;
80|     tx[8] = Tmid+du1;
```

```
81|     strCT = " "
82|     for i in range (0,9):
83|         ct[i] = T1+tx[i]
84|         if tx[i]< 0:
85|             tx[i] = tx[i] + 24.0
86|         if tx[i]> 24.0:
87|             tx[i] = tx[i] - 24.0
88|         cti = htohm(tx[i])
89|         if contact[i] == 0:
90|             cti = "-----"
91|         strCT= strCT + " " + cti
```

## 4.4 Function LEListMsg( )

This function does not take any argument. After the list is prepared this function displays a message on the screen showing the number of different types of lunar eclipses and total number of lunar eclipses during the given period and also informs the name of the file in which the lists are saved.

```
 1|def LEListMsg():
 2|    top = Tk()
 3|    top.geometry("500x200")
 4|    msg1 = "Lunar eclipses from year"\
 5|        +"%d "%year1 +"to " +"%d "%year2
 6|    B1 = Button(top, text = msg1,\
 7|                    font = 'times 16' )
 8|    B1.place(x = 80,y = 30)
 9|    msg2 = "Total=%d "%N_Total \
10|        + "Partial=%d"%N_Partial\
11|        + "Penumbral=%d"%N_Penumbral\
12|        + "All=%d"%N_All
```

```
13|      B2 = Button(top, text = msg2,\
14|                      font = 'times 16' )
15|      B2.place(x = 50,y = 80)
16|      msg3 = "See files 'outfile1.txt'"\
17|          + " and 'outfile2.txt' for results"
18|      B3 = Button(top, text = msg3,\
19|                      font = 'times 16' )
20|      B3.place(x = 50,y = 130)
21|      top.mainloop()
22|      top.quit()
```

The appearance of the message displayed by this function is shown below.

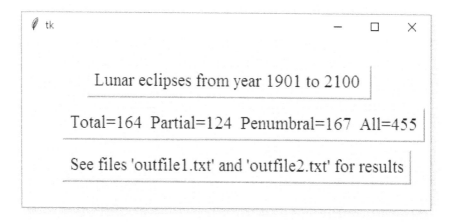

## 4.4 The Main Program

Let us name this program as 'LELIST.Py'.

This program uses a *for* loop for a given period from *year1* to *year2* and checks *argument of Moon* every day, and on coming across a full moon day, checks for possibility of an eclipse. If the possibility is there, function LE_componets() is called to calculate the components such as Time of Mid-eclipse, type of eclipse, magnitude etc. and the lists of lunar eclipses are generated.

```
# main program LELIST.Py
1|def sunrad = 696000.0
2|moonrad = 1737.1
3|earthrad = 6378.14
4|tx = [0.0]*10
5|ct = [0.0]*10
6|strCT = ""
7|gens = ' '; geew = ' '
8|N_Fullmoons = 0
9|N_Total = 0
10|N_Annular = 0
11|N_Partial = 0
12|N_Penumbral = 0
13|N_All = 0
14|letype = "    "
15|[Om,Ms,Mm,D,F,L0,Ls] = [0.0]*7
16|[E,E2,A1,A2,A3] = [0.0]*5
17|f1 = open('outfile1.txt','w')
18|f2 = open('outfile2.txt','w')
19|year1,year2 = GetYears()
20|f2.write("\n"+"-"*99)
21|f2.write("\nList of Lunar Eclipses during" \
22|     +"20th and 21st century with details")
23|f2.write("\n"+"-"*99)
24|f2.write("\nyyyy  mm dd Oppos  EclType"\
25|  +" Magn(U) Magn(P)   U1     U1     P1     P2"\
26|   + "    MID    P3     P4     U3     U4")
27|f2.write("\n"+"-"*99)
28|for year in range (year1,year2):
29|    for month in range(1,13):
30|        n = dim(year)[month]
31|        for dat in range(1,n+1):
```

```
32|          du0 = caldays(dat,month,year)
33|          dt = calDeltaT(dat,month,year)
34|          d = du0 + dt/86400.0
35|          m0 = LonMoon(d-1);
36|          m1 = LonMoon(d);
37|          m2 = LonMoon(d+1);
38|          m3 = LonMoon(d+2);
39|          s0 = LonSun(d-1);
40|          s1 = LonSun(d);
41|          s2 = LonSun(d+1);
42|          s3 = LonSun(d+2);
43|          tt0 = rev(m0-s0)/12.0;
44|          tt1 = rev(m1-s1)/12.0;
45|          tt2 = rev(m2-s2)/12.0;
46|          tt3 = rev(m3-s3)/12.0;
47|          tn1 = (int(tt1)+1);
48|          tn2 = (int(tt2)+1);
49|          k = (tt1-tt0);
50|          m = (tt2-tt1);
51|          l = (tt3-tt2);
52|          l_k = (l - k);
53|          tbal = 15.0 - tt1;
54|          h1 = tbal * 24/m;
55|          h2 = h1*(24-h1)*l_k / (m*96.0);
56|          oppo = h1+h2;
57|          if tn1 ==15 and tn2==16\
58|          or tn1==14 and tn2==16\
59|          or tn1==15 and tn2==17:
60|              LE_Components()
61|              if magn2 > 0.0:
62|                  text1 =("\n%d"%year \
63|                  + "%s"%MonthName(month)\
64|                  + "%02d"%dat \
```

```
65|                              + "%05.2f"%oppo \
66|                              + "%-10s"%letype)
67|                            text2 = ("\n%d"%year \
68|                              + "%s"%MonthName(month)\
69|                              + "%02d"%dat\
70|                              + "%05.2f"%oppo \
71|                              + "%-10s"%letype \
72|                              + "%7.4f"%magn \
73|                              + "%7.4f"%magn2 \
74|                              + "%s"%strCT)
75|                            f1.write(text1)
76|                            f2.write(text2)
77|print("T=", N_Total)
78|print("P=", N_Partial)
79|print("N=", N_Penumbral)
80|print("All=",N_All)
81|f2.write("\nAbstract of Lunar Eclipses"\
82|        + "from the year {:d} to {:d}"\
83|        .format(year1,year2-1))
84|f2.write("\nTotal Elipses      : "\
85|        +"%d"%N_Total)
86|f2.write("\nPartial Elipses    : "\
87|        + "%d"%N_Partial)
88|f2.write("\nPenumbral Elipses : "\
89|        + "%d"%N_Penumbral)
90|f2.write("\nAll Elipses        : "\
91|        + "%d"%N_All)
92|f1.close()
93|f2.close()
94|print("SUCSESS!")
95|print("See files outfile.txt and")
96|print("outfile2.txt for results")
97|LEListMsg()
```

On running this program, two lists are generated.

One list is printed to a file named 'Outfile1.txt' in which each line consists of five columns namely year, month, date, Time of Opposition and type of eclipse. This file, renamed as 'LE_INFILE.TXT', will be used as an 'input-file' for the program of Lunar Eclipses (Chapter 4)

Second list is printed to a file named 'Outfile2.txt'which will be a Catalogue of Lunar Eclipses giving full details of the eclipses such as contact timings, magnitudes and all.

It is suggested that you assign year1 = 2020 and year2 = 2030 at first and check only the file 'Outfile1.txt'. This reduces the run time and consequently saves time. When you find that your program is correct then you go to check the other file 'Outfile2.txt'. If everything goes right you can then modify the values year1 and year2 to any number of years.

Standard output in file for 2020 to 2030 in 'Outfile1.TXT' file is shown below.

**Short List of lunar eclipses from 2020 to 2030**

```
2020 Jan 10 19.36 Penumbral
2020 Jun 05 19.21 Penumbral
2020 Jul 05 04.74 Penumbral
2020 Nov 30 09.50 Penumbral
2021 May 26 11.24 Total
2021 Nov 19 08.96 Partial
2022 May 16 04.23 Total
2022 Nov 08 11.04 Total
2023 May 05 17.57 Penumbral
2023 Oct 28 20.40 Partial
2024 Mar 25 07.02 Penumbral
2024 Sep 18 02.58 Partial
```

```
2025 Mar 14 06.93 Total
2025 Sep 07 18.14 Total
2026 Mar 03 11.65 Total
2026 Aug 28 04.31 Partial
2027 Feb 20 23.40 Penumbral
2027 Jul 18 15.75 Penumbral
2027 Aug 17 07.48 Penumbral
2028 Jan 12 04.05 Partial
2028 Jul 06 18.19 Partial
2028 Dec 31 16.80 Total
2029 Jun 26 03.39 Total
2029 Dec 20 22.77 Total
2030 Jun 15 18.69 Partial
2030 Dec 09 22.68 Penumbral
```

The two complete standard lists of lunar eclipses are given in Appendix-2 and Appendix-6. You have to produce these two files from your program and tally your results with these standard lists until you find them to be correct.

List 1 is important. You have to save it as 'LE_INFILE.TXT' as it is to act as input file for the program of Lunar Eclipses (Chapter 5).

Using this program a catalogue of lunar eclipses can be generated for any number of years. Catalogue of lunar eclipses for 21st century is given in Appendix-6.

# 5. LUNAR ECLIPSES

In this chapter the program of complete solution to lunar eclipses will be given. This program allows the user to select any eclipse from a scrolling list and does all the calculations and produces pictures and videos.

## 5.1 Importing Modules

```
# Importing Modules
1|from AstroMODULE import *
2|import numpy as np
3|import cv2
4|from cv2 import VideoWriter,\
5|                 VideoWriter_fourcc
6|from tkinter import *
```

## 5.2 Function SelectSE( )

This function displays a scrolling list of lunar eclipses on the screen for the user to select one of them and click to process the same.

```
1|def SelectLE():
2|    root = Tk()
3|    root.title("List of Solar Eclipses")
4|    frame = Frame(root)
5|    scroll= Scrollbar(frame)
6|    scroll.pack(side = RIGHT,fill = Y)
```

```
 7|        listbox = Listbox(frame,height = 15,\
 8|           width = 30,font = "Consolas 16",\
 9|              bg = "light yellow",\
10|                 yscrollcommand=scroll.set)
11|        listbox.pack(side = LEFT)
12|        def BasicData():
13|            global LE,date,month,year,oppo
14|            global MonthNum
15|            lecl = listbox.curselection()
16|            for item in lecl:
17|                LE=(listbox.get(item)).split(" ")
18|                year = int(LE[0])
19|                month = MonthNum(LE[1])
20|                date = int(LE[2])
21|                oppo = float(LE[3])
22|                root.destroy()
23|        lbltxt = "List of Lunar Eclipses"
24|        lbl = Label(root, text = lbltxt,\
25|                 font = "times 18",\
26|                   bg = "light yellow")
27|        lbl.pack(side = TOP)
28|        btn = Button(root, \
29|           text = " Click to Process ",\
30|                    bg = "light yellow",\
31|                    command = BasicData)
32|        btn.pack(side = RIGHT)
33|        with open("LE_INFILE.TXT",'r') as f:
34|            for line in f:
35|                listbox.insert(END,line)
36|        scroll.config(command=listbox.yview)
37|        frame.pack()
38|        root.geometry("600x500")
39|        root.mainloop()
```

The scrolling list of lunar eclipses produced by this function is shown below from which user has to make his choice and click on 'Click to Process' button to start processing.

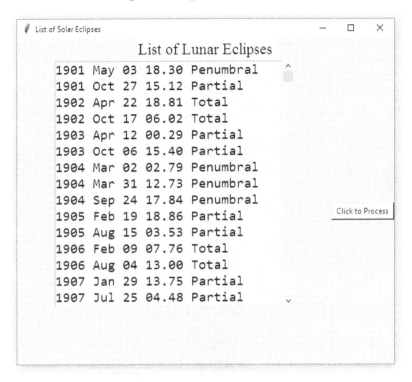

## 5.3  Function EarthShadow( )

This function plots the image of Earth's shadow on the graphic screen at a given position.

```
1|def EarthShadow():
2|    global img,font
3|    img = cv2.circle(img,(x0,y0),\
4|                 int(rP), clrP, -1)
5|    img = cv2.circle(img,(x0,y0),\
6|                 int(rU), clrU, -1)
7|    img = cv2.line(img,(x0,y0-250),\
```

```
 8|                  (x0,y0+250),(255,0,0),1)
 9|      img = cv2.line(img,(x0-350,y0),\
10|                  (x0+350,y0),(255,0,0),1)
```

## 5.4 Function LEframe1( )

This function plots the background frame on the screen on which other images are to be added later by other functions for videos or pictures.

```
1|def LEframe1():
2|     global img,font
3|     img = np.zeros((ht,width,3), np.uint8)
4|     img[:] = [clrB]
5|     LEtext()
6|     EarthShadow()
```

## 5.5 Function Leframe2( )

This function is similar to LEframe1() but produces a different type of background frame on the screen. This is to be used in the other functions.

```
1|def LEframe2():
2|     global img,font
3|     img = np.zeros((ht,width,3), np.uint8)
4|     img[:] = [clrB]
5|     #Creating background picture (unmoving)
6|     img = cv2.circle(img, (x0,y0),int(rM),\
7|                  (255,255,255), -1)
```

## 5.6 Function LEtext( )

This function prepares different text strings to be used in videos and pictures by other functions.

```
 1|def LEtext():
 2|    global img,font
 3|    font = cv2.FONT_HERSHEY_SIMPLEX
 4|    text1 = LE_Title
 5|    text2 = "Touch Penumbra:"\
 6|        + hms(tx[0])\
 7|        + " "*11 + "Middle:"\
 8|        + hms(tx[4]) \
 9|         + " "*6 +"Leave Penumbra:"\
10|        + hms(tx[8]) + "UT"
11|    text3 = "Touch Umbra: "\
12|            + hms(tx[2])
13|    text3a = "  Leave Umbra: "\
14|            + hms(tx[6]) + "UT"
15|    text4 = "Penumbral Magnitude = "\
16|            +"%5.3f"%magn2
17|    text4a = "   Umbral Magnitude = "\
18|            +"%5.3f"%magn
19|    Author ="Computer Program by -"\
20|            +"Manohar Purohit"
21|    img = cv2.putText(img,\
22|            text1,(200,50),\
23|            font,1.0,(0,0,0),\
24|             1,cv2.LINE_AA)
25|    liney = 100
26|    img = cv2.putText(img,\
27|            text2,(40,liney),\
28|             font,0.7,(0,0,0),\
29|             1,cv2.LINE_AA)
30|    if typ <= 2:
31|        liney+=40
32|        img = cv2.putText(img,\
```

```
33|              text3,(40,liney),font,0.7,\
34|                 (0,0,0),1,cv2.LINE_AA)
35|        img = cv2.putText(img,\
36|               text3a,(800,liney),\
37|               font,0.7,(0,0,0),1,\
38|                 cv2.LINE_AA)
39|     img = cv2.putText(img,\
40|            text4,(40,liney+40),\
41|            font,0.7,(0,0,0),1,\
42|              cv2.LINE_AA)
43|     img = cv2.putText(img,\
44|            text4a,(800,liney+40),\
45|            font,0.7,(0,0,0),1,\
46|              cv2.LINE_AA)
47|     img = cv2.putText(img,\
48|            Author,(700,650),\
49|            font,0.6,(0,7,0),1,\
50|              cv2.LINE_AA)
```

## 5.7 Function PlotMoonPath( )

This function plots moon's positions on the background picture of earth's shadow, at Nine different stages of the eclipse.

```
1|def PlotMoonPath():
2|    global img,clrB
3|    clrB = [255,255,255]
4|    LEframe1()
5|    for i in range (9):
6|        ext = 300
7|        img = cv2.circle(img,\
8|            (px[i],py[i]),\
```

```
 9|            int(rM), (0,0,0), 1)
10|        img = cv2.circle(img,\
11|              (px[i],py[i]),\
12|              1, (0,0,0), 1)
13|    x1 = int(px[4] + ext)
14|    y1 = int(py[4] + ext*slope)
15|    x2 = int(px[4] - ext)
16|    y2 = int(py[4] - ext*slope)
17|    cv2.line(img,\
18|        (x1,y1),(x2,y2),(0,0,0),1)#PathLine
19|    cv2.line(img,\
20|        (x2,y2),(x2+30,y2 \
21|        + int(30*slope) -10),\
22|           (0,0,0),1)#arrow
23|    cv2.line(img,\
24|        (x2,y2),(x2+30,y2 \
25|        + int(30*slope) +10),\
26|           (0,0,0),1)#arrow
```

## 5.8 Function AnimateLE1( )

This function produces animation of moon moving across Earth's shadow along with synchronized timings shown on the screen. At the end it shows the plot of different stages of the eclipse. Both the animation and the picture are saved in the current directory as LE_VID1.MP4 and LE_PIC.PNG respectively.

```
1|def AnimateLE1(): # Moon moving wrt Shadow
2|    global img,xm
3|    xm = px[4]; ym = py[4]
4|    #ext = 350
5|    FPS = 60
6|    #Animation and saving as video
```

```
 7|     fourcc = VideoWriter_fourcc(*'MP4v')
 8|     cap = cv2.VideoCapture()
 9|     video = VideoWriter('.\LE_VID1.MP4',\
10|             fourcc,float(FPS), (width,ht))
11|     for i in range(px[0],px[8]-2,-1):
12|         x = i
13|         y = int(py[0] + (i-px[0])*slope)
14|         timex = hms(tx[0] \
15|                 + (px[0]-i)/xdash/scale)
16|         LEframe1()
17|         LEtext()
18|         #variable part of picture
19|         if x >= px[8] and x <= px[0]:
20|             img = cv2.circle(img,\
21|                     (x, y),int(rM),\
22|                     (255,255,255),-1)
23|             img = cv2.rectangle(img,\
24|                     (970,200),(1150,270),\
25|                     (255,255,255),-1)
26|             img = cv2.putText(img,\
27|                 "Time in UT",(1000,230),\
28|                     font,0.6,(0,0,0),\
29|                         1,cv2.LINE_AA)
30|             img = cv2.putText(img,\
31|                     timex,(1000,250),\
32|                     font,0.6,(0,0,0),\
33|                     1,cv2.LINE_AA)
34|         EarthShadow()
35|         img = cv2.circle(img,\
36|                 (x, y),int(rM),\
37|                 (255,255,255), 1)
38|         if x < px[8]:
39|             PlotMoonPath()
```

```
40|          video.write(img)
41|      video.release()
42|      cv2.destroyAllWindows()
43|      cap = cv2.VideoCapture('LE_VID1.MP4')
44|      if (cap.isOpened()== False):
45|          print("Error opening video file")
46|      while(cap.isOpened()):
47|          ret, frame = cap.read()
48|          if ret == True:
49|              cv2.imshow(LE_Title, frame)
50|              #cv2.imshow('Frame', frame)
51|              if cv2.waitKey(25)\
52|              & 0xFF == ord('q'):
53|                  break
54|          else:
55|              break
56|      cap.release()
57|      cv2.destroyAllWindows()
58|      #Draw and Save Image
59|      PlotMoonPath()
60|      img = cv2.rectangle(img,(970,200),\
61|          (1150,270),clrB,-1)#replace rectagle
62|      cv2.imshow(LE_Title,img)
63|      cv2.imwrite("LE_PIC.png", img)
64|      cv2.waitKey(0)
65|      cv2.destroyAllWindows()
```

## 5.9 Function AnimateLE2( )

This function also produces animation of the eclipse differently. It shows the motion of the shadow over the still moon. This animation is also saved in the current directory with file name 'LE_VID2.MP4'.

```
 1|def AnimateLE2(): # Shadow moving wrt Moon
 2|    global img,xm
 3|    print("Please Wait! Processing is ON")
 4|    for i in range (0,9):
 5|        px[i] = int(x0 - u[i]*scale)
 6|        py[i] = int(y0 - v[i]*scale)
 7|    #Animation and saving as video
 8|    FPS = 60
 9|    fourcc = VideoWriter_fourcc(*'MP4v')
10|    cap = cv2.VideoCapture()
11|    video = VideoWriter('.\LE_VID2.MP4',\
12|            fourcc, float(FPS), (width, ht))
13|    x1 = int(px[0]);   x2 = int(px[8])
14|    for i in range(x1 ,x2 ,-1):
15|        x = 2*x0 -i
16|        y = 2*y0 - int(py[0]\
17|                    + (i-px[0])*slope)
18|        timex = hms(tx[0] \
19|                +(px[0]-i)/xdash/scale)
20|        #variable part of picture
21|        LEframe2()
22|        LEtext()
23|        img = cv2.circle(img,(x,y),\
24|                    int(rP), clrP, -1)
25|        img = cv2.circle(img,(x,y),\
26|                    int(rU), clrU, -1)
27|        img = cv2.circle(img, (x0,y0),\
28|                    int(rM),(255,255,255), 1)
29|        if i >= x2 and i <= x1:
30|            img = cv2.rectangle(img,\
31|                    (970,200),(1150,270),\
32|                    (255,255,255),-1)
33|            img = cv2.putText(img,\
```

```
34|                           "Time in UT",\
35|                        (1000,230),font,\
36|                          0.6,(0,0,0),\
37|                          1,cv2.LINE_AA)
38|              img = cv2.putText(img,timex,\
39|                      (1000,250),font,0.6,\
40|                      (0,0,0),1,cv2.LINE_AA)
41|          video.write(img)
42|      video.release()
43|      cv2.destroyAllWindows()
44|      cap = cv2.VideoCapture('LE_VID2.MP4')
45|      if (cap.isOpened()== False):
46|          print("Error opening video file")
47|      while(cap.isOpened()):
48|          ret, frame = cap.read()
49|          if ret == True:
50|              cv2.imshow(LE_Title, frame)
51|              if cv2.waitKey(25)\
52|                  & 0xFF == ord('q'):
53|                  break
54|          else:
55|              break
56|      cap.release()
57|      cv2.destroyAllWindows()
```

## 5.10 Function LE_Components( )

This function does not take any argument and calculates the components of lunar eclipses on a pre-calculated opposition time and date. This function does not return anything. The values of the global variables within this function are retained in memory and will be useful for further processing.

```
 1|def LE_Components():
 2|    global oppo,letype,N_All
 3|    global magn,magn2,strCT
 4|    global N_Total,N_Partial,N_Penumbral
 5|    global rp,ru,sdmoon
 6|    global xdash,ydash,slope
 7|    du1 = 0; du2 = 0; dt1 = 0; dt2 = 0
 8|    contact = [0,0,0,0,1,0,0,0,0]
 9|    T1 = int(oppo)
10|    T2 = T1+1
11|    d1 = d+T1/24.0
12|    d2 = d+T2/24.0
13|    ram1,dcm1 = radcMoon(d1)
14|    ram2,dcm2 = radcMoon(d2)
15|    ras1,dcs1 = radcShadow(d1)
16|    ras2,dcs2 = radcShadow(d2)
17|    dra1 = (ram1 - ras1)
18|    dra2 = (ram2 - ras2)
19|    ddc1 = dcm1 - dcs1
20|    ddc2 = dcm2 - dcs2
21|    x1= (dra1)* cs(dcm1)
22|    y1 = ddc1
23|    x2 = (dra2)* cs(dcm2)
24|    y2 = ddc2
25|    xdash = x2-x1
26|    ydash = y2-y1
27|    slope = ydash/xdash
28|    M = atn2(x1,y1)
29|    N = atn2(xdash,ydash)
30|    m = x1/sn(M)
31|    n = xdash/sn(N)
32|    dTmid = (-m/n) * cs(M - N)
33|    Tmid = T1+dTmid
```

```
34|    msm = m*sn(M-N)
35|    gma = abs(msm)
36|    #fresh calculations at MidEclipse
37|    dmid = d1+dTmid/24.0
38|    rm,pm = rpMoon(dmid)
39|    rs,ps = rpSun(dmid)
40|    sdsun  = asn(sunrad /rs)
41|    sdmoon = asn(moonrad /rm)
42|    rp = 1.01*(ps+pm+sdsun) # Danjon's Method
43|    ru = 1.01*(ps+pm-sdsun)
44|    #limiting values for 'gamma'
45|    n1 = ru + sdmoon
46|    n2 = ru - sdmoon
47|    n3 = rp + sdmoon
48|    n4 = rp - sdmoon
49|    magn = (n1 - abs(msm))/(2*sdmoon)
50|    magn2 = (n3 - abs(msm))/(2*sdmoon)
51|    if n1 > gma:
52|        dt1 = sqrt( n1*n1 - msm*msm)/n
53|        contact[2] = contact[6] = 1
54|    if n2 > gma:
55|        dt2 = sqrt( n2*n2 - msm*msm)/n
56|        contact[3] = contact[5] = 1
57|    if n3 > gma:
58|        du1 = sqrt( n3*n3 - msm*msm)/n
59|        contact[0] = contact[8] = 1
60|    if n4 > gma:
61|        du2 = sqrt( n4*n4 - msm*msm)/n
62|        contact[1] = contact[7] = 1
63|    tx[0] = Tmid-du1
64|    tx[1] = Tmid-du2
65|    tx[2] = Tmid-dt1
66|    tx[3] = Tmid-dt2
```

```
67|     tx[4] = Tmid
68|     tx[5] = Tmid+dt2
69|     tx[6] = Tmid+dt1;
70|     tx[7] = Tmid+du2;
71|     tx[8] = Tmid+du1;
72|     for i in range (0,9):
73|         ct[i] = T1+tx[i]
74|         cthms[i] = hms(tx[i])
75|         u[i] = x1 + (tx[i]-T1)*xdash
76|         v[i] = y1 + (tx[i]-T1)*ydash
77|         q[i] = rev(atn2(u[i],v[i]))
78|         px[i] = int(x0 - u[i]*scale)
79|         py[i] = int(y0 - v[i]*scale)
80|     strCT = " "
81|     for i in range (0,9):
82|         ct[i] = T1+tx[i]
83|         if tx[i]< 0:
84|             tx[i] = tx[i] + 24.0
85|         if tx[i]> 24.0:
86|             tx[i] = tx[i] - 24.0
87|         cti = htohm(tx[i])
88|         if contact[i] == 0:
89|             cti = "------"
90|         strCT= strCT + " " + cti
```

## 5.11 Function LE_Msg( )

This function flashes a message on the screen to inform the user the name of the output files, saved in the current directory as a result of this program.

```
 1|def LE_Msg():
 2|    top = Tk()
 3|    top.geometry("450x160")
 4|    def ShowMsg():
 5|        messagebox.showinfo()
 6|    msg = "See files 'LE_PIC.PNG'"\
 7|          + "\n LE_VID1.MP4"\
 8|          + "and LE_VID2.MP4"\
 9|          + "\n     for results"
10|    B1 = Button(top, text = msg,\
11|            font = 'Consolas 16',\
12|            bg = 'yellow',fg = 'red',\
13|            command = ShowMsg)
14|    B1.place(x = 40,y = 20)
15|    top.mainloop()
16|    top.quit()
```

## 5.12 The Main program

As already mentioned, functions do not operate themselves unless they are called for. That is where the *main* comes into play. Though the 'main' has not been specifically defined, all commands written without the *indent* can be considered as main and the program is executed accordingly. It defines the global variables and calls the functions one by one in a logical sequence and the program is executed accordingly.

```
 1|# Main Program
 2|date = month = year = 0
 3|oppo = 0.0
 4|chkfile('LE_INFILE.TXT')
 5|SelectLE()
 6|if date == 0:
 7|    sys.exit()
```

```
 8|ledat = strdat(date,month,year)
 9|LE_Title = LE[4] \
10|     + " Lunar Eclipse - "+ ledat
11|print(LE_Title)
12|scale = 150
13|x0 = 600; y0 = 400
14|typ = 0
15|tx = [0.0]*9
16|ct = [0.0]*9
17|u = [0.0]*9
18|v = [0.0]*9
19|q = [0.0]*9
20|cthms = [0.0]*9
21|px = [0]*9
22|py = [0]*9
23|du0 = caldays(date,month,year)
24|deltaT = calDeltaT(date,month,year)
25|d = du0 + deltaT/86400.0
26|LE_Components()
27|rP = rp*scale
28|rU = ru*scale
29|rM = sdmoon*scale
30|clrB = (255,255,0)
31|clrU = (0, 90,250)
32|clrP = (0,140,250)
33|clrM = (0,0,0)
34|ht = 700; width = 1200
35|x0 = 600; y0 = 400
36|AnimateLE2()
37|AnimateLE1()
38|PlotMoonPath()
39|LE_Msg()
```

At the end of the program a message is flashed on the screen as shown below.

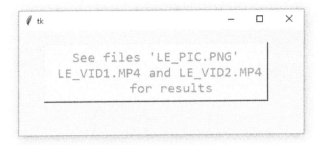

Two video files and a picture file are created by this program. It is not possible to show videos in the book but the picture produced for one of the lunar eclipse is shown below.

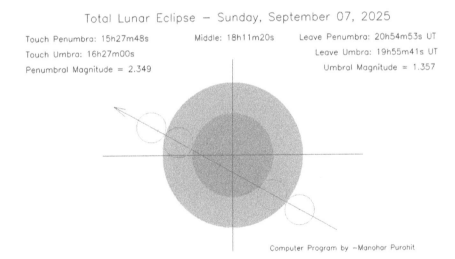

.

# 6. LIST OF SOLAR ECLIPSES

This program produces a list of solar eclipses from *year1* to *year2* chosen by the user. This does not need any input file as the list is prepared from scratch and will be saved in a file named 'SE_LIST1.TXT'. To start with it is advisable to make short list and check the results with the standard list given in Appendix-3. If the results are found correct then it can be extended for longer period.

## 6.1 Importing Modules

Firstly the necessary modules are imported.

```
1|from AstroMODULE import *
2|from tkinter import *
3|import tkinter.messagebox
```

## 6.2 Function caltdq(x)

### Function for calculating Time-Dependant-Quantities (TDQ)

This function takes (time in hours) (on the day under consideration) as argument and calculates many important time-dependent quantities, mainly the ***Bessilian elements*** and other auxiliary values. Though the function does not return any values the global variables evaluated inside the function are automatically retained in the memory for further calculations.

```
 1|def caltdq(x):
 2|    global T1,T2,ATmid
 3|    global f,rosino,rocoso
 4|    global d,d1,d2,deltad
 5|    global tanf11,tanf21
 6|    global z11,xi1,eta1,zeta1
 7|    global x1, y1, x2,y2,dST
 8|    global sin_d1,cos_d1
 9|    global GST1,dmu,mu1,mu2
10|    global xdash,ydash,dxi,deta
11|    global U,V,A,B,N,N2,longi
12|    global sin_h1, cos_h1
13|    global l11,l21,L11,L21
14|    global ras1,dcs1,sds,sdm
15|    td = 0.2
16|    T1 = x; T2 = x+ td
17|    d1 = d+(T1)/24.0
18|    d2 = d+(T2)/24.0
19|    #values at T1
20|    ras1,dcs1,sunr1 = SunValues(d1)
21|    ram1,dcm1,moonr1 = MoonValues(d1)
22|    b1 = moonr1/sunr1
23|    bb1 = moonr1/(sunr1-moonr1)
24|    a1 = ras1 - (bb1*cs(dcm1)\
25|                *(ram1-ras1))/cs(dcs1)
26|    dc1 = dcs1 - bb1*(dcm1 - dcs1)
27|    sin_d1 = sn(dc1)
28|    cos_d1 = cs(dc1)
29|    x1 = sunr1*cs(dcs1)*sn(ras1-a1)
30|    y1 = sunr1*(sn(dcs1)*cos_d1 \
31|            - cs(dcs1)*sin_d1*cs(ras1-a1))
32|    z11 = moonr1*(sn(dcm1)*sin_d1 \
```

```
33|                    + cs(dcm1)*cos_d1*cs(ram1-a1))
34|     sinf11 = (R+K)/(sunr1*(1-b1))
35|     sinf21 = (R-K)/(sunr1*(1-b1))
36|     f11 = asn(sinf11)
37|     f21 = asn(sinf21)
38|     l11 = z11*tn(f11) + K/cs(f11)
39|     l21 = z11*tn(f21) - K/cs(f21)
40|     tanf11 = tn(f11)
41|     tanf21 = tn(f21)
42|     GST1 = Obl_Nut_GST(d1 - deltad)[2]
43|     mu1 = rev(GST1 - a1)
44|     h1 = mu1 - glong
45|     sin_h1 = sn(h1)
46|     cos_h1 = cs(h1)
47|     xi1 = rocoso* sin_h1
48|     eta1 = rosino*cos_d1 \
49|             - rocoso*cos_h1*sin_d1
50|     zeta1 = rosino*sin_d1 \
51|             + rocoso*cos_h1*cos_d1
52|     #Values at T2
53|     ras2,dcs2,sunr2 = SunValues(d2)
54|     ram2,dcm2,moonr2 = MoonValues(d2)
55|     b2 = moonr2/sunr2
56|     bb2 = moonr2/(sunr2-moonr2)
57|     a2 = ras2 - (bb2*cs(dcm2)\
58|             *(ram2-ras2))/cs(dcs2)
59|     dc2 = dcs2 - bb2*(dcm2 - dcs2)
60|     sin_d2 = sn(dc2)
61|     cos_d2 = cs(dc2)
62|     x2 = sunr2*cs(dcs2)*sn(ras2-a2)
63|     y2 = sunr2*(sn(dcs2)*cos_d2 \
64|         - cs(dcs2)*sin_d2*cs(ras2-a2))
65|     z12 = moonr2*(sn(dcm2)*sin_d2 \
```

```
66|          + cs(dcm2)*cos_d2*cs(ram2-a2))
67|      sinf12 = (R+K)/(sunr2*(1-b2))
68|      sinf22 = (R-K)/(sunr2*(1-b2))
69|      f12 = asn(sinf12)
70|      f22 = asn(sinf22)
71|      l12 = z11*tn(f12) + K/cs(f12)
72|      l22 = z11*tn(f22) - K/cs(f22)
73|      tanf12 = tn(f12)
74|      tanf22 = tn(f22)
75|      GST2 = Obl_Nut_GST(d2 - deltad)[2]
76|      mu2 = rev(GST2 - a2)
77|      # values derived from those at T1 and T2
78|      xdash = rev(x2 - x1)/td
79|      ydash = (y2 - y1)/td
80|      dmu = rads(rev(mu2-mu1)/td)
81|      ddc = (dc2 - dc1)/td;
82|      dxi = dmu*rocoso*cos_h1
83|      deta = dmu*xi1*sin_d1 - zeta1*ddc
84|      L11 = l11 - zeta1*tanf11
85|      L21 = l21 - zeta1*tanf21
86|      sds = asn(R/(sunr1-zeta1))
87|      sdm = asn(K/(moonr1-zeta1))
88|      U = (x1 - xi1)
89|      V = (y1 - eta1)
90|      A = xdash - dxi
91|      B = ydash - deta
92|      N2 = A*A + B*B
93|      N = sqrt(N2)
94|      num = x1*xdash +y1*ydash
95|      den = xdash*xdash+ydash*ydash
96|      ATmid = T1 - num/den
```

## 6.3 Function MidEclipse(ATmid)

This function takes ATmid (Approximate Time of Mideclipse) as argument and returns Tmid (Exact Time of Mideclipse).

```
 1|def MidEclipse(ATmid):
 2|    tmp = 0.0
 3|    caltdq(ATmid)
 4|    tx = ATmid
 5|    while abs(tmp) > 0.00000001:
 6|        tmp = (A*U + B*V)/N2
 7|        tx = tx - tmp
 8|        caltdq(tx)
 9|    Tmid = tx
10|    return Tmid
```

## 6.4 Function GetYears( )

This function displays a GUI for the user to enter the years *from* and *to* which it is required to prepare a list of solar eclipses.

```
 1|def GetYears():
 2|    global Entry
 3|    Entry = 0
 4|    year1 ,year2 = 0,0
 5|    Title = "SELECT PERIOD FOR"\
 6|        +"LISTING OF SOLAR ECLIPSES"
 7|    win = tk.Tk()
 8|    win.geometry("700x250+400+250")
 9|    win.resizable(width = False,\
10|                height = False)
11|    win.title(Title)
12|    #Labels
13|    label1 = tk.Label(win,\
```

```
14|                    text = Title,\
15|                    font = 'times 20')
16|    label1.place(x='30',y = '20')
17|    label2 = tk.Label(win,\
18|             text = 'From Year' \
19|             +' '*14 + 'To Year',\
20|               font = 'times 18')
21|    label2.place(x='200',y = '60')
22|    #Entry boxes
23|    Year1_var = tk.StringVar()
24|    Year1_entrybox = tk.Entry(win,\
25|               width = 15, \
26|           textvariable = Year1_var)
27|    Year1_entrybox.place(x = '200',\
28|                    y = '100')
29|    Year1_entrybox.focus()
30|    Year2_var = tk.StringVar()
31|    Year2_entrybox = tk.Entry(win,\
32|               width = 15, \
33|           textvariable = Year2_var)
34|    Year2_entrybox.place(x = '390',\
35|                    y = '100')
36|    def Process():
37|        global yr1,yr2,Entry
38|        yr1 = Year1_var.get()
39|        yr2 = Year2_var.get()
40|        Entry = 1
41|        win.destroy()
42|    def ChkEntry():
43|        warning = "INVALID ENTRIES !"\
44|            + "\nENTER VALID DATA "\
45|            + "AND CLICK SUBMIT"
46|        x1 = Year1_var.get()
```

```
47|            x2 = Year2_var.get()
48|            if x1.isdigit()\
49|              and x2.isdigit()\
50|                and int(x1) < int(x2):
51|                Process()
52|            else:
53|                messagebox.showwarning\
54|                    ("WARNING!", warning)
55|                Year1_var.set("")
56|                Year2_var.set("")
57|                Year1_entrybox.focus()
58|        submit_button = tk.Button(win,\
59|            text = 'Process',\
60|            font = 'Times 14',\
61|                command = ChkEntry)
62|        submit_button.place(x = '300',\
63|                        y = '150')
64|    win.mainloop()
65|    win.quit
66|    if Entry == 0:
67|        sys.exit()
68|    else:
69|        return int(yr1),int(yr2)
```

This function, if a user so desires, can be omitted by just initializing the values of year1 and year2 for simplifying the program. The appearance of GUI displayed by the above function is shown below.

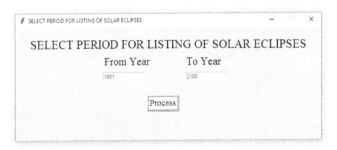

## 6.5 Function SEList1Msg( )

This function does not take any argument. After the list is prepared this function displays a message on the screen showing the number of different types of solar eclipses and total number of solar eclipses during the given period and also informs the name of the file in which the list is saved.

```
 1|def SEList1Msg():
 2|    top = Tk()
 3|    top.geometry("500x200")
 4|    msg1 = "Solar eclipses from year"\
 5|        +"%d"%year1 +"to" +"%d"%year2
 6|    B1 = Button(top, text = msg1,\
 7|                    font = 'times 16')
 8|    B1.place(x = 80,y = 30)
 9|    msg2 = "Total=%d"  %N_T \
10|        +"Annular=%d" %N_A \
11|        +"Partial=%d" %N_P \
12|        +"All=%d"%N_All
13|    B2 = Button(top, text = msg2,\
14|                    font = 'times 16')
15|    B2.place(x = 50,y = 80)
16|    msg3 = "See files 'SE_LIST1.TXT'"
17|    B3 = Button(top, text = msg3,\
18|                    font = 'times 16')
19|    B3.place(x = 150,y = 130)
20|    top.mainloop()
21|    top.quit()
```

The type of the message displayed by this function is shown below.

```
 tk                                    —   □   ×


          Solar eclipses from year 1901 to 2100


       Total=139 Annular=158 Partial=156 All=453


                 See files 'SE_LIST1.TXT'

```

## 6.6 The Main Program

The main program uses all the functions mentions above and finally produces the desired list of solar eclipses.

```
  |#-----------MAIN PROGRAM--------------
 1|def d = 0.0; du0 = 0.0
 2|p_end = 0; tithi_end = 0
 3|Tmid = 0.0; gama = 0.0; L21 = 0.0
 4|rosino = rocoso = longi = 0.0
 5|N_Newmoons = 0
 6|N_T = 0
 7|N_A = 0
 8|N_P = 0
 9|N_All = 0
10|setype = "   "
11|GT = [0.0]*9
12|f1 = open('SE_LIST1.txt','w')
13|year1,year2 = GetYears()
14|for year in range (year1,year2+1):
15|    for month in range(1,13):
16|        n = dim(year)[month]
```

```
17|        for dat in range(1,n+1):
18|            du0 = caldays(dat,month,year)
19|            dt = calDeltaT(dat,month,year)
20|            deltad = dt/86400
21|            d = du0 + deltad
22|            m0 = LonMoon(d-1);
23|            m1 = LonMoon(d);
24|            m2 = LonMoon(d+1);
25|            m3 = LonMoon(d+2);
26|            s0 = LonSun(d-1);
27|            s1 = LonSun(d);
28|            s2 = LonSun(d+1);
29|            s3 = LonSun(d+2);
30|            tt0 = rev(m0-s0)/12.0;
31|            tt1 = rev(m1-s1)/12.0;
32|            tt2 = rev(m2-s2)/12.0;
33|            tt3 = rev(m3-s3)/12.0;
34|            tn1 = (int(tt1)+1);
35|            tn2 = (int(tt2)+1);
36|            tbal = 30.0 - tt1;
37|            k = (tt1-tt0);
38|            if(k<0):
39|                k=k+30;
40|            m = (tt2-tt1)
41|            if(m<0):
42|                m=m+30;
43|            l = (tt3-tt2)
44|            if(l<0):
45|                l=l+30
46|            l_k = (l - k);
47|            h1 = tbal * 24/m;
48|            h2 = h1*(24-h1)*l_k / (m*96.0)
49|            conj = h1+h2;
```

```
50|            if(conj < 0):
51|                conj=+24.0
52|          if tn1 ==30 and tn2==1\
53|          or tn1==29 and tn2==1\
54|          or tn1==30 and tn2==2:
55|              caltdq(conj)
56|              Tmid = MidEclipse(ATmid)
57|              caltdq(Tmid)
58|              gama = sqrt(x1**2 + y1**2)
59|              N_Newmoons +=1
60|              if gama < 1.5467:
61|                  if gama <= 1.0125:
62|                      N_All +=1
63|                      if sdm >= sds:
64|                          setype= "Total"
66|                      if sdm < sds:
67|                          setype= "Annular"
69|                  if gama > 1.0125:
70|                      setype = "Partial"
71|                      N_P += 1
72|                      N_All +=1
73|                  f1.write("%d "%year \
74|          + "%s"%MonthName(month) \
75|          + "%02d"%dat + "%05.2f"%Tmid \
76|          + " %-10s"%setype + "\n")
77|f1.close()
78|print(" SUCCESS!")
79|print(" SOLAR ECLIPSES FROM {:d} TO {:d}"\
80|              .format(year1,year2))
81|print(" Number of Newmoons  {:4d}"\
82|      .format(N_Newmoons))
83|print(" Total Eclipses       {:4d}"\
84|      .format(N_T))
```

```
85|print(" Annular Eclipses      {:4d}"\
86|        .format(N_A))
87|print(" Partial Eclipses      {:4d}"\
88|        .format(N_P))
89|print(" All Eclipses          {:4d}\n\n"\
90|        .format(N_All))
91|print(" See file 'SE_LIST1.TXT' for results")
92|SEList1Msg()
```

The list produced by this program is saved in a file 'SE_LIST1.TXT'. This file will be erased when the program is run again and a new file will be created.

**This list is important** as it is to be used as an input file for other programs given in the next chapters. So after a final list is correctly produced it should also be saved by name **'SE_INFILE.TXT'** as the same name is used in those programs.

# 7. SOLAR ECLIPSES

The program given in this chapter does all the calculations of solar eclipse selected from the list by the user. It produces various outputs like visibility map of the eclipse, video files and picture files mentioned later in this chapter along with a doc file containing the summary of circumstances of the eclipse. You may name this program as 'SOLECL.Py'.

First of all,. it should be noted that the presence of the following two files is essential in the current folder for the execution of this program.

1.  A text file named 'SE_INFILE.TXT' containing the *standard list* of solar eclipses.

    This can be generated by the reader himself by using the program given in Chapter 6. The file should necessarily have the columns as shown in Appendix-3. This file should not contain any other text like headings etc.

2.  A world map of specific dimensions and nature fulfilling the conditions mentioned below.

    i.  This should necessarily be a JPG file with name 'WORLDMAP.JPG'.

    ii. There should be only 3 colors in the map, preferably white color for land and blue color for water and black color for text showing the names of the continents and oceans.

iii. The dimensions of the world map should be (1200×608) pixels with white space of (1200×112) pixels at the top making the total size of the picture (1200×720) pixels.

The program is designed taking into account these properties, hence the map should necessary have them. If the dimensions are not as specified the program may not work properly. Colors can be varied if required. This map is used only in the function of 'VisibilityMap()' and the function itself may be excluded in the beginning if found difficult. *** (*See note at the end of the chapter*)

The following figure shows how the typical world map should be.

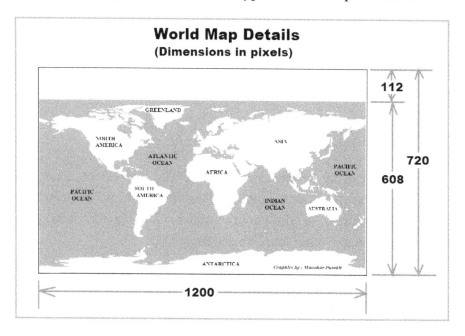

## 7.1 Importing Modules

As usual the modules are imported first.

```
1|from AstroMODULE import *
2|import numpy as np
3|import cv2
4|from cv2 import VideoWriter,\
```

```
 5|          VideoWriter_fourcc
 6|import datetime as dt
 7|import tkinter as tk
 8|from tkinter import *
 9|from tkinter import messagebox
10|import sys
```

## 7.2 Function fprline(n)

This function prints a dashed line in the file that has been opened, of length of n spaces.

```
1|def fprline(n):
2|    f.write("\n"+ "-"*n)
```

## 7.3 Function sp(n)

This function returns a string containing n blank spaces.

```
1|def sp(n):
2|    return " "*n
```

## 7.4 Function fpr3(str,x,y)

This function prints to the open file a string and values of two variables in a line with proper spacing suitable for tabulation.

```
1|def fpr3(str,x,y):
2|    f.write("\n"+"%24s"%str \
3|        + "%16.8f"%x + "%16.8f"%y)
```

## 7.5 Function caltdq(x)

**Function for calculating Time-Dependant-Quantities (TDQ)**

> **This function is the same as given in para 6.2 of the previous chapter**. So it is not reproduced here.

## 7.6 Function IterateTmid( )

This Function, starting from the approximate mid-eclipse-time, calculates the exact time of Mid-Eclipse by iterartion method. It does not take any argument.

```
 1|def IterateTmid():
 2|    global U,V,A,B,N2,Tmid #,MidValue
 3|    caltdq(ATmid)
 4|    tmp = (A*U + B*V)/N2
 5|    tx = ATmid
 6|    while abs(tmp) > 0.00000001:
 7|        tmp = (A*U + B*V)/N2
 8|        tx = tx - tmp
 9|        caltdq(tx)
10|    Tmid = tx
```

## 7.7 Function GEPosition(Tmid)

This function takes Tmid (Time of mideclipse) as argument and finds the position of GE (Greatest Eclipse) in latitude and longitude on the worldmap.

```
 1|def GEPosition(Tmid): #SE_REV
 2|    global x1,y1
 3|    global rsn,rcs,hh
 4|    global gelat, gelong,glong,glat
```

```
 5|    global EWlong,NS,EW
 6|    global Olat,Olong
 7|    caltdq(Tmid)
 8|    gama = sqrt(x1*x1 + y1*y1)
 9|    z2 = 1.0 - (x1*x1 + y1*y1)
10|    if(z2>0):
11|        z = sqrt(z2)
12|    else:
13|        x1 = x1/gama
14|        y1 = y1/gama
15|        z = 0
16|    rsn = y1*cos_d1 + z*sin_d1
17|    hh = atn2(x1, z*cos_d1 - y1*sin_d1)
18|    if abs(rsn/ff)<= 1.0:
19|        rcs = sqrt(1 - rsn*rsn/ff2)
20|        rcs2=cs(asn(rsn/ff))
21|        q2 = asn(rsn/ff)
22|    if abs(rsn/ff)>1.0:
23|        rcs = sqrt(1 - rsn*rsn)
24|        rcs2=cs(asn(rsn))
25|        q2 = asn(rsn)
26|    q =atn2(rsn/ff,rcs)
27|    rsn0 = rsn
28|    rcs0 = rcs
29|    xi0 = x1
30|    eta0 = y1
31|    zeta0 = z
32|    h0 = hh
33|    glat = atn(tn(q)/ff2)
34|    glong = rev(mu1-hh)
35|    if glong > 180.0:
36|        Olong = 360-glong
37|        EW = 'E'
```

```
38|      else:
39|          Olong = glong
40|          EW='W'
41|      if glat < 0:
42|          Olat = -glat; NS = 'S'
43|      else:
44|          Olat = glat; NS = 'N'
```

## 7.8 Function Magnitude( )

This function does not take any argument and using the previously calculated values in memory returns three values namely msr (Moon-Sun-Ratio), magn (Magnitude of the eclipse) and Obs (Obscurity factor) at mid-eclipse.

```
 1|def Magnitude():
 2|    global magn,msr,Obs
 3|    caltdq(CT[2])
 4|    msr = sdm/sds
 5|    dist = sqrt(u[2]**2 +v[2]**2)*sdf
 6|    gama = sqrt(x1*x1 + y1*y1)
 7|    if gama <= 1.0125: #Total or Annular
 8|        magn = msr
 9|        Obs = magn*magn
11|        m = 2*acs((sds*sds + dist*dist\
12|                - sdm*sdm)/(2*sds*dist))
13|        s = 2*acs((sdm*sdm + dist*dist \
14|            - sds*sds)/(2*sdm*dist))
15|        magn = (sds+sdm-dist)/(2*sds)
16|        Olap = 0.5*sdm*sdm*(rads(m) -sn(m))\
17|            + 0.5*sds*sds*(rads(s)-sn(s))
18|        SunArea = pi*sds*sds
19|        Obs = Olap/SunArea
20|    return msr,magn,Obs
```

## 7.9 Function ApproxTimes( )

This function does not take any argument and calculates the Approximate Contact Times at a particular place of observation and also defines a list containing these contact Times.

```
 1|def ApproxTimes():
 2|    global contact,AT
 3|    global AT1,AT2,AT3,AT4,ATm
 4|    global U,V,A,B,N,N2,Tmid,IC23
 5|    AT1 = AT2 = AT3 = AT4 = ATm = 0.0
 6|    tmp1 = tmp2 = 0.0
 7|    contact = [0,0,1,0,0]
 8|    caltdq(Tmid)
 9|    dtm = -(A*U+B*V)/N2
10|    ATm = Tmid + dtm
11|    val1 = (A*V-B*U)/(N*L11)
12|    if val1*val1 < 1.0:
13|        contact[0] = contact[4] = 1
14|        tmp1 = sqrt(1-val1*val1)*L11/N
15|        AT1 = Tmid - tmp1
16|        AT4 = Tmid + tmp1
17|    val2 = (A*V-B*U)/(N*L21)
18|    if val2*val2 < 1.0:
19|        tmp2 = sqrt(1-val2*val2)*L21/N
20|        contact[1] = 1
21|        contact[3] = 1
22|        AT2 = Tmid - tmp2
23|        AT3 = Tmid + tmp2
24|    AT = AT1,AT2,ATm,AT3,AT4
```

## 7.10 Function calT1( )

This function does not take any argument and calculates the exact time of 1$^{st}$ contact CT1, and position-coordinates U1 and V1 at the time of 1$^{st}$ contact. No values are returned.

```
 1|def calT1():
 2|    global CT1,U1,V1
 3|    tx = AT1
 4|    caltdq(tx)
 5|    tmp =  (A*V-B*U)/(N*L11)
 6|    if tmp*tmp < 1.0:
 7|        tmp = -sqrt(1-tmp*tmp)*L11/N
 8|        tmp = (A*U+B*V)/N2 - tmp
 9|        while abs(tmp)> .00000001:
10|            tx-=tmp;
11|            caltdq(tx);
12|            tmp = (A*V - B*U)/N/L11
13|            if tmp*tmp < 1.0:
14|                tmp =-sqrt(1 -tmp*tmp)*L11/N
15|                tmp = (A*U + B*V)/N2 - tmp
16|            else:
17|                break
18|    if tx < 0.0:
19|        tx = tx + 24.00
20|    CT1 = tx
21|    U1 = U
22|    V1 = V
```

## 7.11 Function calT2( )

This function does not take any argument and calculates the exact time of 2$^{st}$ contact CT2, and position-coordinates U2 and V2 at the time of 2$^{st}$ contact. No values are returned.

```
 1|def calT2():
 2|    global CT2,U2,V2
 3|    tx = AT2
 4|    caltdq(AT2)
 5|    tmp =  (A*V-B*U)/(N*L21)
 6|    if tmp*tmp < 1.0:
 7|        tmp = -sqrt(1-tmp*tmp)*L21/N
 8|        tmp = (A*U+B*V)/N2 - tmp*abs(L21)/L21
 9|        while abs(tmp)> .00000001:
10|            tx-=tmp;
11|            caltdq(tx);
12|            tmp = (A*V - B*U)/N/L21
13|            if tmp*tmp < 1.0:
14|                tmp = -sqrt(1 -tmp*tmp)*L21/N
15|                tmp = (A*U + B*V)/N2 \
16|                    - tmp*abs(L21)/L21
17|            else:
18|                break
19|    CT2 = tx
20|    U2 = U
21|    V2 = V
```

## 7.12 Function calT3( )

This function does not take any argument and calculates the exact time of $3^{rd}$ contact CT3, and position-coordinates U3 and V3 at the time of $3^{rd}$ contact. No values are returned.

```
 1|def calT3():
 2|    global CT3,U3,V3
 3|    tx = AT3
 4|    caltdq(AT3)
 5|    tmp =  (A*V-B*U)/(N*L21)
```

```
 6|     if tmp*tmp < 1.0:
 7|         tmp = sqrt(1-tmp*tmp)*L21/N
 8|         tmp = (A*U+B*V)/N2 - tmp*abs(L21)/L21
 9|         while abs(tmp)> .00000001:
10|             tx-=tmp
11|             caltdq(tx)
12|             tmp = (A*V - B*U)/N/L21
13|             if tmp*tmp < 1.0:
14|                 tmp = sqrt(1 - tmp*tmp)*L21/N
15|                 tmp = (A*U + B*V)/N2 \
16|                     - tmp*abs(L21)/L21
17|             else:
18|                 break
19|     CT3 = tx
20|     U3 = U
21|     V3 = V
```

## 7.13 Function calT4( )

This function does not take any argument and calculates the exact time of 4th contact CT2, and position-coordinates U4 and V4 at the time of 4th contact. No values are returned.

```
 1|def calT4():
 2|     global CT4,U4,V4,sdf
 3|     tx = AT4
 4|     caltdq(AT4)
 5|     tmp =  (A*V-B*U)/(N*L11)
 6|     if tmp*tmp < 1.0:
 7|         tmp = sqrt(1-tmp*tmp)*L11/N
 8|         tmp = (A*U+B*V)/N2 - tmp
 9|         while abs(tmp)> .00000001:
10|             tx-=tmp
```

```
11|                caltdq(tx)
12|                tmp = (A*V - B*U)/N/L11
13|                if tmp*tmp < 1.0:
14|                     tmp = sqrt(1 - tmp*tmp)*L11/N
15|                     tmp = (A*U + B*V)/N2 - tmp
16|                else:
17|                     break
18|        CT4 = tx
19|        U4 = U
20|        V4 = V
21|        sdf = (sds+sdm)/sqrt(U4*U4+V4*V4)
```

## 7.14 Function calCT( )

This function does not take any argument and combining all the functions of exact contact times given earlier, produces lists of contact times CT, and lists u and v of position-coordinates. No values are returned.

```
 1|def CalCT():
 2|    global CT,u,v
 3|    caltdq(Tmid)
 4|    ApproxTimes()
 5|    AT = (AT1,AT2,ATm,AT3,AT4)
 6|    Um = U
 7|    Vm = V
 8|    calT1()
 9|    calT2()
10|    calT3()
11|    calT4()
12|    CT = (CT1,CT2,Tmid,CT3,CT4)
13|    u = (U1,U2,Um,U3,U4)
14|    v = (V1,V2,Vm,V3,V4)
```

## 7.15 Function SummaryTable1( )

This function does not take any argument and writes to the file 'SE_SUMMARY.TXT', detailed summary of the circumstances of the eclipse at GE. No values are returned.

```
 1|def SummaryTable1():
 2|    global Header1
 3|    PUMValues()
 4|    Header1 = "Global Circumstances: GE at"\
 5|        + "Lat:" + "%5.2f"%Olat + "%s"%NS\
 6|        + "Long:"+ "%6.2f"%Olong + "%s"%EW
 7|    strct = ("T1","T2","Tm","T3","T4")
 8|    f.write("\n"+ SE_Title.upper())
 9|    f.write("\n\nGlobal Circumstances")
10|    f.write("\n"+ MidValue)
11|    f.write("\n"+ PValues)
12|    f.write("\n"+ UValues)
```

## 7.16 Function SummaryTable2( )

This function does not take any argument and writes to the file 'SE_SUMMARY.TXT', detailed summary of the circumstances of the eclipse at a place chosen by the user. No values are returned.

```
 1|def SummaryTable2():
 2|    global px,Heading
 3|    Heading = "Circumstances at" \
 4|        + "%s"%Place\
 5|        + "Lat:" + "%5.2f"%Olat + "%s"%NS \
 6|        + "Long:"+ "%6.2f"%Olong + "%s"%EW
 7|    f.write("\n\n" + Heading)
 8|    fprline(58)
 9|    f.write("\nContact    UT    Alt    Az")
```

```
10|    f.write("    p      q      v    O'clock")
11|    fprline(58)
12|    for i in range(5):
13|        caltdq(CT[i])
14|        p = rev(atn2(u[i],v[i]))
15|        ra = ras1
16|        ha = rev(GST1 - ra - glong)
17|        dc = dcs1
18|        sinlat = sn(glat)
19|        coslat = cs(glat)
20|        sindc  = sn(dc)
21|        cosdc  = cs(dc)
22|        tandc = sindc/cosdc
23|        sinha = sn(ha)
24|        cosha = cs(ha)
25|        az = rev(atn2(-sinha,\
26|                 tandc*coslat -cosha*sinlat))
27|        alt = asn(sinlat*sindc\
28|                   + coslat*cosdc*cosha)
29|        q = rev(asn(coslat*sinha/cs(alt)))
30|        if eta1< 0:
31|            q = rev(180-q)
32|        vv = rev(p-q)
33|        ocp = (360 - vv)/30
34|        if ocp < 1:
35|            ocp = ocp+12
36|        px[i] = rev(vv+90)
37|        if contact[i] == 1:
38|            text1 = "\n"\
39|              + "%3s"    %TNumber[i]\
40|              + htohm(CT[i]) + "%7.2f"%alt \
41|              + "%7.2f"%az + "%7.2f"%p \
```

```
42|                    + "%7.2f"%q  + "%7.2f"%vv\
43|                    + "%7.2f"%ocp
44|              f.write(text1)
45|        fprline(58)
46|        Magnitude()
47|        f.write("\nValuse at Mid-eclipse:")
48|        fprline(58)
49|        f.write("\n"+sp(6)+"Item"+sp(25)\
50|              + "SUN" + sp(12) + "Moon")
51|        fprline(58)
52|        fpr3("Geocentric Distance (ER)"\
53|                          ,sunr1,moonr1 )
54|        fpr3("Semidiameter (deg)",sds,sdm)
55|        fpr3("Right Ascension (deg)",ras1,ram1)
56|        fpr3("Declination (deg)",dcs1,dcm1)
57|        fprline(58)
58|        f.write("\n  Moon-Sun Ratio   = " \
59|                          + "%6.4f"%msr)
60|        f.write("\n  Magnitude        = " \
61|                          + "%6.4f"%magn)
62|        f.write("\n  Obscurity        = " \
63|                          + "%6.4f"%Obs)
64|        fprline(58)
65|        f.write("\n\n")
```

The type of information saved in the file 'SE_SUMMARY.TXT' produced by the above two functions is shown in the next page.

ANNULAR SOLAR ECLIPSE - THURSDAY, DECEMBER 26, 2019

Global Circumstances
  Tmid = 05:18
  P1=02:30 P2=05:01 P3=05:35 P4=08:06
  U1=03:35 U2=03:38 U3=06:58 U4=07:01

Circumstances at GE Lat: 1.00N Long:102.14E

| Contact | UT | Alt | Az | p | q | v | O'clock |
|---|---|---|---|---|---|---|---|
| T1 | 03:23 | 54.09 | 134.48 | 282.23 | 309.00 | 333.23 | 12.89 |
| T2 | 05:16 | 65.60 | 182.54 | 277.07 | 2.77 | 274.30 | 2.86 |
| TMid | 05:18 | 65.58 | 183.55 | 4.02 | 3.87 | 0.16 | 11.99 |
| T3 | 05:20 | 65.55 | 184.55 | 96.88 | 4.96 | 91.92 | 6.94 |
| T4 | 07:14 | 51.53 | 228.72 | 91.13 | 54.94 | 36.19 | 10.79 |

Values at Mid-eclipse:

| Item | SUN | Moon |
|---|---|---|
| Geocentric Distance (ER) | 23067.68269842 | 60.24375110 |
| Semidiameter (deg) | 0.27105215 | 0.26300118 |
| Right Ascension (deg) | 274.49087546 | 274.51959874 |
| Declination (deg) | -23.37191640 | -22.98076023 |

  Moon-Sun Ratio = 0.9703
  Magnitude      = 0.9703
  Obscurity      = 0.9415

Circumstances at MUMBAI Lat:18.83N Long: 72.97E

| Contact | UT | Alt | Az | p | q | v | O'clock |
|---|---|---|---|---|---|---|---|
| T1 | 03:29 | 40.95 | 148.32 | 254.24 | 327.22 | 287.02 | 2.43 |
| TMid | 05:12 | 47.79 | 180.04 | 186.43 | 0.04 | 186.39 | 5.79 |
| T4 | 06:55 | 40.80 | 212.00 | 119.76 | 33.11 | 86.65 | 9.11 |

Values at Mid-eclipse:

| Item | SUN | Moon |
|---|---|---|
| Geocentric Distance (ER) | 23067.68736727 | 60.24110354 |
| Semidiameter (deg) | 0.27105011 | 0.26226697 |
| Right Ascension (deg) | 274.48604269 | 274.45706843 |
| Declination (deg) | -23.37205454 | -22.97725459 |

  Moon-Sun Ratio = 0.9676
  Magnitude      = 0.5321
  Obscurity      = 0.4245

## 7.17 Function SelectSE( )

This function displays a scrolling list of lunar eclipses on the screen for the user to select one of them and click to process the same.

```
 1| def SelectSE():
 2|     root = Tk()
 3|     root.title("Solar Eclipses")
 4|     frame = Frame(root)
 5|     scroll= Scrollbar(frame)
 6|     scroll.pack(side = RIGHT,fill = Y)
 7|     listbox = Listbox(frame,height = 15,\
 8|         width = 30,font = "Consolas 16",\
 9|                     bg = "light yellow",\
10|                 yscrollcommand=scroll.set)
11|     listbox.pack(side = LEFT)
12|     def BasicData():
13|         global SE,date,month,year,conj,setype
14|         secl = listbox.curselection()
15|         for item in secl:
16|             SE=(listbox.get(item)).split(" ")
17|             year = int(SE[0])
18|             month = MonthNum(SE[1])
19|             date = int(SE[2])
20|             conj = float(SE[3])
21|             setype = SE[4]
22|             root.destroy()
23|     lbltxt = "List of Solar Eclipses"\
24|             + "\n of 20th and 21st Century"
25|     lbl = Label(root, text = lbltxt,\
26|             font = "times 18",\
27|                 bg = "light yellow")
28|     lbl.pack(side = TOP)
29|     btn = Button(root,text="Click Process",\
```

```
30|                    bg = "light yellow",\
31|                    command = BasicData)
32|     btn.pack(side = RIGHT)
33|     with open("SE_INFILE.TXT",'r') as f:
34|         for line in f:
35|             listbox.insert(END,line)
36|     scroll.config(command=listbox.yview)
37|     frame.pack()
38|     root.geometry("600x500")
39|     root.mainloop()
```

The scrolling list of solar eclipses produced by this function is shown below. The user has to make his choice and click on 'Click to Process' button to start processing.

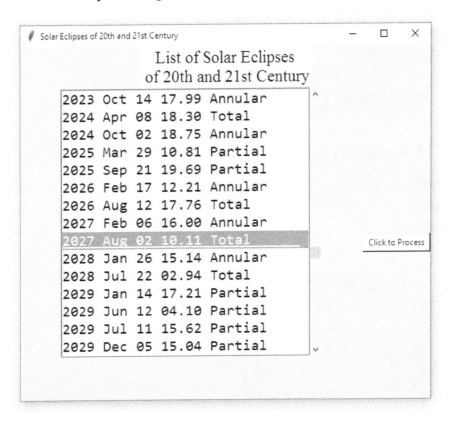

## 7.18 Function grx(lon)

This function takes longitude of a place as argument and returns the equivalent x coordinate of the point in pixels for plotting on the world map present on the screen. This function is used as a sub-function in the function VisibilityMap().

```
 1|def grx(lon):
 2|    xp = 0
 3|    global Mapx0
 4|    if lon > 180 :
 5|        lon = 360 - lon
 6|        ew = 'E'
 7|    else:
 8|        ew = 'W'
 9|    if ew == 'E':
10|        xp = Mapx0 + lon*3.33333
11|    else:
12|        xp = Mapx0 - lon*3.33333
13|    return int(xp)
```

## 7.19 Function gry(lon)

This function takes latitude of a place as argument and returns the equivalent y coordinate of the point in pixels for plotting on the world map present on the screen. This function is used as a sub-function in the function VisibilityMap().

```
 1|def gry(lat):
 2|    yp = 0
 3|    global Mapy0
 4|    if lat < 0 :
 5|        lat = -lat
 6|        ns = 'S'
```

```
 7|     else:
 8|         ns = 'N'
 9|     if ns == 'N':
10|         yp = Mapy0 - lat*3.375
11|     else:
12|         yp = Mapy0 + lat*3.375
13|     return int(yp)
```

## 7.20 Function calGlobalTimes( )

The eclipse starts at one location and ends at another. Global times are actual times corresponding to the following Nine events when the eclipse occurs. These times do not refer to a specific location but indicate the times of different stages of the eclipse on a global scale, each referring to a different location. It is not necessary that all these events are present in a particular eclipse.

1. Penumbra of Moon's shadow first touches the earth externally at a point. That is the first location to see the partial eclipse begin. This time is denoted by P1

2. Umbra of Moon's shadow first touches the earth externally at a point. That is the first location to see the full eclipse begin. This time is denoted by U1.

3. Umbra of Moon's shadow first touches the earth internally at a point. This time is denoted by U2.

4. Penumbra of Moon's shadow first touches the earth internally at a point. This time is denoted by P2.

5. Maximum Eclipse. A point on earth when the Moon's shadow is nearest to the center of the earth. This time is denoted by Tmid.

6. Penumbra of Moon's shadow lastly touches the earth internally at a point. This time is denoted by P3.

7. Umbra of Moon's shadow lastly touches the earth internally at a point. This time is denoted by U3.

8. Umbra of Moon's shadow lastly touches the earth externally at a point. That is the last location to see the full eclipse end. This time is denoted by U4.

9. Penumbra of Moon's shadow first touches the earth externally at a point. That is the last location to see the partial eclipse end. This time is denoted by P4

This function calculates all the global times 1 to 9 described above and it also it calculates the graphic coordinates of all these points GTx[9] and GTy[9] to be plotted on the fundamental plane on the screen in the function PlotGT( )

```
1|def CalGlobalTimes():
2|    cc = [0.0]*9
3|    caltdq(Tmid)
4|    xmid = int(x0 + x1*scale)
5|    ymid = int(y0 - y1*scale)
6|    GTx[4] = xmid; GTy[4] = ymid
7|    GM2 = x1*x1 + y1*y1
8|    L = [1+L11,1+L21,1-L21,1-L11]
9|    m = ydash/xdash
10|   ang = atn(m)
11|   for i in range(4):
12|       OP = L[i]
13|       OP2 = OP*OP
14|       if OP2 >=GM2:
15|           dif = sqrt(OP2 - GM2)
16|           GC[i] = 1
17|       else:
18|           GC[i] = 0
```

```
19|          xdif = dif*cs(ang)
20|          ydif = dif*sn(ang)
21|          xs = x1 - xdif
22|          ys = y1 - ydif
23|          cc[i] = sqrt(xs*xs + ys*ys)
24|          GT[i] = Tmid - xdif/xdash
25|          GT[8-i] = Tmid + xdif/xdash
26|          GTx[i] = int(x0 + xs*scale)
27|          GTy[i] = int(y0 - ys*scale)
28|          xs = x1 + xdif
29|          ys = y1 + ydif
30|          GTx[8-i] = int(x0 + xs*scale)
31|          GTy[8-i] = int(y0 - ys*scale)
32|    if setype == 'Total': #NEW
33|          GT[1],GT[2] = swap (GT[1],GT[2])
34|          GT[6],GT[7] = swap (GT[6],GT[7])
```

## 7.21 Function VisibilityMap( )

This function plots the Visibility Map showing the path of Moon's shadow on the world map highlighting the zones of partial and full eclipses with different colors.

It firstly loads the world map file 'WORLDMAP.JPG' on the screen. And then plots the visibility map over it. As mentioned before the required file should be present in the current directory. The resulting final map is saved in the current directory by name 'SE_MAP.JPG'.

```
1|def VisibilityMap():
2|    global t0,Mapx0,Mapy0
3|    global x1,y1
4|    Mapx0 = 600; Mapy0 = 416
5|    clrPW = (0, 0,255)
```

```
 6|      clrUW = (0,200,250)
 7|      worldmap = cv2.imread("WORLDMAP.JPG")
 8|      title1 = "Visibility Map of" + SE_Title
 9|      font = cv2.FONT_HERSHEY_COMPLEX
10|      worldmap = cv2.putText(worldmap,\
11|              title1,(200,40),\
12|              font,0.7,(0,0,0),1,cv2.LINE_AA)
13|      worldmap = cv2.putText(worldmap,\
14|              Header1,(300,70),\
15|              font,0.7,(0,0,0),1,cv2.LINE_AA)
16|      output = worldmap.copy()
17|      alpha = 0.4
18|      overlay = worldmap.copy()
19|      int1 = 0.001; int2 = 0.5; # Best but slow
20|      #int1 = 0.05; int2 = 0.5 #Quik but rough
21|      xpc = 0; ypc = 0
22|      for Ti in np.arange(GT[0],GT[8],int1):
23|          caltdq(Ti)
24|          xm = x1
25|          ym = y1
26|          ang2 = asn(L21/L11)
27|          for angle in np.arange(0,360,int2):
28|              x1 = xm + L11*cs(angle)
29|              y1 = ym + L11*sn(angle)
30|              z2 = 1 -x1*x1-y1*y1
31|              if z2 > 0:
32|                  z = sqrt(z2)
33|              else:
34|                  continue
35|              rsn = y1*cos_d1 + z* sin_d1
36|              hh = atn2(x1,z*cos_d1 - y1*sin_d1)
37|              rcs = sqrt(1 - rsn*rsn)
38|              q = atn2(rsn/ff,rcs)
```

```
39|                lat = atn(tn(q)/ff2)
40|                lon = rev(mu1-hh)
41|                x = grx(lon)
42|                y = gry(lat)
43|                if x > 1199 or y > 719:
44|                    continue
45|                overlay[y,x]= clrPW
46|        for Ti in np.arange(GT[0],GT[8],int1):
47|            caltdq(Ti)
48|            xm = x1
49|            ym = y1
50|            for angle in np.arange(0,360,int2):
51|                x1 = xm + L21*cs(angle)
52|                y1 = ym + L21*sn(angle)
53|                z2 = 1 -x1*x1-y1*y1
54|                if z2 > 0:
55|                    z = sqrt(z2)
56|                else:
57|                    continue
58|                rsn = y1*cos_d1 + z* sin_d1
59|                hh = atn2(x1,z*cos_d1 - y1*sin_d1)
60|                rcs = sqrt(1 - rsn*rsn)
61|                q = atn2(rsn/ff,rcs)
62|                lat = atn(tn(q)/ff2)
63|                lon = rev(mu1-hh)
64|                x = grx(lon)
65|                y = gry(lat)
66|                if x > 1199 or y > 719:
67|                    continue
68|                overlay[y,x]=clrUW #Clr4
69|        xpc = grx(glong)
70|        ypc = gry(glat)
71|        overlay = cv2.circle(overlay,\
```

```
72|            (xpc,ypc), 10, (255,0,0), -1)
73|      overlay = cv2.circle(overlay,\
74|            (xpc,ypc), 5, (250,250,0), -1)
75|      overlay = cv2.line(overlay,(0,Mapy0),\
76|              (1200,Mapy0),(255,255,0),1)
77|      overlay = cv2.line(overlay,(600,112),\
78|              (600,720),(255,255,0),1)
79|      cv2.addWeighted(overlay, alpha,output,\
80|              1 - alpha, 0, output)
81|      cv2.imshow("Visibility Map",output)
82|      cv2.imwrite("SE_MAP.JPG", output)
83|      cv2.waitKey(0)
84|      cv2.destroyAllWindows()
```

This function calculates the position of shadow at minute intervals of time and plots the points of the shadow pixel by pixel onto the map. Shorter the intervals taken better is the result but longer the time it takes for execution.

Two intervals are involved in this function, int1 (Time interval in hours) and int2 (interval in degrees). If we take int1 = 0.05 and int2 = 0.5, it takes about 90 seconds to plot the map. The pixels are thinly populated. Initially it is advisable to adopt these intervals for trial performances and when the program works satisfactorily, closer intervals may be used to get better results.

When the intervals int1=0.001 and int2 = 0.5 are adopted better plot is obtained and suitable for getting prints. However the process becomes slow and takes about 6 minutes for plotting the map.The maps obtained by both these methods are shown below.

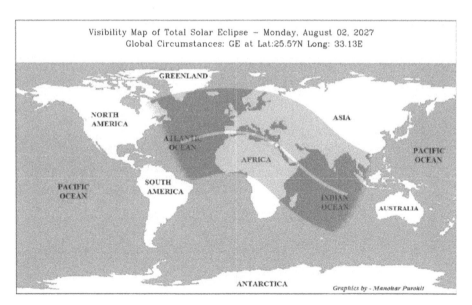

Visibility map plotted with int1 = 0.05 and int2 = 0.5

Visibility map plotted with int1 = 0.001 and int2 = 0.5

## 7.22 Function PUMValues( )

This function prepares the text strings of timings of global timings of penumbral P1,P2,P3,P4, umbral contacts U1,U2,U3,U4 and MidValue for printing them on the background frames of pictures and videos.

```
 1|def PUMValues():
 2|    global MidValue, PValues,UValues
 3|    if GC[3] == 1:
 4|        PValues = "P1="+ "%s"%htohm(GT[0])\
 5|                + "P2="+ "%s"%htohm(GT[3])\
 6|                + "P3="+ "%s"%htohm(GT[5])\
 7|                + "P4="+ "%s"%htohm(GT[8])
 8|    else:
 9|        PValues = "P1="+ "%s"%htohm(GT[0])\
10|                + "P4="+ "%s"%htohm(GT[8])
11|    if GC[2] == 1:
12|        UValues = "U1="+ "%s"%htohm(GT[1])\
13|                + "U2="+ "%s"%htohm(GT[2])\
14|                + "U3="+ "%s"%htohm(GT[6])\
15|                + "U4="+ "%s"%htohm(GT[7])
16|    if GC[2] == 0 and GC[1] == 1:
17|        PValues = "U1="+ "%s"%htohm(GT[1])\
18|                + "U2="+ "%s"%htohm(GT[7])
19|    if GC[1] == 0:
20|        UValues = "%45s"%"No Umbral contacts"
21|    MidValue = "Tmid = " + "%s"%htohm(GT[4])
```

## 7.23 Function SEframe( )

This function plots the background frame on the screen on which other images are to be added later by other functions for videos or pictures.

```
 1|def SEframe():
 2|    global img
 3|    # Create a background image
 4|    img = np.zeros((720,1200,3),\
 5|                   np.uint8)
 6|    img[:] = clrB #frame color
 7|    font = cv2.FONT_HERSHEY_COMPLEX
 8|    EarthClr = (0,180,255)
 9|    sedat = strdat(date,month,year)
10|    title1 = SE_Title = setype\
11|              +"Solar Eclipse -"+ sedat
12|    title2a = "Path of Moon's shadow over"\
13|          + "the Earth's fundamental plane"
14|    txtEarth = "EARTH"
15|    img = cv2.circle(img,\
16|              (x0,y0), scale, EarthClr,-1)
17|    img = cv2.putText(img,txtEarth,\
18|              (x0-150,y0+20),font,2.8,\
19|               (150,150,250),1,cv2.LINE_AA)
20|    PUMValues()
21|    img = cv2.putText(img,\
22|              SE_Title,(300,30),\
23|              font,0.7,(0,0,0),1,cv2.LINE_AA)
24|    img = cv2.putText(img,\
25|              Header1,(300,60),\
26|              font,0.7,(0,0,0),1,cv2.LINE_AA)
27|    img = cv2.putText(img,\
28|              PValues,(10,90),\
29|              font,0.6,(0,0,0),1,cv2.LINE_AA)
30|    img = cv2.putText(img,\
31|              MidValue,(550,90),\
32|              font,0.6,(0,0,0),1,cv2.LINE_AA)
```

```
33|      img = cv2.putText(img,\
34|            UValues,(750,90),\
35|            font,0.6,(0,0,0),1,cv2.LINE_AA)
36|      img = cv2.putText(img,\
37|            title2a,(150,120),\
38|            font,0.8,(0,0,0),1,cv2.LINE_AA)
```

## 7.24 Function SEframe2( )

This function plots a different background frame on the screen on which other images are to be added later by other functions for videos or pictures.

```
 1|def SEframe2():
 2|    global img,font,CT
 3|    # Create a background image
 4|    img = np.zeros((720,1200,3), np.uint8)
 5|    img[:] = [250,200,150] #frame color
 6|    font = cv2.FONT_HERSHEY_COMPLEX
 7|    title1 = SE_Title
 8|    magn = Magnitude()[1]
 9|    title2a = "Magn={:6.4f}".format(magn)
10|    title3 = "Path of Moon's disc over Sun"
11|    img = cv2.putText(img,\
12|          SE_Title,(100,30),font,1.2,\
13|          (0,0,0),1,cv2.LINE_AA)
14|    img = cv2.putText(img,\
15|          Heading,(100,65), font,0.8,\
16|          (0,0,0),1,cv2.LINE_AA)
17|    img = cv2.putText(img,\
18|          title2a,(900,65),font,0.8,\
19|          (0,0,0),1,cv2.LINE_AA)
20|    img = cv2.putText(img,\
```

```
21|            title3,(350,100),font,0.8,\
22|            (0,0,0),1,cv2.LINE_AA)
23|    img = cv2.putText(img,\
24|            strCT(),(100,135),font,0.6,\
25|            (0,0,0),1,cv2.LINE_AA)
```

## 7.25 Function AnimateMoonPath( )

This functions simulates the motion of Moon's disc over the sun during the eclipse from 1st contact to the last contact and saves the video as 'SE_VID2.MP4'

```
 1|def AnimateMoonPath(): # Saving as video
 2|    global img
 3|    MoonClr = (0,100,0)
 4|    rM = int(sdm*scale2)
 5|    SunClr = (255,255,255)
 6|    rS = int(sds*scale2)
 7|    FPS = 60
 8|    fourcc = VideoWriter_fourcc(*'MP4v')
 9|    cap = cv2.VideoCapture()
10|    if Place == "GE":
11|        vfile2 = 'SE_VID2.MP4'
12|    else:
13|        vfile2 = 'SE_VID3.MP4'
14|    video = VideoWriter(vfile2,\
15|                    fourcc, float(FPS),\
16|                    (1200, 720))
17|    SEframe2()
18|    img = cv2.circle(img,\
19|                (x0,y0), rS, SunClr,-1)
20|    T1 = CT[0]; T2 = CT[4]
```

```
21|     for Ti in np.arange(T1,T2,0.01):
22|         caltdq(Ti)
23|         p = rev(atn2(U,V))
24|         ra = ras1
25|         ha = rev(GST1 - ra - glong)
26|         dc = dcs1
27|         sinlat = sn(glat)
28|         coslat = cs(glat)
29|         sindc  = sn(dc)
30|         cosdc  = cs(dc)
31|         tandc = sindc/cosdc
32|         sinha = sn(ha)
33|         cosha = cs(ha)
34|         az = rev(atn2(-sinha,tandc*coslat\
35|                         - cosha*sinlat))
36|         alt = asn(sinlat*sindc \
37|                     + coslat*cosdc*cosha)
38|         q = (asn(coslat*sinha/cs(alt)))
39|         if eta1< 0:
40|             q =(180-q)
41|         px = rev(p-q+90)
42|         gm = sqrt(U*U+V*V)
43|         xm = int(x0 + gm*cs(px)*scale2*sdf)
44|         ym = int(y0 - gm*sn(px)*scale2*sdf)
45|         SEframe2()
46|         img = cv2.circle(img,\
47|                     (x0,y0), rS, SunClr,-1)
48|         img = cv2.circle(img,\
49|                     (xm,ym), rM, MoonClr,-1)
50|         #display Time
51|         img = cv2.rectangle(img,(970,200),\
52|                     (1150,270),(255,255,255),-1)
```

```
53|          img = cv2.putText(img,"Time in UT",\
54|              (1000,230),font,0.6,(0,0,0),1,\
55|                            cv2.LINE_AA)
56|        hmsTi = hms(Ti)
57|        img = cv2.putText(img,hms(Ti),\
58|              (1000,250),font,0.6,\
59|              (0,0,0),1,cv2.LINE_AA)
60|        #display Az and Alt
61|        img = cv2.rectangle(img,\
62|              (970,300),(1150,390),\
63|              (255,255,255),-1)
64|        img = cv2.putText(img,\
65|              "SUN POSITION",(990,330),\
66|               font,0.6,(0,0,0),1,\
67|                            cv2.LINE_AA)
68|        azi = str("Az = %05.2f"%az)
69|        img = cv2.putText(img,\
70|              azi,(1000,350),font,0.6,\
71|                (0,0,0),1,cv2.LINE_AA)
72|        alti = str("Alt = %04.2f"%alt)
73|        img = cv2.putText(img,\
74|              alti,(1000,370),font,0.6,\
75|                (0,0,0),1,cv2.LINE_AA)
76|        video.write(img)
77|    video.release()
78|    cv2.destroyAllWindows()
79|    cap = cv2.VideoCapture(vfile2)
80|    if (cap.isOpened()== False):
81|        print("Error opening video  file")
82|    while(cap.isOpened()):
83|      ret, frame = cap.read()
84|      if ret == True:
85|        cv2.imshow(vfile2, frame)
```

```
86|              if cv2.waitKey(25) & 0xFF==ord('q'):
87|                  break
88|          else:
89|              break
90|      cap.release()
91|      cv2.destroyAllWindows()
```

The video generated will show the movement of Moon's disk over that of Sun simultaneously showing the corresponding universal time, altitude and azimuth of Sun at a place under consideration.

The video can be played backward and forward to review the position of the eclipse at any desired instant of time.

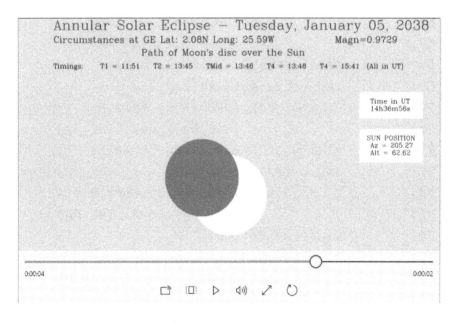

## 7.26 Function DrawMoonPath( )

This functions plots the path of Moon's disc over the Sun showing the Moon position at short intervals so that its path can be visualized. This is saved in a picture file 'SE_PIC2.PNG'.

```
 1|def DrawMoonPath():
 2|    global img
 3|    MoonClr = (0,100,0)
 4|    rM = int(sdm*scale2)
 5|    SunClr = (255,255,255)
 6|    rS = int(sds*scale2)
 7|    SEframe2()
 8|    img= cv2.circle(img,(x0,y0),rS,SunClr,-1)
 9|    T1 = CT1; T2 = CT4
10|    cnt = 0
11|    n = int((T2-T1)*100) # Number of cycles
12|    for Ti in np.arange(T1,T2,0.01):
13|        cnt += 1
14|        caltdq(Ti)
15|        p = rev(atn2(U,V))
16|        ra = ras1
17|        ha = rev(GST1 - ra - glong)
18|        dc = dcs1
19|        sinlat = sn(glat)
20|        coslat = cs(glat)
21|        sindc  = sn(dc)
22|        cosdc  = cs(dc)
23|        tandc = sindc/cosdc
24|        sinha = sn(ha)
25|        cosha = cs(ha)
26|        az = rev(atn2(-sinha,\
27|            tandc*coslat -cosha*sinlat))
28|        alt = asn(sinlat*sindc\
29|             + coslat*cosdc*cosha)
30|        q = (asn(coslat*sinha/cs(alt)))
31|        if eta1< 0:
32|            q =(180-q)
33|        px = rev(p-q+90)
```

```
33|         px = rev(p-q+90)
34|         gm = sqrt(U*U+V*V)
35|         xm = int(x0 + gm*cs(px)*scale2*sdf)
36|         ym = int(y0 - gm*sn(px)*scale2*sdf)
37|         img = cv2.circle(img,\
38|                     (xm,ym), 1, MoonClr,1)
39|         if cnt%10 == 0:
40|             img = cv2.circle(img,\
41|                 (xm,ym), rM, MoonClr,1)
42|         if cnt == n- 5:
43|             a = xm; b = ym
44|     #Arrow mark at the end of path line
45|     ang = rev(atn2(b-ym,a-xm))
46|     p1 = int(xm + 20*cs(ang+20))
47|     p2 = int(xm + 20*cs(ang-20))
48|     q1 = int(ym + 20*sn(ang+20))
49|     q2 = int(ym + 20*sn(ang-20))
50|     img = cv2.line(img,(xm,ym),\
51|                 (p1,q1),(0,0,0),2)
52|     img = cv2.line(img,(xm,ym),\
53|                 (p2,q2),(0,0,0),2)
54|     if Place == "GE":
55|         pfile2 = 'SE_PIC2.PNG'
56|     else:
57|         pfile2 = 'SE_PIC4.PNG'
58|     cv2.imshow(pfile2,img)
59|     cv2.imwrite(pfile2, img)
60|     cv2.waitKey(0)
61|     cv2.destroyAllWindows()
```

A sample of the picture produced by this function is shown below.

Total Solar Eclipse – Monday, August 02, 2027
Circumstances at GE Lat:25.57N Long: 33.13E          Magn=1.0793
Path of Moon's disc over the Sun
Timings:    T1 = 08:42    T2 = 10:04    TMid = 10:07    T4 = 10:10    T4 = 11:28   (All in UT)

## 7.27 Function PlotGT( )

This functions plots the positions of Moon's shadow as seen on the fundamental plane of the earth at different times on a global scale showing all the global timings.

```
 1|def PlotGT():
 2|    global img
 3|    SEframe()
 4|    for i in range(9):
 5|        m =(GTy[8] - GTy[0])/(GTx[8]-GTx[0])
 6|        p1 = GTx[4] - 450
 7|        p2 = GTx[4] + 450
 8|        q1 = int(GTy[4] - m*450)
 9|        q2 = int(GTy[4] + m*450)
10|        q3 = int(q2-20*m-5)
11|        q4 = int(q2-20*m+5)
12|        img = cv2.line(img,(p1,q1),\
13|                   (p2,q2),(0,0,0),1)
14|        img = cv2.line(img,(p2-20,q3),\
```

```
15|                    (p2,q2),(0,0,0),1)
16|        img = cv2.line(img,(p2-20,q4),\
17|                    (p2,q2),(0,0,0),1)
18|        img = cv2.circle(img,(int(GTx[i]),\
19|             int(GTy[i])), rP, (0,0,0), 1)
20|        img = cv2.circle(img,(int(GTx[i]),\
21|             int(GTy[i])), rU, (0,0,0), -1)
```

A sample of the picture produced by this function is shown below.

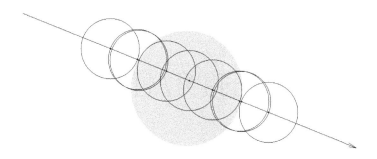

Total Solar Eclipse – Monday, August 02, 2027
Global Circumstances: GE at Lat:25.57N Long: 33.13E
P1=07:30 P2=09:21 P3=10:53 P4=12:43    Tmid = 10:07    U1=08:24 U2=08:27 U3=11:47 U4=11:50
Path of Moon's shadow over the Earth's fundamental plane

## 7.28  Function strGT()

This function produces strings of texts to be printed on screen and to the output file in different situations.

```
1|def strCT():
2|    gap = " " *15
3|    tmp = CT1
4|    if tmp < 0:
5|        tmp += 24.0
6|    sCT1  = "    T1 = " + htohm(tmp)
7|    sCTMid = "   TMid = " + htohm(CT[2])
```

```
 7|     sCTMid = "    TMid = " + htohm(CT[2])
 8|     sCT5  = "     T4 = " + htohm(CT4)
 9|     if contact[1] ==1:
10|         sCT2 = "    T2 = " + htohm(CT2)
11|         sCT4 = "    T4 = " + htohm(CT3)
12|     else:
13|         sCT2 = sCT4 = gap
14|     ctimes = "Timings:"+ sCT1 + sCT2 \
15|             + sCTMid +sCT4 + sCT5 \
16|             + "(All in UT)"
17|     return ctimes
```

## 7.29 Function AnimateGlobalTimes( )

This function simulates on the screen, a view from space, the motion of Moon's shadow on over the earth's fundamental plane from start to end of the eclipse. This motion is saved in a video file named 'SE_VID1.MP4'.

```
 1|def AnimateGlobalTimes():
 2|    global img,rP,rU
 3|    caltdq(Tmid)
 4|    rP = int(l11*scale)
 5|    rU = int(abs(l21*scale)) #Avoid -ve value
 6|    xmid = x0 + x1*scale
 7|    ymid = y0 - y1*scale
 8|    GM2 = x1*x1+y1*y1
 9|    GM = sqrt(GM2)
10|    m = ydash/xdash
11|    ang = atn(m)
12|    # Animation and saving as video
13|    FPS = 60
14|    fourcc = VideoWriter_fourcc(*'MP4v')
```

```
15|     cap = cv2.VideoCapture()
16|     video = VideoWriter('SE_VID1.MP4',\
17|            fourcc,float(FPS),(1200, 720))
18|     SEframe()
19|     for Ti in np.arange(GT[0],\
20|                    GT[8]+0.02,0.01):
21|         caltdq(Ti)
22|         xm = int(x0 + x1*scale)
23|         ym = int(y0 - y1*scale)
24|         SEframe()
25|         img = cv2.circle(img,(xm,ym),\
26|                 rP, (160,160,160), -1)
27|         img = cv2.circle(img,(xm,ym),\
28|                   rU, (0,0,0), -1)
29|         img = cv2.putText(img,"Moon's",\
30|                 (xm-35,ym-20),font,0.6,\
31|              (190,190,190),1,cv2.LINE_AA)
32|         img = cv2.putText(img,"Shadow",\
33|                 (xm-35,ym+30),font,0.6,\
34|             (190,190,190),1,cv2.LINE_AA)
35|         img = cv2.circle(img,(x0,y0),\
36|                 scale, (250,0,150),1)
37|         img = cv2.rectangle(img,(970,200),\
38|             (1150,270),(255,255,255),-1)
39|         img = cv2.putText(img,"Time in UT",\
40|                 (1000,230),font,0.6,(0,0,0),1,\
41|                         cv2.LINE_AA)
42|         hmsTi = hms(Ti)
43|         img = cv2.putText(img,hmsTi,\
44|                 (1000,250),font,0.6,(0,0,0),\
45|                 1,cv2.LINE_AA)
46|         if Ti > GT[8]:
```

```
47|              PlotGT()
48|          video.write(img)
49|      cv2.waitKey(0)
50|      video.release()
51|      cv2.destroyAllWindows()
52|      cap = cv2.VideoCapture('SE_VID1.MP4')
53|      if (cap.isOpened()== False):
54|          print("Error opening video file")
55|      while(cap.isOpened()):
56|        ret, frame = cap.read()
57|        if ret == True:
58|          cv2.imshow('SE_VID1.MP4', frame)
59|          if cv2.waitKey(25) & 0xFF==ord('q'):
60|            break
61|        else:
62|          break
63|      cap.release()
64|      cv2.destroyAllWindows()
65|      PlotGT()
66|      cv2.imshow("SE_PIC1.png",img)
67|      cv2.imwrite("SE_PIC1.png", img)
68|      cv2.waitKey(0)
69|      cv2.destroyAllWindows()
```

The following figure shows how the video-file produced by this function will look like. It shows the movement of Moon's shadow on the Earth's fundamental plane, simultaneously showing the corresponding universal time.

The video can be played backward and forward to review the position of the shadow at any desired instant of time.

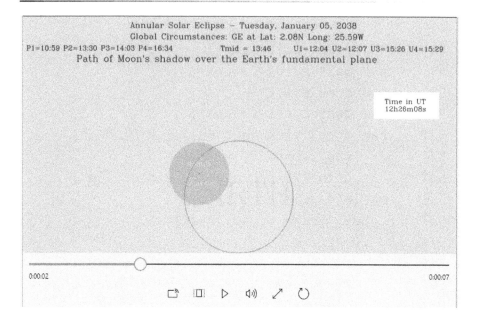

## 7.30 Function SE_Process( )

This can be assumed to be the function that manages the execution of all the processes involved in this program using all the different functions. It does all the calculations of the selected eclipse, produces following 4 pictures 2 videos and a text file concerning global circumstances and the circumstances at the Greatest-Eclipse-spot of the selected solar eclipse.

1. Visibility world map of the eclipse (file SE_MAP.JPG)

2. Annimation of Moon's shadow moving over earth's Fundamental plane (file SE_VID1.MP4)

3. Picture of different global positions of shadow with respect to earth on the fundamental plane. (file SE_PIC1.PNG)

4. Animation of Path of Moon's disc over the Sun at Greatest Eclipse (file SE_VID2.MP4)

5. Picture of Path of Moon's disc over the Sun at Greatest Eclipse (file SE_PIC2.PNG)

6. Pictures of different stages of the eclipse at GE (file SE_PIC3. PNG)

7. A text file 'SE_SUMMARY.TXT', containing a summary of the circumstances of the eclipse

```
 1|def SE_Process():
 2|    global CT,u,v
 3|    global Place,rosino,rocoso
 4|    global glong,glat,NS,EW
 5|    global Olong,Olat
 6|    Longd = int(Ent1); Longm = int(Ent2);
 7|    Latd = int(Ent3); Latm = int(Ent4);
 8|    Olong = float(Longd) + float(Longm)/60.0
 9|    Olat = float(Latd) + float(Latm)/60.0
10|    Heading="Circumstances at"+"%s"%Place\
11|        + "Lat:" + "%5.2f"%Olat + "%s"%NS \
12|        + "Long:"+ "%6.2f"%Olong + "%s"%EW
13|    if NS == 'S':
14|        glat = - glat
15|    if NS == 'N':
16|        glat = Olat
17|    q = atn(ff*tn(glat))
18|    rosino = ff*sn(q)
19|    rocoso = cs(q)
20|    caltdq(Tmid)
21|    ApproxTimes()
22|    AT = (AT1,AT2,ATm,AT3,AT4)
23|    caltdq(ATm)
24|    Um = U
25|    Vm = V
26|    calT1()
27|    if contact[1] == 1:
```

```
28|          calT2()
29|          calT3()
30|      calT4()
31|      CT = (CT1,CT2,ATm,CT3,CT4)
32|      u = (U1,U2,Um,U3,U4)
33|      v = (V1,V2,Vm,V3,V4)
34|      def SE_Msg():
35|          top = Tk()
36|          top.geometry("500x200")
37|          def NoEclipse():
38|              messagebox.showinfo()
39|          B1 = Button(top, text = SE_Title,\
40|                      font = 'times 16' )
41|          B1.place(x = 20,y = 20)
42|          B2 = Button(top, text = Heading,\
43|                      font = 'times 16',)
44|          B2.place(x = 20,y = 70)
45|          B2txt = "Eclipse Not Visible here"
46|          B3 = Button(top, text = B2txt,\
47|                  font = 'times 20',\
48|                  bg = 'yellow',fg = 'red',\
49|                      command = NoEclipse)
50|          B3.place(x = 80,y = 120)
51|          top.mainloop()
52|          top.quit()
53|      if contact[0]==1:
54|          SummaryTable2()
55|          DrawMoonPath()
56|          PlotStages()
57|          AnimateMoonPath()
58|      else:
59|          print("Eclipse Not Visible")
60|          f.write("\n\n This Eclipse is")
```

```
61|            f.write("\n  NOT VISIBLE at")
62|            f.write("%s"%Place + "\n\n")
63|            SE_Msg()
64|     return
```

## 7.31 Function UserInterface( )

This function produces a GUI for entering the longitude and latitude of a place of user's interest for getting the circumstances of the eclipse at that place.

```
 1|def UserInterface():
 2|    global SE_Process
 3|    win = tk.Tk()
 4|    win.geometry("600x300+400+250")
 5|    win.resizable(width = False,\
 6|                  height = False)
 7|    win.title("CIRCUMSTANCES AT"\
 8|                  +"A GIVEN PLACE")
 9|    label1 = tk.Label(win,\
10|        text = 'If you want'\
11|            +'circumstances at'\
12|            + 'any other place',
13|            font = 'times 16')
14|    label1.place(x="120',y = '20')
15|    label2 = tk.Label(win,\
16|        text = 'Please Enter Place'\
17|            + 'Longitude and Latitude'\
18|                ,font = 'times 14')
19|    label2.place(x='150',y = '45')
20|    label3 = tk.Label(win,\
21|            text = ' '*23 + 'Longitude'\
22|              + ' '*13 + 'Latitude',\
```

```
23|                          font = 'times 14')
24|    label3.place(x='180',y = '75')
25|    label4 = tk.Label(win, \
26|        text = 'Place'+ ' '* 19 \
27|             + 'Deg  Min E/W'\
28|          + ' '* 8 +'Deg  Min N/S',\
29|                          font = 'times 14')
30|    label4.place(x='140',y = '95')
31|    Place_var = tk.StringVar()
32|    Place_entrybox= tk.Entry(win,width = 25,\
33|                 textvariable = Place_var)
34|    Place_entrybox.place(x = '100',y = '120')
35|    Place_entrybox.focus_set()
36|    Ent1_var = tk.StringVar()
37|    Ent1_entrybox = tk.Entry(win, width = 5,\
38|                   textvariable = Ent1_var)
39|    Ent1_entrybox.place(x='280', y='120')
40|    Ent2_var =tk.StringVar()
41|    Ent2_entrybox = tk.Entry(win, width = 5,\
42|                   textvariable = Ent2_var)
43|    Ent2_entrybox.place(x = '320', y = '120')
44|    EW_var = tk.StringVar()
45|    EW_entrybox = tk.Entry(win, width = 3,\
46|                    textvariable = EW_var)
47|    EW_entrybox.place(x = '360', y = '120')
48|    Ent3_var =tk.StringVar()
49|    Ent3_entrybox = tk.Entry(win, width = 5,\
50|                   textvariable = Ent3_var)
51|    Ent3_entrybox.place(x = '420', y = '120')
52|    Ent4_var =tk.StringVar()
53|    Ent4_entrybox = tk.Entry(win, width = 5,\
54|                   textvariable = Ent4_var)
55|    Ent4_entrybox.place(x = '460', y = '120')
```

```
56|    NS_var = tk.StringVar()
57|    NS_entrybox = tk.Entry(win, width = 3,\
58|                    textvariable = NS_var)
59|    NS_entrybox.place(x = '500', y = '120')
60|    def errMessage():
61|        label5 = tk.Label(win, \
62|        text = 'Please reset and '\
63|                + 'make valid entries',\
64|        font = 'times 16', \
65|                bg = 'yellow',fg = 'red')
66|        label5.place(x='180',y = '200')
67|    def EraseMessage():
68|        label5 = tk.Label(win, \
69|        text = ' '*60,font = 'times 16')
70|        label5.place(x='180',y = '200')
71|        Place_entrybox.focus_set()
72|    def reset():
73|        Place_var.set("")
74|        Ent1_var.set("")
75|        Ent2_var.set("")
76|        EW_var.set("")
77|        Ent3_var.set("")
78|        Ent4_var.set("")
79|        NS_var.set("")
80|        EraseMessage()
81|    def Exit():
82|        win.quit()
83|        win.destroy()
84|    def action():
85|        global Place,Ent1,Ent2,EW
86|        global Ent3,Ent4,NS
87|        Place = Place_var.get()
88|        Ent1 = Ent1_var.get()
```

```
 89|         Ent2 = Ent2_var.get()
 90|         EW = EW_var.get().upper()
 91|         Ent3 = Ent3_var.get()
 92|         Ent4 = Ent4_var.get()
 93|         NS = NS_var.get().upper()
 94|         if Ent1.isdigit()\
 95|             and Ent1.isdigit()\
 96|             and Ent3.isdigit()\
 97|             and  Ent4.isdigit()\
 98|             and (EW == 'E' or EW == 'W')\
 99|             and (NS =='N'  or NS == 'S'):
100|             Exit()
101|             SE_Process()
102|             SE_Msg()
103|         else:
104|             errMessage()
105|     Ent1 = 0; Ent2 = 0; Ent3 = 0; Ent4 = 0
106|     submit_button = tk.Button(win,\
107|         text = 'Process',command = action)
108|     submit_button.place(x = '225', y = '150')
109|     reset_button = tk.Button(win,\
110|             text = ' Reset ',command = reset)
111|     reset_button.place(x = '300', y = '150')
112|     exit_button = tk.Button(win,\
113|             text = ' EXIT ',command = Exit)
114|     exit_button.place(x = '375', y = '150')
115|     Place_entrybox.focus_set()
116|     win.mainloop()
117|     win.quit
```

The following figure shows the interface produced by this function.

User has to enter the valid data in the proper boxes and click Process.

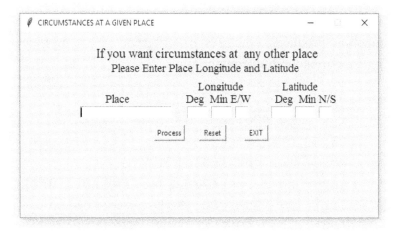

If the eclipse is visible from that place this function will produce the following additional output files concerning the circumstances of the eclipse at the place of user's choice.

1. Animation of Path of Moon's disc over the Sun at the place of user's choice (file SE_VID3.MP4)

2. Picture of Path of Moon's disc over the Sun at the place of user's choice (file SE_PIC4.PNG)

3. Pictures of different stages of the eclipse at the place of user's choice (file SE_PIC5.PNG)

4. Summary of the eclipse at the place chosen by the user.

If the eclipse is not visible from that place a message to that effect will flash on the screen as shown below.

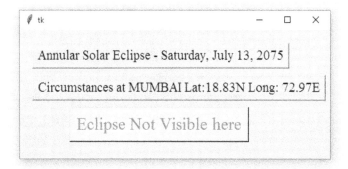

## 7.32 Function PlotStages( )

This function produces pictures of different stages of the eclipse showing the corresponding contact times.

```
 1|def PlotStages():
 2|    x = [200,400,600,800,1000]
 3|    rS = int(sds*scale)
 4|    rM =  int(sdm*scale)
 5|    img = np.zeros((720,1200,3), np.uint8)
 6|    img[:] = [250,200,150] #frame color
 7|    font = cv2.FONT_HERSHEY_COMPLEX
 8|    title1 = SE_Title
 9|    magn = Magnitude()[1]
10|    title2 = "Circumstances at"\
11|         + "%s"%Place\
12|         + "Lat:" + "%5.2f"%Olat + "%s"%NS \
13|         + "Long:"+ "%6.2f"%Olong + "%s"%EW
14|    title2a = "Magn={:6.4f}".format(magn)
15|    title3 = "Different Stages"\
16|            +"at the Greatest Eclipse"
17|    title4 = 'All timings in Universal Time'
18|    img = cv2.putText(img,SE_Title,(100,30),\
19|            font,1.2,(0,0,0),1,cv2.LINE_AA)
20|    img = cv2.putText(img,title2,(150,65),\
21|            font,0.8,(0,0,0),1,cv2.LINE_AA)
22|    img = cv2.putText(img,title2a,(900,65),\
23|            font,0.8,(0,0,0),1,cv2.LINE_AA)
24|    img = cv2.putText(img,title3,(350,100),\
25|            font,0.8,(0,0,0),1,cv2.LINE_AA)
26|    img = cv2.putText(img,strCT(),(100,135),\
27|            font,0.6,(0,0,0),1,cv2.LINE_AA)
28|    img = cv2.putText(img,title4,(400,280),\
```

```
29|              font,0.8,(0,0,0),1,cv2.LINE_AA)
30|    for i in range(5):
31|        gm[i] = sqrt(u[i]*u[i]+v[i]*v[i])
32|        xm[i] = int(x[i]\
33|            + gm[i]*cs(px[i])*scale*sdf)
34|        ym[i] = int(y0 \
35|            - gm[i]*sn(px[i])*scale*sdf)
36|        if contact[i] != 0:
37|            img = cv2.circle(img,\
38|                    (x[i],y0),\
39|                    rS, (255,255,255), -1)
40|            img = cv2.circle(img,\
41|                    (xm[i],ym[i]),\
42|                    rM, (0,0,0), -1)
43|            img = cv2.circle(img,\
44|                    (x[i],y0 + 200),\
45|                    20, (0,0,0), 1)
46|            img = cv2.putText(img,\
47|                    str(i+1),\
48|                    (x[i]-10,y0+210),\
49|                font,0.8,(0,0,0),1,\
50|                    cv2.LINE_AA)
51|            img = cv2.putText(img,\
52|                    htohm(CT[i]),\
53|                (x[i]-30,y0+150),\
54|                font,0.8,(0,0,0),\
55|                    1,cv2.LINE_AA)
56|    if Place == "GE":
57|        pfile3 = 'SE_PIC3.PNG'
58|    else:
59|        pfile3 = 'SE_PIC5.PNG'
60|    cv2.imshow(pfile3,img)
```

```
61|     cv2.imwrite(pfile3, img)
62|     cv2.waitKey(0)
63|     cv2.destroyAllWindows()
```

A sample of the picture produced by this function is shown below.

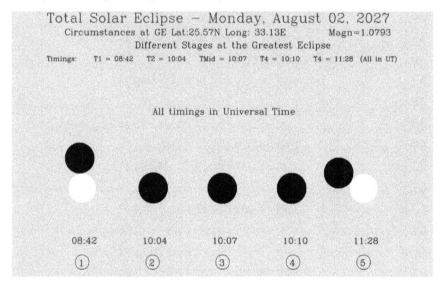

## 7.33 Function SE_Msg( )

This function is used to flash a message on the screen to inform the user ,at the end of the program, which files to refer for seeing the results there off.

```
1|def SE_Msg():
2|    top = Tk()
3|    top.geometry("500x160")
4|    def ShowMsg():
5|        messagebox.showinfo()
6|    msg = "See PNG files 'SE_MAP',"\
7|    + "\n SE_PIC1, SE_PIC2, SE_PIC3"\
8|    + "\n and MP4 files SE_VID1 to SE_VID5"\
9|                    + "\n    for results"
```

```
10|      B1 = Button(top, text = msg,\
11|                  font = 'Consolas 16',\
12|                  bg = 'yellow',fg = 'red',\
13|                  command = ShowMsg)
14|      B1.place(x = 45,y = 20)
15|      top.mainloop()
16|      top.quit()
```

A picture of the message produced by this function is shown below.

## 7.34 The Main Program

As already known, functions do not operate themselves unless they are called for. That is where the *main* comes into play. Though the 'main' has not been specifically defined, all commands written without the *indent* are considered as main and the program is executed accordingly. It defines the global variables and calls the functions one by one in a logical sequence and the program is executed accordingly.

```
 |#----------MAIN PROGRAM--------------
1|def chkfile('SE_INFILE.TXT')
2|chkfile('WORLDMAP.JPG')
3|date = 0; month = 0; year = 0
4|conj = 0.0
5|x0 = 600; y0 = 480
```

```
 6│scale = 150
 7│scale2 = 400
 8│TNumber =["T1","T2","TMid","T3","T4"]
 9│font = cv2.FONT_HERSHEY_COMPLEX
10│px = [0.0]*5
11│gm = [0.0]*5
12│xm = [0.0]*5
13│ym = [0.0]*5
14│f = open('SE_SUMMARY.TXT','w')
15│SelectSE()
16│if year == 0:
17│    sys.exit()
18│sedat = strdat(year,month,date)
19│SE_Title = setype \
20│            +"Solar Eclipse -"+ sedat
21│T1 = int(conj)
22│T2 = T1 +1.0
23│print(SE_Title)
24│du0 = caldays(date,month,year)
25│deltaT = calDeltaT(date,month,year)
26│deltad = deltaT/86400.0
27│d = du0 + deltad
28│d1 = d+T1/24.0
29│d2 = d +(T1+1)/24.0
  │#Part1. Global Circumstances
30│rosino = 0.0
31│rocoso = 0.0
32│glong = 0.0
33│caltdq(T1)
34│IterateTmid()
35│GEPosition(Tmid)
36│xmid = 0;ymid = 0
```

```
37|GC = [0.0]*9
38|GT = [0.0,0.0,0.0,0.0,Tmid,0.0,0.0,0.0,0.0]
39|GTx = [0,0,0,0,xmid,0,0,0,0]
40|GTy = [0,0,0,0,ymid,0,0,0,0]
41|CalGlobalTimes()
42|SummaryTable1()
43|AnimateGlobalTimes()
44|VisibilityMap()
  |#Part2. Circumstances at GE
45|Place = "GE"
46|rosino = rsn
47|rocoso = rcs
48|CalCT()
49|SummaryTable2()
50|AnimateMoonPath()
51|DrawMoonPath()
52|PlotStages()
  |#Part3. Circumstances at a Given Place
53|UserInterface()
54|f.close()
55|print("PROGRAM SUCCESSFUL")
```

*** *Special Note regarding VisibilityMap() function*

*As a specially designed world map has to be prepared for this function. It is most likely that the reader may find it difficult to produce this map. Keeping this in view, a picture of this world map has been posted in Facebook. It can be downloaded from 'Manohar Purohit photos' from Facebook.*

*What you have to do is, open 'facebook.com' and search for 'Manohar world map'. You can easily find the map with blue and white colors and download this map. As the size is (720 X 576) you will have to resize it increasing by 125 percent and save it in your python working folder by name "worldmap.jpg".*

# 8. CATALOGUE OF SOLAR ECLIPSES

In this chapter a program for generating a more detailed list of solar eclipses with more columns of information such as value of *gamma* (γ), all the nine global timings, latitude and longitude of greatest eclipse and magnitude, which can be called as catalogue of solar eclipses. A catalogue of solar eclipses during 21$^{st}$ century is given in Appendix-7.

First of all, it should be noted that the presence of a text file named 'SE_LIST1.TXT' containing the *standard list* of solar eclipses is necessary for the execution of this program. This file has been already descried in chapter 7.

## 8.1 Importing the Required Modules

```
1|from AstroMODULE import *
2|from tkinter import *
3|from tkinter import messagebox
```

## 8.2 Function caltdq(x)

**Function for calculating Time-Dependant-Quantities (TDQ)**

This is the same function which has been fully explained 6.2. and has been used in the programs of chapter 6 and 7 . So it is not reproduced here.

## 8.3 Function MidEclipse(ATmid )

This function, taking ATmid (approximate mid-eclipse-time), calculates the exact time of Mid-Eclipse by iteration method.

```
 1|def MidEclipse(ATmid):
 2|    tmp = 0.0
 3|    caltdq(ATmid)
 4|    tx = ATmid
 5|    while abs(tmp) > 0.00000001:
 6|        tmp = (A*U + B*V)/N2
 7|        tx = tx - tmp
 8|        caltdq(tx)
 9|    Tmid = tx
10|    return Tmid
```

## 8.4 Function CalGlobalTimes( )

This function is similar to the function of the same name given in chapter 7, but with some difference.

The term *GlobalTimes* has been fully explained in Chapter 7.

```
 1|def CalGlobalTimes():
 2|    global GC,GT,L,sGT
 3|    GC = [1,0,0,0,1,0,0,0,1]
 4|    caltdq(Tmid)
 5|    GT[4]= Tmid
 6|    sGT[4] = " " + htohm(Tmid)
 7|    GM2 = x1*x1+y1*y1
 8|    gama = sqrt(GM2)
 9|    L = [1+L11,1+L21,1-L21,1-L11]
10|    m = ydash/xdash
11|    ang = atn(m)
12|    dif = 0
```

```
13|     for i in range(4):
14|         OP = L[i]
15|         OP2 = OP*OP
16|         if OP2 >= GM2:
17|             dif = sqrt(OP2 - GM2)
18|             GC[i] = 1
19|             xdif = dif*cs(ang)
20|             GT[i] = Tmid - xdif/xdash
21|             GT[8-i] = Tmid + xdif/xdash
22|             sGT[i] = " " + htohm(GT[i])
23|             sGT[8-i] = " " + htohm(GT[8-i])
24|         if GC[1] == 0:
25|             sGT[1] = sGT[7] = " -----"
26|         if GC[2] == 0:
27|             sGT[2] = sGT[6] = " -----"
28|         if GC[3] == 0:
29|             sGT[3] = sGT[5] = " -----"
30|     if setype == 'Total':
31|         GT[1],GT[2] = swap (GT[1],GT[2])
32|         GT[6],GT[7] = swap (GT[6],GT[7])
```

## 8.5 Function GEPosition(x)

This function is the same as that given in chapter 7 with slight difference.

```
1|def GEPosition(x):
2|    global prGEPos, glong, glat
3|    global x1,y1,gama
4|    global rsn,rcs,hh
5|    global gelat, gelong,gens,geew
6|    caltdq(x)
7|    gama = sqrt(x1*x1 + y1*y1)
```

```
 8|     z2 = 1.0 - (x1*x1 + y1*y1)
 9|     if(z2>0):
10|         z = sqrt(z2)
11|     else:
12|         x1 = x1/gama
13|         y1 = y1/gama
14|         z = 0
15|     rsn = y1*cos_d1 + z*sin_d1
16|     hh = atn2(x1, z*cos_d1 - y1*sin_d1)
17|     if abs(rsn/ff)<= 1.0:
18|         rcs = sqrt(1 - rsn*rsn/ff2)
19|         rcs2=cs(asn(rsn/ff))
20|         q2 = asn(rsn/ff)
21|     if abs(rsn/ff)>1.0:
22|         rcs = sqrt(1 - rsn*rsn)
23|         rcs2=cs(asn(rsn))
24|         q2 = asn(rsn)
25|     q =atn2(rsn/ff,rcs)
26|     rsn0 = rsn
27|     rcs0 = rcs
28|     xi0 = x1
29|     eta0 = y1
30|     zeta0 = z
31|     h0 = hh
32|     glat = atn(tn(q)/ff2)
33|     glong = rev(mu1-hh)
34|     if glong > 180.0:
35|         gelong = 360-glong
36|         geew = 'E'
37|     else:
38|         gelong = glong; geew='W'
39|     if glat < 0:
```

```
40|              gelat = -glat; gens = 'S'
41|      else:
42|              gelat = glat; gens='N'
```

## 8.6 Function ApproxTimes( )

This function is the same as that given in chapter 7.

```
 1|def ApproxTimes():
 2|    global contact,AT
 3|    global AT1,AT2,AT3,AT4,ATm
 4|    global U,V,A,B,N,N2,Tmid,IC23
 5|    AT1 = AT2 = AT3 = AT4 = ATm = 0.0
 6|    tmp1 = tmp2 = 0.0
 7|    contact = [0,0,1,0,0]
 8|    caltdq(Tmid)
 9|    dtm = -(A*U+B*V)/N2
10|    ATm = Tmid + dtm
11|    val1 = (A*V-B*U)/(N*L11)
12|    if val1*val1 < 1.0:
13|        contact[0] = contact[4] = 1
14|        tmp1 = sqrt(1-val1*val1)*L11/N
15|        AT1 = Tmid - tmp1
16|        AT4 = Tmid + tmp1
17|    val2 = (A*V-B*U)/(N*L21)
18|    if val2*val2 < 1.0:
19|        tmp2 = sqrt(1-val2*val2)*L21/N
20|        contact[1] = 1
21|        contact[3] = 1
22|        AT2 = Tmid - tmp2
23|        AT3 = Tmid + tmp2
24|    AT = AT1,AT2,ATm,AT3,AT4
```

## 8.7 Function calT1( )

This function is the same as that given in chapter 7.

```
 1|def calT1():
 2|    cnt1 = 0
 3|    global CT1,U1,V1,tx,tmp
 4|    tx = AT1
 5|    caltdq(AT1)
 6|    tmp =  (A*V-B*U)/(N*L11)
 7|    if tmp*tmp < 1.0:
 8|        tmp = -sqrt(1-tmp*tmp)*L11/N
 9|        tmp = (A*U+B*V)/N2 - tmp
10|        while abs(tmp) > .00000001:
11|            cnt1 += 1
12|            tx-=tmp;
13|            caltdq(tx);
14|            tmp = (A*V - B*U)/N/L11
15|            if tmp*tmp < 1.0:
16|                tmp = -sqrt(1 -tmp*tmp)*L11/N
17|                tmp = (A*U + B*V)/N2 - tmp
18|            else:
19|                break
20|    CT1 = tx
21|    U1 = U
22|    V1 = V
```

## 8.8 Function calT4( )

This function is the same as that given in chapter 7.

```
 1|def calT4():
 2|    global CT4,U4,V4,tx
 3|    tx = AT4
```

```
 4|     caltdq(AT4)
 5|     tmp = (A*V-B*U)/(N*L11)
 6|     if tmp*tmp < 1.0:
 7|         tmp = sqrt(1-tmp*tmp)*L11/N
 8|         tmp = (A*U+B*V)/N2 - tmp
 9|         while abs(tmp)> .00000001:
10|             tx-=tmp
11|             caltdq(tx)
12|             tmp = (A*V - B*U)/N/L11
13|             if tmp*tmp < 1.0:
14|                 tmp = sqrt(1 - tmp*tmp)*L11/N
15|                 tmp = (A*U + B*V)/N2 - tmp
16|             else:
17|                 break
18|     CT4 = tx
19|     U4 = U
20|     V4 = V
21|     sdf = (sds+sdm)/sqrt(U4*U4+V4*V4)
```

## 8.9  Function Magnitude( )

This function is the same as that given in chapter 7.

```
1|def Magnitude():
2|    global rosino,rocoso,longi
3|    caltdq(Tmid)
4|    msr = sdm/sds
5|    sdf = (sds+sdm)/sqrt(U4*U4+V4*V4)
6|    dist = sqrt(U*U + V*V)*sdf
7|    gama = sqrt(x1*x1 + y1*y1)
8|    if gama <= 1.0125: #Total or Annular
9|        magn = msr
```

```
10|          Obs = magn*magn
11|      if gama > 1.0125: # Partial Eclipse
12|          m = 2*acs((sds*sds + dist*dist \
13|                  - sdm*sdm)/(2*sds*dist))
14|          s = 2*acs((sdm*sdm + dist*dist \
15|                  - sds*sds)/(2*sdm*dist))
16|          magn = (sds+sdm-dist)/(2*sds)
17|          Ovrlap = 0.5*sdm*sdm*(rads(m)-sn(m))\
18|                  + 0.5*sds*sds*(rads(s)-sn(s))
19|          SunArea = pi*sds*sds
20|          Obs = Ovrlap/SunArea
21|      return magn
```

## 8.10  Function SEList2Msg( )

This function produces a message at the end of the program.

```
 1|def SEList2Msg():
 2|    top = Tk()
 3|    top.geometry("500x200")
 4|    msg1 = "Solar eclipses from year"\
 5|        +"%d" "%year1 +"to " +"%d "%year2
 6|    B1 = Button(top, text = msg1,\
 7|                    font = 'times 16' )
 8|    B1.place(x = 80,y = 30)
 9|    msg2 = "Total=%d"%Totcnt \
10|            +"Annular=%d"%Anucnt\
11|            +"Partial=%d"%Parcnt\
12|            +"All=%d"%Allcnt
13|    B2 = Button(top, text = msg2,\
14|                    font = 'times 16' )
15|    B2.place(x = 50,y = 80)
16|    msg3 = "See file 'SE_LIST2.TXT'"
```

```
17|     B3 = Button(top, text = msg3,\
18|                     font = 'times 16' )
19|     B3.place(x = 150,y = 130)
20|     top.mainloop()
21|     top.quit()
```

This function flashes the message on the screen similar to one shown below.

## 8.11 Main Program

As mentioned in the previous chapter all commands outside the functions may be considered as *main*.

```
# -----------main program---------------
1|f1 = open("SE_LIST1.TXT",'r')
2|f2 = open("SE_LIST2.TXT",'w')
3|f2.write("\nLIST OF SOLAR ECLIPSES" \
4|         + "DURING 20TH AND 21ST CENTURIES"\
5|         + "WITH GLOBAL TIMINGS IN 'UT'")
6|f2.write("\n" + "-"*108)
7|f2.write("\nYYYY  MM DD  Conj SE_Type Gamma"\
8|+"   P1    U1    U2    P2    MID    P3"\
```

```
 9|+"    U3      U4      P4        GE Position    Magn.")
10|f2.write("\n" + "-"*108)
11|du0 = 0.0
12|GT = [0.0]*9
13|sGT = ["-----"]*9
14|Allcnt = 0
15|Parcnt = 0
16|Totcnt = 0
17|Anucnt = 0
18|for line in f1:
19|    Allcnt = Allcnt+1
20|    ln = line.split(' ')
21|    year  = int(ln[0])
22|    month = MonthNum(ln[1])
23|    date = int(ln[2])
24|    conj = float(ln[3])
25|    setype = ln[4]
26|    if Allcnt ==1:
27|        year1 = year
28|    if setype == 'Annular':
29|        Anucnt = Anucnt + 1
30|    if setype == 'Total':
31|        Totcnt = Totcnt + 1
32|    if setype == 'Partial':
33|        Parcnt = Parcnt + 1
34|    du0 = caldays(date,month,year)
35|    deltaT = calDeltaT(date,month,year)
36|    deltad = deltaT/86400.0
37|    d = du0 + deltad
38|    T1 = conj
39|    d1 = d+T1/24.0
40|    d2 = d +(T1+1)/24.0
41|    rosino = rocoso = longi = 0.0
```

```
42|    glong = 0
43|    caltdq(T1)
44|    Tmid = MidEclipse(ATmid)
45|    caltdq(Tmid)
46|    CalGlobalTimes()
47|    GEPosition(Tmid)
48|    txt1 = "%d"%year \
49|        + "%s"%MonthName(month)\
50|         + "%02d"%date + "%s"%htohm(conj)\
51|          + "%-7s"%setype + "%6.4f"%gama
52|    txt2 =  str(sGT[0]) + str(sGT[1])\
53|             + str(sGT[2]) + str(sGT[3])\
54|             + str(sGT[4]) + str(sGT[5])\
55|             + str(sGT[6]) + str(sGT[7])\
56|          + str(sGT[8])
57|    txt3 = "%5.2f"%gelat + "%s"%gens \
58|             + "%6.2f"%gelong + "%s"%geew
59|    rosino = rsn
60|    rocoso = rcs
61|    longi = glong
62|    EWlong = gelong
63|    ApproxTimes()
64|    calT4()
65|    magn = Magnitude()
66|    txt4 = "%6.4f"%magn
67|    f2.write("\n"+txt1+txt2+txt3+txt4)
68|year2 = year
69|f2.write("\n" + "-"*108)
70|f2.write("\nAbstract of Solar Eclipses")
71|f2.write("\nTotal Eclipses    : {:3d}"\
72|         .format(Totcnt))
73|f2.write("\nAnnular Eclipses   : {:3d}"\
74|         .format(Anucnt))
```

```
75|f2.write("\nPartial Eclipses   : {:3d}"\
76|          .format(Parcnt))
77|f2.write("\nAll Eclipses       : {:3d}"\
78|          .format(Allcnt))
79|f1.close()
80|f2.close()
81|print("See file 'SE_LIST2.TXT' for results")
82|SEList2Msg()
```

# APPENDIX – 1

Table of DeltaT for the year    1600 to 2400

---

| Year | 1 | 2 | 3 | 4 | 5 | 6 | 7 | 8 | 9 |
|------|-----|-----|-----|-----|-----|-----|-----|-----|-----|
| 1600 | 118.4 | 117.4 | 116.4 | 115.3 | 114.2 | 113.1 | 112.0 | 110.9 | 109.7 | 108.5 |
| 1610 | 107.3 | 106.0 | 104.7 | 103.5 | 102.1 | 100.8 | 99.5 | 98.1 | 96.7 | 95.3 |
| 1620 | 93.9 | 92.5 | 91.1 | 89.6 | 88.2 | 86.7 | 85.2 | 83.7 | 82.2 | 80.7 |
| 1630 | 79.2 | 77.7 | 76.2 | 74.6 | 73.1 | 71.6 | 70.1 | 68.5 | 67.0 | 65.5 |
| 1640 | 63.9 | 62.4 | 60.9 | 59.4 | 57.9 | 56.4 | 54.9 | 53.4 | 51.9 | 50.4 |
| 1650 | 49.0 | 47.5 | 46.1 | 44.7 | 43.3 | 41.9 | 40.5 | 39.1 | 37.8 | 36.5 |
| 1660 | 35.2 | 33.9 | 32.6 | 31.4 | 30.2 | 29.0 | 27.8 | 26.6 | 25.5 | 24.4 |
| 1670 | 23.3 | 22.3 | 21.3 | 20.3 | 19.3 | 18.4 | 17.5 | 16.7 | 15.9 | 15.1 |
| 1680 | 14.3 | 13.6 | 12.9 | 12.3 | 11.7 | 11.1 | 10.6 | 10.2 | 9.7 | 9.3 |
| 1690 | 9.0 | 8.7 | 8.4 | 8.2 | 8.1 | 8.0 | 7.9 | 7.9 | 7.9 | 8.0 |
| 1700 | 8.0 | 8.2 | 8.3 | 8.4 | 8.6 | 8.7 | 8.8 | 8.9 | 9.0 | 9.1 |
| 1710 | 9.2 | 9.3 | 9.3 | 9.4 | 9.5 | 9.6 | 9.6 | 9.7 | 9.8 | 9.8 |
| 1720 | 9.9 | 9.9 | 10.0 | 10.1 | 10.1 | 10.2 | 10.3 | 10.3 | 10.4 | 10.5 |
| 1730 | 10.6 | 10.6 | 10.7 | 10.8 | 10.9 | 11.0 | 11.1 | 11.2 | 11.3 | 11.4 |
| 1740 | 11.5 | 11.6 | 11.7 | 11.9 | 12.0 | 12.1 | 12.3 | 12.4 | 12.5 | 12.7 |
| 1750 | 12.8 | 13.0 | 13.1 | 13.3 | 13.4 | 13.6 | 13.7 | 13.9 | 14.1 | 14.2 |
| 1760 | 14.4 | 14.5 | 14.7 | 14.9 | 15.0 | 15.2 | 15.3 | 15.4 | 15.6 | 15.7 |
| 1770 | 15.9 | 16.0 | 16.1 | 16.2 | 16.3 | 16.4 | 16.5 | 16.6 | 16.6 | 16.7 |
| 1780 | 16.7 | 16.7 | 16.7 | 16.7 | 16.7 | 16.7 | 16.6 | 16.6 | 16.5 | 16.4 |
| 1790 | 16.2 | 16.1 | 15.9 | 15.7 | 15.4 | 15.2 | 14.9 | 14.6 | 14.2 | 13.9 |
| 1800 | 13.4 | 13.1 | 12.8 | 12.6 | 12.4 | 12.3 | 12.2 | 12.1 | 12.1 | 12.2 |
| 1810 | 12.2 | 12.3 | 12.3 | 12.4 | 12.4 | 12.4 | 12.3 | 12.2 | 12.1 | 11.9 |
| 1820 | 11.6 | 11.3 | 11.0 | 10.6 | 10.2 | 9.8 | 9.3 | 8.9 | 8.4 | 7.9 |
| 1830 | 7.5 | 7.0 | 6.7 | 6.3 | 6.0 | 5.7 | 5.5 | 5.4 | 5.3 | 5.3 |
| 1840 | 5.3 | 5.4 | 5.5 | 5.6 | 5.8 | 6.0 | 6.2 | 6.4 | 6.6 | 6.8 |
| 1850 | 7.0 | 7.1 | 7.1 | 7.2 | 7.2 | 7.1 | 7.1 | 7.0 | 7.1 | 7.2 |
| 1860 | 7.5 | 7.8 | 7.8 | 7.4 | 6.7 | 5.9 | 5.0 | 4.0 | 2.9 | 1.9 |
| 1870 | 0.8 | -0.1 | -1.0 | -1.8 | -2.5 | -3.2 | -3.7 | -4.2 | -4.5 | -4.8 |
| 1880 | -5.1 | -5.3 | -5.4 | -5.5 | -5.6 | -5.7 | -5.8 | -5.9 | -6.0 | -6.1 |

```
            Table of DeltaT for the year   1600 to 2400
--------------------------------------------------------------------------------

Year    1      2      3      4      5      6      7      8      9
--------------------------------------------------------------------------------

1890   -6.2   -6.3   -6.3   -6.4   -6.4   -6.2   -6.0   -5.6   -4.9   -4.0
1900   -2.8   -1.4   -0.0    1.3    2.5    3.8    5.1    6.4    7.7    9.0
1910   10.4   11.7   13.1   14.5   15.8   17.1   18.2   19.3   20.1   20.8
1920   21.2   22.0   22.6   23.1   23.5   23.8   24.0   24.1   24.2   24.2
1930   24.1   24.1   24.0   23.9   23.9   23.8   23.8   23.9   24.0   24.1
1940   24.4   24.8   25.3   25.9   26.4   26.9   27.3   27.8   28.2   28.7
1950   29.1   29.5   29.9   30.3   30.7   31.0   31.4   31.8   32.3   32.7
1960   33.1   33.6   34.0   34.5   35.1   35.8   36.6   37.4   38.3   39.2
1970   40.2   41.2   42.3   43.3   44.4   45.5   46.5   47.6   48.6   49.6
1980   50.5   51.4   52.3   53.0   53.7   54.3   54.9   55.3   55.8   56.3
1990   56.9   57.6   58.3   59.1   60.0   60.8   61.6   62.3   62.9   63.5
2000   63.9   64.1   64.3   64.4   64.5   64.7   65.0   65.4   65.8   66.2
2010   66.7   67.1   67.6   68.0   68.5   69.0   69.5   70.0   70.5   71.0
2020   71.5   72.1   72.7   73.2   73.8   74.4   75.0   75.6   76.3   76.9
2030   77.5   78.2   78.9   79.6   80.3   81.0   81.7   82.4   83.1   83.9
2040   84.7   85.4   86.2   87.0   87.8   88.6   89.5   90.3   91.2   92.0
2050   92.9   94.9   97.0   99.0  101.1  103.1  105.2  107.3  109.4  111.4
2060  113.5  115.6  117.7  119.8  122.0  124.1  126.2  128.4  130.5  132.7
2070  134.8  137.0  139.1  141.3  143.5  145.7  147.9  150.1  152.3  154.5
2080  156.7  159.0  161.2  163.4  165.7  167.9  170.2  172.4  174.7  177.0
2090  179.3  181.6  183.9  186.2  188.5  190.8  193.1  195.5  197.8  200.1
2100  202.5  204.8  207.2  209.6  211.9  214.3  216.7  219.1  221.5  223.9
2110  226.3  228.7  231.1  233.6  236.0  238.5  240.9  243.4  245.8  248.3
2120  250.8  253.3  255.7  258.2  260.7  263.2  265.8  268.3  270.8  273.3
2130  275.9  278.4  281.0  283.5  286.1  288.7  291.2  293.8  296.4  299.0
2140  301.6  304.2  306.8  309.5  312.1  314.7  317.4  320.0  322.7  325.3
2150  328.0  330.1  332.2  334.3  336.5  338.6  340.8  342.9  345.1  347.2
2160  349.4  351.6  353.7  355.9  358.1  360.3  362.5  364.7  367.0  369.2
2170  371.4  373.6  375.9  378.1  380.4  382.7  384.9  387.2  389.5  391.8
2180  394.1  396.4  398.7  401.0  403.3  405.6  408.0  410.3  412.7  415.0
2190  417.4  419.7  422.1  424.5  426.9  429.3  431.7  434.1  436.5  438.9
2200  441.3  443.7  446.2  448.6  451.1  453.5  456.0  458.4  460.9  463.4
2210  465.9  468.4  470.9  473.4  475.9  478.4  480.9  483.5  486.0  488.5
2220  491.1  493.7  496.2  498.8  501.4  503.9  506.5  509.1  511.7  514.3
2230  516.9  519.6  522.2  524.8  527.5  530.1  532.8  535.4  538.1  540.8
2240  543.4  546.1  548.8  551.5  554.2  556.9  559.6  562.4  565.1  567.8
2250  570.6  573.3  576.1  578.8  581.6  584.4  587.1  589.9  592.7  595.5
2260  598.3  601.1  604.0  606.8  609.6  612.4  615.3  618.1  621.0  623.9
```

### Table of DeltaT for the year   1600 to 2400

---

| Year | 1 | 2 | 3 | 4 | 5 | 6 | 7 | 8 | 9 |
|------|---|---|---|---|---|---|---|---|---|

---

| 2270 | 626.7 | 629.6 | 632.5 | 635.4 | 638.3 | 641.2 | 644.1 | 647.0 | 649.9 | 652.8 |
| 2280 | 655.8 | 658.7 | 661.6 | 664.6 | 667.6 | 670.5 | 673.5 | 676.5 | 679.5 | 682.4 |
| 2290 | 685.4 | 688.4 | 691.4 | 694.5 | 697.5 | 700.5 | 703.5 | 706.6 | 709.6 | 712.7 |
| 2300 | 715.7 | 718.8 | 721.9 | 725.0 | 728.1 | 731.1 | 734.2 | 737.3 | 740.5 | 743.6 |
| 2310 | 746.7 | 749.8 | 753.0 | 756.1 | 759.3 | 762.4 | 765.6 | 768.7 | 771.9 | 775.1 |
| 2320 | 778.3 | 781.5 | 784.7 | 787.9 | 791.1 | 794.3 | 797.5 | 800.8 | 804.0 | 807.3 |
| 2330 | 810.5 | 813.8 | 817.0 | 820.3 | 823.6 | 826.9 | 830.2 | 833.4 | 836.7 | 840.1 |
| 2340 | 843.4 | 846.7 | 850.0 | 853.4 | 856.7 | 860.0 | 863.4 | 866.8 | 870.1 | 873.5 |
| 2350 | 876.9 | 880.3 | 883.6 | 887.0 | 890.4 | 893.9 | 897.3 | 900.7 | 904.1 | 907.6 |
| 2360 | 911.0 | 914.5 | 917.9 | 921.4 | 924.8 | 928.3 | 931.8 | 935.3 | 938.8 | 942.3 |
| 2370 | 945.8 | 949.3 | 952.8 | 956.3 | 959.9 | 963.4 | 967.0 | 970.5 | 974.1 | 977.6 |
| 2380 | 981.2 | 984.8 | 988.4 | 991.9 | 995.5 | 999.1 | 1002.7 | 1006.4 | 1010.0 | 1013.6 |
| 2390 | 1017.2 | 1020.9 | 1024.5 | 1028.2 | 1031.8 | 1035.5 | 1039.2 | 1042.9 | 1046.5 | 1050.2 |
| 2400 | 1053.9 | | | | | | | | | |

# APPENDIX - 2

**List of Lunar Eclipses from year 1901 to 2100 (as per 'Outfile1.txt')**

```
1901 May 03 18.30 Penumbral
1901 Oct 27 15.12 Partial
1902 Apr 22 18.81 Total
1902 Oct 17 06.02 Total
1903 Apr 12 00.29 Partial
1903 Oct 06 15.40 Partial
1904 Mar 02 02.79 Penumbral
1904 Mar 31 12.73 Penumbral
1904 Sep 24 17.84 Penumbral
1905 Feb 19 18.86 Partial
1905 Aug 15 03.53 Partial
1906 Feb 09 07.76 Total
1906 Aug 04 13.00 Total
1907 Jan 29 13.75 Partial
1907 Jul 25 04.48 Partial
1908 Jan 18 13.62 Penumbral
1908 Jun 14 13.92 Penumbral
1908 Jul 13 21.80 Penumbral
1908 Dec 07 21.73 Penumbral
1909 Jun 04 01.41 Total
1909 Nov 27 08.86 Total
1910 May 24 05.64 Total
1910 Nov 17 00.42 Total
1911 May 13 06.15 Penumbral
1911 Nov 06 15.80 Penumbral
```

```
1912 Apr 01 22.06 Partial
1912 Sep 26 11.58 Partial
1913 Mar 22 11.92 Total
1913 Sep 15 12.76 Total
1914 Mar 12 04.29 Partial
1914 Sep 04 14.01 Partial
1915 Jan 31 04.68 Penumbral
1915 Mar 01 18.53 Penumbral
1915 Jul 26 12.17 Penumbral
1915 Aug 24 21.67 Penumbral
1916 Jan 20 08.48 Partial
1916 Jul 15 04.66 Partial
1917 Jan 08 07.69 Total
1917 Jul 04 21.67 Total
1917 Dec 28 09.86 Partial
1918 Jun 24 10.63 Partial
1918 Dec 17 19.29 Penumbral
1919 May 15 01.02 Penumbral
1919 Nov 07 23.59 Partial
1920 May 03 01.77 Total
1920 Oct 27 14.15 Total
1921 Apr 22 07.81 Total
1921 Oct 16 22.99 Partial
1922 Mar 13 11.23 Penumbral
1922 Apr 11 20.72 Penumbral
1922 Oct 06 00.97 Penumbral
1923 Mar 03 03.38 Partial
1923 Aug 26 10.49 Partial
1924 Feb 20 16.11 Total
1924 Aug 14 20.32 Total
1925 Feb 08 21.80 Partial
1925 Aug 04 11.99 Partial
1926 Jan 28 21.58 Penumbral
1926 Jun 25 21.20 Penumbral
```

```
1926 Jul 25 05.21 Penumbral
1926 Dec 19 06.15 Penumbral
1927 Jun 15 08.31 Total
1927 Dec 08 17.54 Total
1928 Jun 03 12.21 Total
1928 Nov 27 09.10 Total
1929 May 23 12.83 Penumbral
1929 Nov 17 00.23 Penumbral
1930 Apr 13 05.82 Partial
1930 Oct 07 18.93 Partial
1931 Apr 02 20.09 Total
1931 Sep 26 19.75 Total
1932 Mar 22 12.62 Partial
1932 Sep 14 21.10 Partial
1933 Feb 10 13.00 Penumbral
1933 Mar 12 02.75 Penumbral
1933 Aug 05 19.54 Penumbral
1933 Sep 04 05.08 Penumbral
1934 Jan 30 16.52 Partial
1934 Jul 26 12.14 Partial
1935 Jan 19 15.73 Total
1935 Jul 16 05.01 Total
1936 Jan 08 18.23 Total
1936 Jul 04 17.58 Partial
1936 Dec 28 04.00 Penumbral
1937 May 25 07.62 Penumbral
1937 Nov 18 08.16 Partial
1938 May 14 08.64 Total
1938 Nov 07 22.39 Total
1939 May 03 15.24 Total
1939 Oct 28 06.70 Partial
1940 Mar 23 19.55 Penumbral
1940 Apr 22 04.61 Penumbral
1940 Oct 16 08.26 Penumbral
```

```
1941 Mar 13 11.78 Partial
1941 Sep 05 17.60 Partial
1942 Mar 03 00.33 Total
1942 Aug 26 03.76 Total
1943 Feb 20 05.75 Partial
1943 Aug 15 19.57 Partial
1944 Feb 09 05.49 Penumbral
1944 Jul 06 04.45 Penumbral
1944 Aug 04 12.66 Penumbral
1944 Dec 29 14.64 Penumbral
1945 Jun 25 15.14 Partial
1945 Dec 19 02.28 Total
1946 Jun 14 18.70 Total
1946 Dec 08 17.87 Total
1947 Jun 03 19.44 Partial
1947 Nov 28 08.76 Penumbral
1948 Apr 23 13.47 Partial
1948 Oct 18 02.40 Penumbral
1949 Apr 13 04.13 Total
1949 Oct 07 02.89 Total
1950 Apr 02 20.81 Total
1950 Sep 26 04.36 Total
1951 Mar 23 10.83 Penumbral
1951 Aug 17 02.99 Penumbral
1951 Sep 15 12.64 Penumbral
1952 Feb 11 00.47 Partial
1952 Aug 05 19.67 Partial
1953 Jan 29 23.74 Total
1953 Jul 26 12.35 Total
1954 Jan 19 02.61 Total
1954 Jul 16 00.49 Partial
1955 Jan 08 12.74 Penumbral
1955 Jun 05 14.14 Penumbral
1955 Nov 29 16.84 Partial
```

```
1956 May 24 15.43 Partial
1956 Nov 18 06.74 Total
1957 May 13 22.57 Total
1957 Nov 07 14.54 Total
1958 Apr 04 03.74 Penumbral
1958 May 03 12.39 Partial
1958 Oct 27 15.68 Penumbral
1959 Mar 24 20.04 Partial
1959 Sep 17 00.86 Penumbral
1960 Mar 13 08.42 Total
1960 Sep 05 11.32 Total
1961 Mar 02 13.57 Partial
1961 Aug 26 03.22 Partial
1962 Feb 19 13.30 Penumbral
1962 Jul 17 11.68 Penumbral
1962 Aug 15 20.16 Penumbral
1963 Jan 09 23.14 Penumbral
1963 Jul 06 21.92 Partial
1963 Dec 30 11.08 Total
1964 Jun 25 01.13 Total
1964 Dec 19 02.69 Total
1965 Jun 14 02.00 Partial
1965 Dec 08 17.36 Penumbral
1966 May 04 21.02 Penumbral
1966 Oct 29 10.00 Penumbral
1967 Apr 24 12.06 Total
1967 Oct 18 10.18 Total
1968 Apr 13 04.86 Total
1968 Oct 06 11.77 Total
1969 Apr 02 18.75 Penumbral
1969 Aug 27 10.55 Penumbral
1969 Sep 25 20.35 Penumbral
1970 Feb 21 08.31 Partial
1970 Aug 17 03.26 Partial
```

```
1971 Feb 10 07.68 Total
1971 Aug 06 19.71 Total
1972 Jan 30 10.97 Total
1972 Jul 26 07.40 Partial
1973 Jan 18 21.47 Penumbral
1973 Jun 15 20.58 Penumbral
1973 Jul 15 11.94 Penumbral
1973 Dec 10 01.59 Partial
1974 Jun 04 22.15 Partial
1974 Nov 29 15.17 Total
1975 May 25 05.84 Total
1975 Nov 18 22.48 Total
1976 May 13 20.07 Partial
1976 Nov 06 23.25 Penumbral
1977 Apr 04 04.16 Partial
1977 Sep 27 08.29 Penumbral
1978 Mar 24 16.35 Total
1978 Sep 16 19.02 Total
1979 Mar 13 21.24 Partial
1979 Sep 06 10.98 Total
1980 Mar 01 21.00 Penumbral
1980 Jul 27 18.91 Penumbral
1980 Aug 26 03.71 Penumbral
1981 Jan 20 07.65 Penumbral
1981 Jul 17 04.67 Partial
1982 Jan 09 19.88 Total
1982 Jul 06 07.53 Total
1982 Dec 30 11.55 Total
1983 Jun 25 08.53 Partial
1983 Dec 20 02.00 Penumbral
1984 May 15 04.48 Penumbral
1984 Jun 13 14.70 Penumbral
1984 Nov 08 17.73 Penumbral
1985 May 04 19.88 Total
```

```
1985 Oct 28 17.63 Total
1986 Apr 24 12.78 Total
1986 Oct 17 19.36 Total
1987 Apr 14 02.51 Penumbral
1987 Oct 07 04.21 Penumbral
1988 Mar 03 16.02 Penumbral
1988 Aug 27 10.93 Partial
1989 Feb 20 15.53 Total
1989 Aug 17 03.11 Total
1990 Feb 09 19.27 Total
1990 Aug 06 14.32 Partial
1991 Jan 30 06.17 Penumbral
1991 Jun 27 02.98 Penumbral
1991 Jul 26 18.41 Penumbral
1991 Dec 21 10.39 Partial
1992 Jun 15 04.83 Partial
1992 Dec 09 23.68 Total
1993 Jun 04 13.05 Total
1993 Nov 29 06.51 Total
1994 May 25 03.66 Partial
1994 Nov 18 06.95 Penumbral
1995 Apr 15 12.13 Partial
1995 Oct 08 15.87 Penumbral
1996 Apr 04 00.11 Total
1996 Sep 27 02.85 Total
1997 Mar 24 04.75 Partial
1997 Sep 16 18.85 Total
1998 Mar 13 04.58 Penumbral
1998 Aug 08 02.16 Penumbral
1998 Sep 06 11.35 Penumbral
1999 Jan 31 16.13 Penumbral
1999 Jul 28 11.41 Partial
2000 Jan 20 04.68 Total
2000 Jul 16 13.92 Total
```

```
2001 Jan 09 20.42 Total
2001 Jul 05 15.07 Partial
2001 Dec 30 10.68 Penumbral
2002 May 26 11.87 Penumbral
2002 Jun 24 21.72 Penumbral
2002 Nov 20 01.57 Penumbral
2003 May 16 03.60 Total
2003 Nov 09 01.23 Total
2004 May 04 20.57 Total
2004 Oct 28 03.12 Total
2005 Apr 24 10.12 Penumbral
2005 Oct 17 12.23 Partial
2006 Mar 14 23.60 Penumbral
2006 Sep 07 18.70 Partial
2007 Mar 03 23.29 Total
2007 Aug 28 10.59 Total
2008 Feb 21 03.50 Total
2008 Aug 16 21.28 Partial
2009 Feb 09 14.82 Penumbral
2009 Jul 07 09.36 Penumbral
2009 Aug 06 00.92 Penumbral
2009 Dec 31 19.22 Partial
2010 Jun 26 11.51 Partial
2010 Dec 21 08.23 Total
2011 Jun 15 20.22 Total
2011 Dec 10 14.62 Total
2012 Jun 04 11.20 Partial
2012 Nov 28 14.77 Penumbral
2013 Apr 25 19.97 Partial
2013 May 25 04.43 Penumbral
2013 Oct 18 23.63 Penumbral
2014 Apr 15 07.72 Total
2014 Oct 08 10.84 Total
2015 Apr 04 12.11 Partial
```

```
2015 Sep 28 02.84 Total
2016 Mar 23 12.02 Penumbral
2016 Sep 16 19.10 Penumbral
2017 Feb 11 00.56 Penumbral
2017 Aug 07 18.19 Partial
2018 Jan 31 13.45 Total
2018 Jul 27 20.34 Total
2019 Jan 21 05.26 Total
2019 Jul 16 21.64 Partial
2020 Jan 10 19.36 Penumbral
2020 Jun 05 19.21 Penumbral
2020 Jul 05 04.74 Penumbral
2020 Nov 30 09.50 Penumbral
2021 May 26 11.24 Total
2021 Nov 19 08.96 Partial
2022 May 16 04.23 Total
2022 Nov 08 11.04 Total
2023 May 05 17.57 Penumbral
2023 Oct 28 20.40 Partial
2024 Mar 25 07.02 Penumbral
2024 Sep 18 02.58 Partial
2025 Mar 14 06.93 Total
2025 Sep 07 18.14 Total
2026 Mar 03 11.65 Total
2026 Aug 28 04.31 Partial
2027 Feb 20 23.40 Penumbral
2027 Jul 18 15.75 Penumbral
2027 Aug 17 07.48 Penumbral
2028 Jan 12 04.05 Partial
2028 Jul 06 18.19 Partial
2028 Dec 31 16.80 Total
2029 Jun 26 03.39 Total
2029 Dec 20 22.77 Total
2030 Jun 15 18.69 Partial
```

```
2030 Dec 09 22.68 Penumbral
2031 May 07 03.67 Penumbral
2031 Jun 05 11.98 Penumbral
2031 Oct 30 07.55 Penumbral
2032 Apr 25 15.16 Total
2032 Oct 18 18.98 Total
2033 Apr 14 19.30 Total
2033 Oct 08 10.97 Total
2034 Apr 03 19.33 Penumbral
2034 Sep 28 02.94 Partial
2035 Feb 22 08.91 Penumbral
2035 Aug 19 01.00 Partial
2036 Feb 11 22.16 Total
2036 Aug 07 02.82 Total
2037 Jan 31 14.07 Total
2037 Jul 27 04.26 Partial
2038 Jan 21 04.00 Penumbral
2038 Jun 17 02.51 Penumbral
2038 Jul 16 11.80 Penumbral
2038 Dec 11 17.51 Penumbral
2039 Jun 06 18.80 Partial
2039 Nov 30 16.82 Partial
2040 May 26 11.79 Total
2040 Nov 18 19.10 Total
2041 May 16 00.88 Partial
2041 Nov 08 04.72 Partial
2042 Apr 05 14.28 Penumbral
2042 Sep 29 10.57 Penumbral
2043 Mar 25 14.43 Total
2043 Sep 19 01.79 Total
2044 Mar 13 19.69 Total
2044 Sep 07 11.41 Total
2045 Mar 03 07.88 Penumbral
2045 Aug 27 14.13 Penumbral
```

```
2046 Jan 22 12.86 Partial
2046 Jul 18 00.91 Partial
2047 Jan 12 01.37 Total
2047 Jul 07 10.56 Total
2048 Jan 01 06.95 Total
2048 Jun 26 02.14 Partial
2048 Dec 20 06.66 Penumbral
2049 May 17 11.24 Penumbral
2049 Jun 15 19.45 Penumbral
2049 Nov 09 15.63 Penumbral
2050 May 06 22.45 Total
2050 Oct 30 03.26 Total
2051 Apr 26 02.32 Total
2051 Oct 19 19.22 Total
2052 Apr 14 02.49 Penumbral
2052 Oct 08 10.90 Partial
2053 Mar 04 17.17 Penumbral
2053 Aug 29 07.89 Penumbral
2054 Feb 22 06.78 Total
2054 Aug 18 09.36 Total
2055 Feb 11 22.81 Total
2055 Aug 07 10.95 Partial
2056 Feb 01 12.59 Penumbral
2056 Jun 27 09.80 Penumbral
2056 Jul 26 18.91 Penumbral
2056 Dec 22 01.57 Penumbral
2057 Jun 17 02.31 Partial
2057 Dec 11 00.77 Partial
2058 Jun 06 19.26 Total
2058 Nov 30 03.28 Total
2059 May 27 08.06 Partial
2059 Nov 19 13.16 Partial
2060 Apr 15 21.38 Penumbral
2060 Oct 09 18.68 Penumbral
```

```
2060 Nov 08 04.29 Penumbral
2061 Apr 04 21.81 Total
2061 Sep 29 09.53 Total
2062 Mar 25 03.61 Total
2062 Sep 18 18.60 Total
2063 Mar 14 16.25 Partial
2063 Sep 07 20.88 Penumbral
2064 Feb 02 21.62 Partial
2064 Jul 28 07.68 Partial
2065 Jan 22 09.89 Total
2065 Jul 17 17.76 Total
2066 Jan 11 15.12 Total
2066 Jul 07 09.58 Partial
2066 Dec 31 14.68 Penumbral
2067 May 28 18.69 Penumbral
2067 Jun 27 02.87 Penumbral
2067 Nov 20 23.83 Penumbral
2068 May 17 05.58 Partial
2068 Nov 09 11.67 Total
2069 May 06 09.20 Total
2069 Oct 30 03.58 Total
2070 Apr 25 09.52 Penumbral
2070 Oct 19 18.98 Partial
2071 Mar 16 01.31 Penumbral
2071 Sep 09 14.85 Penumbral
2072 Mar 04 15.30 Total
2072 Aug 28 15.99 Total
2073 Feb 22 07.45 Total
2073 Aug 17 17.74 Total
2074 Feb 11 21.10 Penumbral
2074 Jul 08 17.09 Penumbral
2074 Aug 07 02.09 Penumbral
2075 Jan 02 09.66 Penumbral
2075 Jun 28 09.78 Partial
```

```
2075 Dec 22 08.80 Partial
2076 Jun 17 02.64 Total
2076 Dec 10 11.57 Total
2077 Jun 06 15.13 Partial
2077 Nov 29 21.71 Partial
2078 Apr 27 04.33 Penumbral
2078 Oct 21 02.91 Penumbral
2078 Nov 19 12.88 Penumbral
2079 Apr 16 05.05 Partial
2079 Oct 10 17.39 Total
2080 Apr 04 11.41 Total
2080 Sep 29 01.90 Total
2081 Mar 25 00.50 Partial
2081 Sep 18 03.75 Penumbral
2082 Feb 13 06.29 Partial
2082 Aug 08 14.54 Penumbral
2083 Feb 02 18.35 Total
2083 Jul 29 01.00 Total
2084 Jan 22 23.26 Total
2084 Jul 17 17.03 Partial
2085 Jan 10 22.71 Penumbral
2085 Jun 08 02.05 Penumbral
2085 Jul 07 10.25 Penumbral
2085 Dec 01 08.16 Penumbral
2086 May 28 12.59 Partial
2086 Nov 20 20.20 Partial
2087 May 17 15.93 Total
2087 Nov 10 12.08 Total
2088 May 05 16.43 Partial
2088 Oct 30 03.16 Partial
2089 Mar 26 09.35 Penumbral
2089 Sep 19 21.92 Penumbral
2090 Mar 15 23.71 Total
2090 Sep 08 22.74 Total
```

```
2091 Mar 05 15.98 Total
2091 Aug 29 00.65 Total
2092 Feb 23 05.49 Penumbral
2092 Jul 19 00.40 Penumbral
2092 Aug 17 09.37 Penumbral
2093 Jan 12 17.73 Penumbral
2093 Jul 08 17.24 Partial
2094 Jan 01 16.86 Partial
2094 Jun 28 09.97 Total
2094 Dec 21 19.94 Total
2095 Jun 17 22.10 Partial
2095 Dec 11 06.35 Partial
2096 May 07 11.13 Penumbral
2096 Jun 06 02.99 Penumbral
2096 Oct 31 11.27 Penumbral
2096 Nov 29 21.57 Penumbral
2097 Apr 26 12.17 Partial
2097 Oct 21 01.37 Total
2098 Apr 15 19.09 Total
2098 Oct 10 09.32 Total
2099 Apr 05 08.62 Partial
2099 Sep 29 10.75 Penumbral
2100 Feb 24 14.87 Penumbral
2100 Aug 19 21.49 Penumbral
```

*Note. This is a data-file hence nothing other than data such as title etc. is included.*

# APPENDIX - 3

**List of Solar Eclipses (file 'SE_LIST1.TXT')**
1901 May 18 05.62 Total
1901 Nov 11 07.58 Annular
1902 Apr 08 13.82 Partial
1902 May 07 22.74 Partial
1902 Oct 31 08.23 Partial
1903 Mar 29 01.43 Annular
1903 Sep 21 04.51 Total
1904 Mar 17 05.64 Annular
1904 Sep 09 20.72 Total
1905 Mar 06 05.32 Annular
1905 Aug 30 13.22 Total
1906 Feb 23 07.95 Partial
1906 Jul 21 12.99 Partial
1906 Aug 20 01.46 Partial
1907 Jan 14 05.94 Total
1907 Jul 10 15.28 Annular
1908 Jan 03 21.73 Total
1908 Jun 28 16.52 Annular
1908 Dec 23 11.82 Annular
1909 Jun 17 23.47 Annular
1909 Dec 12 19.98 Partial
1910 May 09 05.54 Total
1910 Nov 02 01.93 Partial
1911 Apr 28 22.41 Total
1911 Oct 22 04.16 Annular
1912 Apr 17 11.65 Annular

```
1912 Oct 10 13.68 Total
1913 Apr 06 17.78 Partial
1913 Aug 31 20.63 Partial
1913 Sep 30 04.94 Partial
1914 Feb 25 00.02 Annular
1914 Aug 21 12.44 Total
1915 Feb 14 04.51 Annular
1915 Aug 10 22.87 Annular
1916 Feb 03 16.09 Total
1916 Jul 30 02.25 Annular
1916 Dec 24 20.52 Partial
1917 Jan 23 07.66 Partial
1917 Jun 19 13.03 Partial
1917 Jul 19 03.00 Partial
1917 Dec 14 09.29 Annular
1918 Jun 08 22.04 Total
1918 Dec 03 15.32 Annular
1919 May 29 13.20 Total
1919 Nov 22 15.33 Annular
1920 May 18 06.41 Partial
1920 Nov 10 16.09 Partial
1921 Apr 08 09.08 Annular
1921 Oct 01 12.43 Total
1922 Mar 28 13.05 Annular
1922 Sep 21 04.64 Total
1923 Mar 17 12.84 Annular
1923 Sep 10 20.88 Total
1924 Mar 05 15.95 Partial
1924 Jul 31 19.70 Partial
1924 Aug 30 08.62 Partial
1925 Jan 24 14.74 Total
1925 Jul 20 21.67 Annular
1926 Jan 14 06.58 Total
1926 Jul 09 23.09 Annular
```

```
1927 Jan 03 20.47 Annular
1927 Jun 29 06.52 Total
1927 Dec 24 04.22 Partial
1928 May 19 13.22 Total
1928 Jun 17 20.69 Partial
1928 Nov 12 09.59 Partial
1929 May 09 06.12 Total
1929 Nov 01 12.01 Annular
1930 Apr 28 19.15 Annular
1930 Oct 21 21.79 Total
1931 Apr 18 00.99 Partial
1931 Sep 12 04.44 Partial
1931 Oct 11 13.10 Partial
1932 Mar 07 07.73 Annular
1932 Aug 31 19.92 Total
1933 Feb 24 12.73 Annular
1933 Aug 21 05.81 Annular
1934 Feb 14 00.72 Total
1934 Aug 10 08.76 Annular
1935 Jan 05 05.33 Partial
1935 Feb 03 16.45 Partial
1935 Jun 30 19.74 Partial
1935 Jul 30 09.54 Partial
1935 Dec 25 17.82 Annular
1936 Jun 19 05.24 Total
1936 Dec 13 23.42 Annular
1937 Jun 08 20.72 Total
1937 Dec 02 23.18 Annular
1938 May 29 13.99 Total
1938 Nov 22 00.09 Partial
1939 Apr 19 16.57 Annular
1939 Oct 12 20.51 Total
1940 Apr 07 20.30 Annular
1940 Oct 01 12.69 Total
```

```
1941 Mar 27 20.23 Annular
1941 Sep 21 04.64 Total
1942 Mar 16 23.84 Partial
1942 Aug 12 02.45 Partial
1942 Sep 10 15.87 Partial
1943 Feb 04 23.49 Total
1943 Aug 01 04.10 Annular
1944 Jan 25 15.40 Total
1944 Jul 20 05.71 Annular
1945 Jan 14 05.11 Annular
1945 Jul 09 13.59 Total
1946 Jan 03 12.49 Partial
1946 May 30 20.83 Partial
1946 Jun 29 04.10 Partial
1946 Nov 23 17.39 Partial
1947 May 20 13.72 Total
1947 Nov 12 20.02 Annular
1948 May 09 02.50 Annular
1948 Nov 01 06.05 Total
1949 Apr 28 08.03 Partial
1949 Oct 21 21.39 Partial
1950 Mar 18 15.33 Annular
1950 Sep 12 03.48 Total
1951 Mar 07 20.85 Annular
1951 Sep 01 12.83 Annular
1952 Feb 25 09.27 Total
1952 Aug 20 15.35 Annular
1953 Jan 15 14.14 Partial
1953 Feb 14 01.17 Partial
1953 Jul 11 02.47 Partial
1953 Aug 09 16.17 Partial
1954 Jan 05 02.35 Annular
1954 Jun 30 12.43 Total
1954 Dec 25 07.56 Annular
```

```
1955 Jun 20 04.19 Total
1955 Dec 14 07.13 Annular
1956 Jun 08 21.49 Total
1956 Dec 02 08.21 Partial
1957 Apr 29 23.90 Annular
1957 Oct 23 04.72 Total
1958 Apr 19 03.39 Annular
1958 Oct 12 20.87 Total
1959 Apr 08 03.48 Annular
1959 Oct 02 12.52 Total
1960 Mar 27 07.61 Partial
1960 Sep 20 23.22 Partial
1961 Feb 15 08.16 Total
1961 Aug 11 10.59 Annular
1962 Feb 05 00.17 Total
1962 Jul 31 12.39 Annular
1963 Jan 25 13.70 Annular
1963 Jul 20 20.71 Total
1964 Jan 14 20.73 Partial
1964 Jun 10 04.37 Partial
1964 Jul 09 11.52 Partial
1964 Dec 04 01.30 Partial
1965 May 30 21.22 Total
1965 Nov 23 04.17 Annular
1966 May 20 09.71 Annular
1966 Nov 12 14.44 Total
1967 May 09 14.93 Partial
1967 Nov 02 05.81 Total
1968 Mar 28 22.80 Partial
1968 Sep 22 11.14 Total
1969 Mar 18 04.86 Annular
1969 Sep 11 19.94 Annular
1970 Mar 07 17.71 Total
1970 Aug 31 22.03 Annular
```

```
1971 Feb 25 09.80 Partial
1971 Jul 22 09.25 Partial
1971 Aug 20 22.89 Partial
1972 Jan 16 10.87 Annular
1972 Jul 10 19.65 Total
1973 Jan 04 15.71 Annular
1973 Jun 30 11.65 Total
1973 Dec 24 15.13 Annular
1974 Jun 20 04.92 Total
1974 Dec 13 16.42 Partial
1975 May 11 07.08 Partial
1975 Nov 03 13.08 Partial
1976 Apr 29 10.33 Annular
1976 Oct 23 05.17 Total
1977 Apr 18 10.60 Annular
1977 Oct 12 20.51 Total
1978 Apr 07 15.27 Partial
1978 Oct 02 06.67 Partial
1979 Feb 26 16.76 Total
1979 Aug 22 17.17 Annular
1980 Feb 16 08.85 Total
1980 Aug 10 19.17 Annular
1981 Feb 04 22.23 Annular
1981 Jul 31 03.88 Total
1982 Jan 25 04.93 Partial
1982 Jun 21 11.87 Partial
1982 Jul 20 18.95 Partial
1982 Dec 15 09.30 Partial
1983 Jun 11 04.63 Total
1983 Dec 04 12.43 Annular
1984 May 30 16.80 Annular
1984 Nov 22 22.96 Total
1985 May 19 21.69 Partial
1985 Nov 12 14.35 Total
```

```
1986 Apr 09 06.14 Partial
1986 Oct 03 18.91 Annular
1987 Mar 29 12.76 Annular
1987 Sep 23 03.14 Annular
1988 Mar 18 02.04 Total
1988 Sep 11 04.82 Annular
1989 Mar 07 18.32 Partial
1989 Aug 31 05.75 Partial
1990 Jan 26 19.34 Annular
1990 Jul 22 02.90 Total
1991 Jan 15 23.84 Annular
1991 Jul 11 19.11 Total
1992 Jan 04 23.16 Annular
1992 Jun 30 12.31 Total
1992 Dec 24 00.71 Partial
1993 May 21 14.12 Partial
1993 Nov 13 21.57 Partial
1994 May 10 17.12 Annular
1994 Nov 03 13.59 Total
1995 Apr 29 17.60 Annular
1995 Oct 24 04.61 Total
1996 Apr 17 22.81 Partial
1996 Oct 12 14.25 Partial
1997 Mar 09 01.24 Total
1997 Sep 01 23.87 Partial
1998 Feb 26 17.44 Total
1998 Aug 22 02.05 Annular
1999 Feb 16 06.66 Annular
1999 Aug 11 11.14 Total
2000 Feb 04 13.06 Partial
2000 Jul 01 19.34 Partial
2000 Jul 31 02.42 Partial
2000 Dec 25 17.37 Partial
2001 Jun 21 11.97 Total
```

```
2001 Dec 14 20.80 Annular
2002 Jun 10 23.79 Annular
2002 Dec 04 07.58 Total
2003 May 31 04.33 Annular
2003 Nov 23 22.99 Total
2004 Apr 19 13.36 Partial
2004 Oct 14 02.80 Partial
2005 Apr 08 20.54 Annular
2005 Oct 03 10.47 Annular
2006 Mar 29 10.26 Total
2006 Sep 22 11.75 Annular
2007 Mar 19 02.71 Partial
2007 Sep 11 12.74 Partial
2008 Feb 07 03.74 Annular
2008 Aug 01 10.21 Total
2009 Jan 26 07.93 Annular
2009 Jul 22 02.58 Total
2010 Jan 15 07.20 Annular
2010 Jul 11 19.68 Total
2011 Jan 04 09.05 Partial
2011 Jun 01 21.04 Partial
2011 Jul 01 08.90 Partial
2011 Nov 25 06.17 Partial
2012 May 20 23.79 Annular
2012 Nov 13 22.14 Total
2013 May 10 00.49 Annular
2013 Nov 03 12.84 Annular
2014 Apr 29 06.25 Annular
2014 Oct 23 21.95 Partial
2015 Mar 20 09.61 Total
2015 Sep 13 06.69 Partial
2016 Mar 09 01.91 Total
2016 Sep 01 09.06 Annular
2017 Feb 26 14.98 Annular
```

```
2017 Aug 21 18.51 Total
2018 Feb 15 21.09 Partial
2018 Jul 13 02.80 Partial
2018 Aug 11 09.97 Partial
2019 Jan 06 01.47 Partial
2019 Jul 02 19.27 Total
2019 Dec 26 05.23 Annular
2020 Jun 21 06.69 Annular
2020 Dec 14 16.28 Total
2021 Jun 10 10.88 Annular
2021 Dec 04 07.73 Total
2022 Apr 30 20.46 Partial
2022 Oct 25 10.81 Partial
2023 Apr 20 04.22 Annular
2023 Oct 14 17.92 Annular
2024 Apr 08 18.36 Total
2024 Oct 02 18.82 Annular
2025 Mar 29 10.98 Partial
2025 Sep 21 19.89 Partial
2026 Feb 17 12.03 Annular
2026 Aug 12 17.61 Total
2027 Feb 06 15.94 Annular
2027 Aug 02 10.09 Total
2028 Jan 26 15.21 Annular
2028 Jul 22 03.04 Total
2029 Jan 14 17.41 Partial
2029 Jun 12 03.86 Partial
2029 Jul 11 15.87 Partial
2029 Dec 05 14.87 Partial
2030 Jun 01 06.36 Annular
2030 Nov 25 06.78 Total
2031 May 21 07.29 Annular
2031 Nov 14 21.17 Annular
2032 May 09 13.60 Annular
```

```
2032 Nov 03 05.76 Partial
2033 Mar 30 17.87 Total
2033 Sep 23 13.66 Partial
2034 Mar 20 10.26 Total
2034 Sep 12 16.22 Annular
2035 Mar 09 23.17 Annular
2035 Sep 02 01.99 Total
2036 Feb 27 05.00 Partial
2036 Jul 23 10.28 Partial
2036 Aug 21 17.59 Partial
2037 Jan 16 09.58 Partial
2037 Jul 13 02.54 Total
2038 Jan 05 13.70 Annular
2038 Jul 02 13.54 Annular
2038 Dec 26 01.04 Total
2039 Jun 21 17.36 Annular
2039 Dec 15 16.54 Total
2040 May 11 03.47 Partial
2040 Nov 04 18.93 Partial
2041 Apr 30 11.79 Total
2041 Oct 25 01.50 Annular
2042 Apr 20 02.33 Total
2042 Oct 14 02.05 Annular
2043 Apr 09 19.11 Total
2043 Oct 03 03.21 Annular
2044 Feb 28 20.21 Annular
2044 Aug 23 01.10 Total
2045 Feb 16 23.86 Annular
2045 Aug 12 17.66 Total
2046 Feb 05 23.18 Annular
2046 Aug 02 10.42 Total
2047 Jan 26 01.75 Partial
2047 Jun 23 10.59 Partial
2047 Jul 22 22.82 Partial
```

```
2047 Dec 16 23.64 Partial
2048 Jun 11 12.84 Annular
2048 Dec 05 15.51 Total
2049 May 31 14.01 Annular
2049 Nov 25 05.59 Annular
2050 May 20 20.86 Annular
2050 Nov 14 13.69 Partial
2051 Apr 11 01.99 Partial
2051 Oct 04 20.77 Partial
2052 Mar 30 18.46 Total
2052 Sep 22 23.54 Annular
2053 Mar 20 07.20 Annular
2053 Sep 12 09.60 Total
2054 Mar 09 12.77 Partial
2054 Aug 03 17.80 Partial
2054 Sep 02 01.30 Partial
2055 Jan 27 17.66 Partial
2055 Jul 24 09.79 Total
2056 Jan 16 22.18 Annular
2056 Jul 12 20.34 Annular
2057 Jan 05 09.83 Total
2057 Jul 01 23.79 Annular
2057 Dec 26 01.38 Total
2058 May 22 10.39 Partial
2058 Jun 21 00.58 Partial
2058 Nov 16 03.15 Partial
2059 May 11 19.26 Total
2059 Nov 05 09.19 Annular
2060 Apr 30 10.19 Total
2060 Oct 24 09.42 Annular
2061 Apr 20 03.10 Total
2061 Oct 13 10.69 Annular
2062 Mar 11 04.23 Partial
2062 Sep 03 08.70 Partial
```

```
2063 Feb 28 07.64 Annular
2063 Aug 24 01.29 Total
2064 Feb 17 07.05 Annular
2064 Aug 12 17.83 Total
2065 Feb 05 10.04 Partial
2065 Jul 03 17.27 Partial
2065 Aug 02 05.77 Partial
2065 Dec 27 08.45 Partial
2066 Jun 22 19.26 Annular
2066 Dec 17 00.29 Total
2067 Jun 11 20.68 Annular
2067 Dec 06 14.09 Annular
2068 May 31 04.06 Total
2068 Nov 24 21.70 Partial
2069 Apr 21 09.98 Partial
2069 May 20 18.11 Partial
2069 Oct 15 04.05 Partial
2070 Apr 11 02.51 Total
2070 Oct 04 07.01 Annular
2071 Mar 31 15.07 Annular
2071 Sep 23 17.35 Total
2072 Mar 19 20.38 Partial
2072 Sep 12 09.11 Total
2073 Feb 07 01.68 Partial
2073 Aug 03 17.06 Total
2074 Jan 27 06.63 Annular
2074 Jul 24 03.12 Annular
2075 Jan 16 18.62 Total
2075 Jul 13 06.20 Annular
2076 Jan 06 10.24 Total
2076 Jun 01 17.24 Partial
2076 Jul 01 07.09 Partial
2076 Nov 26 11.46 Partial
2077 May 22 02.64 Total
```

```
2077 Nov 15 17.00 Annular
2078 May 11 17.95 Total
2078 Nov 04 16.94 Annular
2079 May 01 10.95 Total
2079 Oct 24 18.33 Annular
2080 Mar 21 12.10 Partial
2080 Sep 13 16.42 Partial
2081 Mar 10 15.29 Annular
2081 Sep 03 09.01 Total
2082 Feb 27 14.83 Annular
2082 Aug 24 01.29 Total
2083 Feb 16 18.27 Partial
2083 Jul 14 23.90 Partial
2083 Aug 13 12.75 Partial
2084 Jan 07 17.29 Partial
2084 Jul 03 01.64 Annular
2084 Dec 27 09.11 Total
2085 Jun 22 03.32 Annular
2085 Dec 16 22.64 Annular
2086 Jun 11 11.21 Total
2086 Dec 06 05.80 Partial
2087 May 02 17.86 Partial
2087 Jun 01 01.65 Partial
2087 Oct 26 11.48 Partial
2088 Apr 21 10.43 Total
2088 Oct 14 14.65 Annular
2089 Apr 10 22.78 Annular
2089 Oct 04 01.23 Total
2090 Mar 31 03.82 Partial
2090 Sep 23 17.04 Total
2091 Feb 18 09.64 Partial
2091 Aug 15 00.36 Total
2092 Feb 07 15.05 Annular
2092 Aug 03 09.91 Annular
```

```
2093 Jan 27 03.37 Total
2093 Jul 23 12.61 Annular
2094 Jan 16 19.10 Total
2094 Jun 13 00.05 Partial
2094 Jul 12 13.61 Partial
2094 Dec 07 19.84 Partial
2095 Jun 02 09.97 Total
2095 Nov 27 00.90 Annular
2096 May 22 01.60 Total
2096 Nov 15 00.60 Annular
2097 May 11 18.69 Total
2097 Nov 04 02.13 Annular
2098 Apr 01 19.81 Partial
2098 Sep 25 00.27 Partial
2098 Oct 24 10.80 Partial
2099 Mar 21 22.79 Annular
2099 Sep 14 16.84 Total
2100 Mar 10 22.49 Annular
2100 Sep 04 08.82 Total
```

# APPENDIX – 4

## Names of Variables and Constants

| | |
|---|---|
| a | [Array of Mean distance from Sun] |
| A | rate of change of U |
| a0 | [Array of a at J2000 for planets] |
| AT | [Array of approx. contact times] |
| ATmid | Approximate Mid-eclipse time |
| AU | Astronomical Unit |
| Ayan | Ayanamsha |
| B | rate of change of V |
| b_array | [Array of Terms of Moon's latitude] |
| Bm | Latitude of Moon |
| clrB | Background color for pictures and videos |
| clrM | Moon color in pictures and videos |
| clrP | Penumbra color in pictures and videos |
| clrPL | color of penumbral shadow on land portion |
| clrPW | color of penumbral shadow on water portion |
| clrU | Umbra color in pictures and videos |
| clrUL | color of umbral shadow on land portion |
| clrUW | color of umbral shadow on water portion |
| contact | [Array of Contacts status] |
| cos_d1 | cos(declination of shadow-centre) |
| cos_h1 | cos(Hou rAngle of Shadow) |
| ct = CT1,CT2... | [Array of Contact Times] in solar eclipse |
| cthms | Contact Times (h:m:s) |
| D | Mean Elongation of Moon from Sun |
| d, d1, d2 | Number of days since J2000 |

| | |
|---|---|
| da | [Array of change in a] |
| date | date of the event |
| dc | Declination |
| dcm1,dcm2 | Declination of Moon |
| dcs1,dcs2 | Declination of Sun |
| de | [Array of change in e] |
| deltad | deltaT in days |
| deltaT | deltaT in seconds |
| deta | change in eta |
| di | [Array of change in i] |
| dim | [Array of days in Months] |
| dl | Sum of Moon's longitude array |
| dl_array | [Array of Moon's longitude terms] |
| dl00 to dl60 | Terms of Moon's longitude |
| dl1 | Change in Moon's longitude |
| dM | [Array of change in M] |
| dmu | Change in HA of Moon's shadow |
| dN | [Array of change in N] |
| dObl | change in obliquity |
| dphi | Nutation in Moon's longitude |
| dpsi | Nutation in longitude |
| dr | sum of Moon's distance array |
| dr_array | [Array of Moon's distance terms] |
| dr01 to dr60 | Moon's distance terms |
| dST | Change in Sidereal Time |
| du0 | Number of days at 0:0 UT |
| dw | [Array of change in w] |
| dxi | change in xi |
| e | [Array of eccentricity of planet's orbit] |
| E,E0,E1 | Eccentric Anomoly values |
| E,E2,A1,A2,A3 | Auxiliaries in Moon Calculation |
| e0 | [Array of e at J2000 for planets] |
| earthrad | Radius of Earth (6378.137km) |
| ep | [Array of Earth to Planet distance] |

| | |
|---|---|
| eta1 | Value of eta at time T1 |
| EW | East/West notation |
| EWlong | East/West notation |
| F | Mean argument of Moon's latitude |
| f1 | semi-vertical angle of penumbral cone |
| f2 | semi-vertical angle of umbral cone |
| ff | Earth's flattening factor |
| ff2 | square of flattening factor |
| gama | Nearest distance of shadow from Earth |
| GC | [Array of Global contact status] |
| geew | East /West notation for GE |
| gelat | latitude of Greatest Eclipse |
| gelong | longitude of Greatest Eclipse |
| gens | North/South notation for GE |
| glat | latitude of a place |
| glong | longitude of a place |
| GMST0 | GST at Greenwich at 0:0 UT |
| GST,GST1, | Greenwich Sidereal Time at a place |
| GT | Array of Global Timings |
| GTx | X coordinates Global positions |
| GTy | Y coordinates Global positions |
| hh | Hour Angle of Moon's shadow |
| i | [Array of inclination of planet's orbit] |
| i0 | [Array of i at J2000 for planets] |
| j_array | Perturbations in Jupiter |
| K | Moon/Earth Ratio |
| L | pixel color (rgb) in Map in land portion |
| L0 | Mean longitude of Sun |
| l11 | Radius of Penumbra on Fundamental plane |
| L11 | Radius of Penumbra on Observer's plane |
| l21 | Radius of Umbra on Fundamental plane |
| L21 | Radius of Umbra on Observer's plane |
| Land | pixel color (rgb) in Map in land portion |
| lat | latitude |

| | |
|---|---|
| LE_Title | Title string for lunar eclipse |
| ledat | string for date in a required format |
| letype | Type of lunar eclipse |
| Lm | Longitude of Moon |
| lon | longitude |
| Ls | Mean Ecliptic longitude of Sun |
| M | [Array of Mean Anomaly of planets] |
| M0 | [Array of M at J2000 for planets] |
| magn | Magnitude of eclipse |
| magn2 | Penumbral Magnitude of eclipse |
| md[] | Days till end of previous month |
| MidValue | Time of mid-eclipse |
| Mj | Mean Anomaly of Jupiter |
| Mm | Mean Anomaly of Moon |
| month | Month of the event |
| moonr1,moonr2 | Distance of Moon |
| moonrad | Radius of Moon in km |
| Ms | Mean Anomaly of Saturn |
| Ms | Mean Anomaly of Sun |
| Mu | Mean Anomaly of Uranus |
| mu,mu1,mu2 | Hour Angle of Moon's shadow |
| N | [Array of Longitude of planets asc. node] |
| N | vector Sum of (U+V) |
| N_All | Total number of lunar eclipses |
| N_Partial | Number of Partial eclipses |
| N_Penumbral | Number of Penumbral eclipses |
| N_Total | Number of Total eclipses |
| N0 | [Array of N at J2000 for planets] |
| N2 | Square of N |
| Ndays | Number of days since J2000 |
| NS | North/South notation |
| Obl | Obliquity of ecliptic |
| Obl0 | Mean obliquity |
| Obs | Obscurity in eclipse |

| | |
|---|---|
| Olap | Overlap of Moon over Sun |
| Olat | Observer's latitude |
| Olong | Observer's longitude |
| Om | Omega, longitude of Moon's Asc. Node |
| oppo | Time of opposition of Sun and Moon |
| pcLatSat | perturbations in Saturn's latitude |
| pcLonJup | perturbations in Jupiter's longitude |
| pcLonSat | perturbations in Saturn's longitude |
| pcLonUrn | perturbations in Uranus's longitude |
| pDecl | [Array of declinations of planets] |
| ph | [Array of phases of planets] |
| pLat | [Array of latitudes of planets] |
| plnt | [Array of planet-names] |
| pLong | [Array of longitudes of planets] |
| pm | Parallax of Moon |
| pRA | Array of Right Ascensions of planets |
| PValues | string of Penumbral contact times |
| px | [Array of x-coordinates] |
| py | [Array of x-coordinates] |
| q | [Array of q-values] |
| R | Ratio of Sun/Earth |
| r0 | Mean distance of Moon |
| ra | Right Ascension |
| ram1,ram2 | Rignt Ascension of Moon |
| ras1,ras2 | Rignt Ascension of Sun |
| rcs | Earth Radius * cos(latitude) |
| re | Geocentric Distance of planet |
| res | Earth-Sun distance |
| rh | Heliocentric distance of planet |
| rm | Distance of Moon |
| rM | Radius of Moon in pixels |
| rocoso | Earth Radius * cos(latitude) |
| rosino | Earth Radius * sin(latitude) |
| rp | Radius of Penumbra in ER units |

| | |
|---|---|
| rP | Radius of Penumbra in pixels |
| rsn | Earth Radius * sin(latitude) |
| ru | Radius of Umbra in ER units |
| rU | Radius of Umbra in pixels |
| s_array | [Array of Perturbations in Saturn] |
| scale, scale2 | scale for plotting on screen |
| sdf | Scale Difference Factor |
| sdm | Semi-diameter of Moon in ER Units |
| sdmoon | Semi-diameter of Moon in ER units |
| sds | Semi-diameter of Sun in ER units |
| sdsun | Semi-diameter of Sun in ER units |
| sin_d1 | sin(declination of shadow-centre) |
| sin_h1 | sin(Hour Angle of Shadow) |
| slope | slope of line on screen |
| sp | [Array of Sun to Planet Distance] |
| strCT | string of all contact times |
| sunr1,sunr2 | Distance of Sun |
| sunrad = 696000.0 | Radius of Sun in km |
| T1,T2 | Two chosen instants of time |
| td = 0.2 | Time-Difference between T1 and T2 |
| Tmid | Time of Mid-eclipse |
| tx | [Array of Contact times] in lunar eclipse |
| typ | Integer representing eclipse-type |
| u | [Array of u-values] |
| U | x-coordinate of shadow from Observer |
| u_array | [Array of Perturbations in Uranus] |
| UValues | string of Umbral contact times |
| v | [Array of v-values] |
| V | y-coordinate of shadow from Observer |
| W,Water | pixel color (rgb) in Map in water portion |
| w | [Array of Argument of perihelion] |
| w0 | [Array of w at J2000 for planets] |
| x0 | Zero x-coordinate in pixels on screen |
| x1 | x-coordinate of shadow on funda. plane |

| | |
|---|---|
| xdash | change in x-coordinate |
| xe | Geocentric x-coordinate of planet |
| xh | Heliocentric x-coordinate of planet |
| xi,eta,zeta | Cartesian coordinates of Observer |
| xi1 | Value of xi at time T1 |
| xmid | x-coordinate of shadow at mid-eclipse |
| xsun | Geocentric x-coordinate of Sun |
| y0 | Zero y-coordinate in pixels on screen |
| y1 | y-coordinate of shadow on funda. plane |
| ydash | change in y-coordinate |
| ye | Geocentric y-coordinate of planet |
| year | Year of the event |
| yh | Heliocentric y-coordinate of planet |
| ymid | y-coordinate of shadow at mid-eclipse |
| ysun | Geocentric y-coordinate of Sun |
| z11 | z-coordinate of Moon |
| ze | Geocentric z-coordinate of planet |
| zeta1 | Value of zeta at time T1 |
| zh | Heliocentric z-coordinate of planet |
| zsun | Geocentric z-coordinate of Sun |

## List of User-made Functions

acs(x)

AnimateGlobalTimes()

AnimateLE1()

AnimateLE2()

AnimateMoonPath()

ApproxTimes()

asn(x)

atn(x)

atn2(y,x)

cal_d(date,month,year)

CalCT()

caldays(d,m,y)

calDeltaT(date,month,year)

calGETimes()

CalGlobalTimes()

CalGlobalTimes()

calPlanets(d)

CalPluto(x)

calT1()

calT2()

calT3()

calT4()

caltdq(x)

chkfile(filename)

cs(x)

degs(x)

dim(y)

DistMoon(x)

DrawMoonPath()

EarthShadow()

fpr3(str,x,y)

fprline(n)

GEPosition(x)

GetYears()

grx(lon)

gry(lat)

hms(hr)

htohm(hr)

IterateTmid()

LatMoon(x)

LE_Components()

LE_Msg()

LEframe1()

LEframe2()

LEListMsg()

LEtext()

LonMoon(x)

LonSun(d)

LuniSolar(x)

Magnitude()

MidEclipse(ATmid)

MonthName(x)

MonthNum(MonthName)

MoonValues(x)

Obl_Nut_GST(x)

OpeningFrame()

OpeningPage()

Perturb(x)

PlntMsg()

PlntPos(d,m,y,h,m)

PlotGT()

PlotMoonPath()

PlotStages()

pr_b_array(x)

pr_dl_array(x)

pr_dr_array(x)

pr8dec(x)

ProcessPlanets()

prPerturb()

prPlanets(d,m,y,h,m)

PUMValues()

radc(lon,lat)

radcMoon(x)

radcShadow(x)

rads(x)

rev(x)

rpMoon(x)

rpSun(x)

SE_Msg()

SE_Process()

SEframe()

SEframe2()

SelectLE()

SEList1Msg()

SEList2Msg()

sn(x)

sp(n)

sqrt(x)

strCT()

strdat(y,m,d)

SummeryTable1()

SummeryTable2()

SunValues(x)

Sunxyzr(d)

swap(num1,num2)

TableDeltaT()

tn(x)

UserInterface()

VisibilityMap()

APPENDIX – 6

CATALOGUE

OF

LUNAR

ECLIPSES

DURING

21$^{ST}$ CENTURY

## CATALOGUE OF LUNAR ECLIPSES

| yyyy | mm | dd | Oppos | EclType | Magn(U) | Magn(P) | U1 |
|------|-----|----|-------|-----------|---------|---------|-------|
| 2001 | Jan | 09 | 20.43 | Total | 1.1844 | 2.1675 | 17:46 |
| 2001 | Jul | 05 | 15.09 | Partial | 0.4894 | 1.5532 | 12:14 |
| 2001 | Dec | 30 | 10.70 | Penumbral | -0.1195 | 0.8999 | 08:29 |
| 2002 | May | 26 | 11.89 | Penumbral | -0.2937 | 0.6946 | 10:17 |
| 2002 | Jun | 24 | 21.73 | Penumbral | -0.7983 | 0.2141 | 20:23 |
| 2002 | Nov | 20 | 01.58 | Penumbral | -0.2326 | 0.8652 | 23:35 |
| 2003 | May | 16 | 03.62 | Total | 1.1228 | 2.0799 | 01:08 |
| 2003 | Nov | 09 | 01.24 | Total | 1.0129 | 2.1204 | 22:18 |
| 2004 | May | 04 | 20.58 | Total | 1.2992 | 2.2684 | 17:54 |
| 2004 | Oct | 28 | 03.14 | Total | 1.3035 | 2.3701 | 00:08 |
| 2005 | Apr | 24 | 10.14 | Penumbral | -0.1485 | 0.8707 | 07:53 |
| 2005 | Oct | 17 | 12.25 | Partial | 0.0575 | 1.0639 | 09:54 |
| 2006 | Mar | 14 | 23.60 | Penumbral | -0.0657 | 1.0361 | 21:24 |
| 2006 | Sep | 07 | 18.70 | Partial | 0.1786 | 1.1378 | 16:44 |
| 2007 | Mar | 03 | 23.29 | Total | 1.2280 | 2.3254 | 20:18 |
| 2007 | Aug | 28 | 10.59 | Total | 1.4718 | 2.4589 | 07:54 |
| 2008 | Feb | 21 | 03.50 | Total | 1.1015 | 2.1512 | 00:36 |
| 2008 | Aug | 16 | 21.28 | Partial | 0.8012 | 1.8410 | 18:25 |
| 2009 | Feb | 09 | 14.82 | Penumbral | -0.0962 | 0.9018 | 12:39 |
| 2009 | Jul | 07 | 09.36 | Penumbral | -0.9180 | 0.1626 | 08:37 |
| 2009 | Aug | 06 | 00.92 | Penumbral | -0.6733 | 0.4059 | 23:04 |
| 2009 | Dec | 31 | 19.22 | Partial | 0.0724 | 1.0620 | 17:18 |
| 2010 | Jun | 26 | 11.51 | Partial | 0.5325 | 1.5840 | 08:57 |
| 2010 | Dec | 21 | 08.23 | Total | 1.2521 | 2.2874 | 05:30 |
| 2011 | Jun | 15 | 20.22 | Total | 1.6949 | 2.6922 | 17:24 |
| 2011 | Dec | 10 | 14.62 | Total | 1.0991 | 2.1903 | 11:34 |
| 2012 | Jun | 04 | 11.20 | Partial | 0.3646 | 1.3224 | 08:48 |
| 2012 | Nov | 28 | 14.77 | Penumbral | -0.1946 | 0.9197 | 12:15 |
| 2013 | Apr | 25 | 19.97 | Partial | 0.0113 | 0.9933 | 18:04 |
| 2013 | May | 25 | 04.43 | Penumbral | -0.9412 | 0.0179 | 03:53 |
| 2013 | Oct | 18 | 23.63 | Penumbral | -0.2760 | 0.7716 | 21:50 |
| 2014 | Apr | 15 | 07.72 | Total | 1.2872 | 2.3255 | 04:54 |
| 2014 | Oct | 08 | 10.84 | Total | 1.1615 | 2.1515 | 08:15 |
| 2015 | Apr | 04 | 12.11 | Partial | 0.9943 | 2.0839 | 09:02 |
| 2015 | Sep | 28 | 02.84 | Total | 1.2725 | 2.2358 | 00:12 |
| 2016 | Mar | 23 | 12.02 | Penumbral | -0.3185 | 0.7795 | 09:39 |

## DURING 21ST CENTURY

| U2 | P1 | P2 | MID | P3 | P4 | U3 | U4 |
|-------|-------|-------|-------|-------|-------|-------|-------|
| 18:45 | 18:44 | 19:52 | 20:22 | 20:52 | 22:00 | 21:59 | 22:58 |
| 13:32 | 13:38 | ----- | 14:57 | ----- | 16:16 | 16:22 | 17:40 |
| ----- | ----- | ----- | 10:31 | ----- | ----- | ----- | 12:33 |
| ----- | ----- | ----- | 12:05 | ----- | ----- | ----- | 13:54 |
| ----- | ----- | ----- | 21:29 | ----- | ----- | ----- | 22:34 |
| ----- | ----- | ----- | 01:48 | ----- | ----- | ----- | 04:01 |
| 02:07 | 02:05 | 03:16 | 03:41 | 04:07 | 05:18 | 05:15 | 06:15 |
| 23:27 | 23:34 | 01:10 | 01:20 | 01:29 | 03:05 | 03:13 | 04:22 |
| 18:52 | 18:50 | 19:54 | 20:32 | 21:09 | 22:13 | 22:11 | 23:10 |
| 01:12 | 01:16 | 02:25 | 03:05 | 03:45 | 04:54 | 04:58 | 06:02 |
| ----- | ----- | ----- | 09:57 | ----- | ----- | ----- | 11:60 |
| 11:36 | 11:38 | ----- | 12:04 | ----- | 12:31 | 12:33 | 14:15 |
| 23:24 | ----- | ----- | 23:48 | ----- | ----- | 00:12 | 02:12 |
| 18:12 | 18:07 | ----- | 18:51 | ----- | 19:36 | 19:31 | 20:59 |
| 21:24 | 21:31 | 22:45 | 23:21 | 23:57 | 01:11 | 01:18 | 02:24 |
| 08:52 | 08:52 | 09:53 | 10:37 | 11:22 | 12:23 | 12:23 | 13:21 |
| 01:40 | 01:43 | 03:02 | 03:26 | 03:50 | 05:08 | 05:11 | 06:16 |
| 19:34 | 19:37 | ----- | 21:11 | ----- | 22:44 | 22:47 | 23:56 |
| ----- | ----- | ----- | 14:39 | ----- | ----- | ----- | 16:38 |
| ----- | ----- | ----- | 09:39 | ----- | ----- | ----- | 10:41 |
| ----- | ----- | ----- | 00:40 | ----- | ----- | ----- | 02:15 |
| 18:56 | 18:54 | ----- | 19:23 | ----- | 19:53 | 19:50 | 21:29 |
| 10:13 | 10:18 | ----- | 11:39 | ----- | 12:59 | 13:04 | 14:20 |
| 06:31 | 06:33 | 07:42 | 08:17 | 08:53 | 10:01 | 10:04 | 11:05 |
| 18:23 | 18:23 | 19:23 | 20:12 | 21:02 | 22:02 | 22:02 | 23:01 |
| 12:40 | 12:47 | 14:08 | 14:32 | 14:57 | 16:18 | 16:24 | 17:31 |
| 10:05 | 10:01 | ----- | 11:03 | ----- | 12:06 | 12:02 | 13:19 |
| ----- | ----- | ----- | 14:33 | ----- | ----- | ----- | 16:52 |
| ----- | 19:57 | ----- | 20:08 | ----- | 20:20 | ----- | 22:13 |
| ----- | ----- | ----- | 04:11 | ----- | ----- | ----- | 04:29 |
| ----- | ----- | ----- | 23:50 | ----- | ----- | ----- | 01:50 |
| 05:57 | 05:60 | 07:08 | 07:47 | 08:25 | 09:34 | 09:36 | 10:39 |
| 09:16 | 09:15 | 10:26 | 10:54 | 11:23 | 12:34 | 12:33 | 13:34 |
| 10:11 | 10:17 | ----- | 12:01 | ----- | 13:45 | 13:52 | 15:00 |
| 01:10 | 01:08 | 02:12 | 02:47 | 03:23 | 04:27 | 04:25 | 05:23 |
| ----- | ----- | ----- | 11:48 | ----- | ----- | ----- | 13:56 |

## CATALOGUE OF LUNAR ECLIPSES

| yyyy | mm | dd | Oppos | EclType | Magn(U) | Magn(P) | U1 |
|------|-----|-----|-------|-----------|---------|---------|-------|
| 2016 | Sep | 16 | 19.10 | Penumbral | -0.0694 | 0.9123 | 16:55 |
| 2017 | Feb | 11 | 00.56 | Penumbral | -0.0396 | 0.9949 | 22:34 |
| 2017 | Aug | 07 | 18.19 | Partial | 0.2415 | 1.2946 | 15:50 |
| 2018 | Jan | 31 | 13.45 | Total | 1.3123 | 2.3013 | 10:51 |
| 2018 | Jul | 27 | 20.34 | Total | 1.6036 | 2.6853 | 17:15 |
| 2019 | Jan | 21 | 05.26 | Total | 1.1913 | 2.1746 | 02:36 |
| 2019 | Jul | 16 | 21.64 | Partial | 0.6491 | 1.7107 | 18:43 |
| 2020 | Jan | 10 | 19.36 | Penumbral | -0.1202 | 0.9019 | 17:08 |
| 2020 | Jun | 05 | 19.21 | Penumbral | -0.4117 | 0.5721 | 17:45 |
| 2020 | Jul | 05 | 04.74 | Penumbral | -0.6490 | 0.3597 | 03:07 |
| 2020 | Nov | 30 | 09.50 | Penumbral | -0.2678 | 0.8341 | 07:32 |
| 2021 | May | 26 | 11.24 | Total | 1.0049 | 1.9594 | 08:48 |
| 2021 | Nov | 19 | 08.96 | Partial | 0.9699 | 2.0793 | 06:02 |
| 2022 | May | 16 | 04.23 | Total | 1.4104 | 2.3793 | 01:32 |
| 2022 | Nov | 08 | 11.04 | Total | 1.3537 | 2.4203 | 08:02 |
| 2023 | May | 05 | 17.57 | Penumbral | -0.0497 | 0.9702 | 15:14 |
| 2023 | Oct | 28 | 20.40 | Partial | 0.1178 | 1.1243 | 18:01 |
| 2024 | Mar | 25 | 07.02 | Penumbral | -0.1376 | 0.9620 | 04:53 |
| 2024 | Sep | 18 | 02.58 | Partial | 0.0794 | 1.0418 | 00:41 |
| 2025 | Mar | 14 | 06.93 | Total | 1.1745 | 2.2669 | 03:58 |
| 2025 | Sep | 07 | 18.14 | Total | 1.3568 | 2.3492 | 15:28 |
| 2026 | Mar | 03 | 11.65 | Total | 1.1441 | 2.1881 | 08:45 |
| 2026 | Aug | 28 | 04.31 | Partial | 0.9246 | 1.9700 | 01:24 |
| 2027 | Feb | 20 | 23.40 | Penumbral | -0.0652 | 0.9287 | 21:12 |
| 2027 | Jul | 18 | 15.75 | Penumbral | -1.0728 | 0.0078 | 15:50 |
| 2027 | Aug | 17 | 07.48 | Penumbral | -0.5326 | 0.5496 | 05:24 |
| 2028 | Jan | 12 | 04.05 | Partial | 0.0624 | 1.0533 | 02:08 |
| 2028 | Jul | 06 | 18.19 | Partial | 0.3860 | 1.4343 | 15:45 |
| 2028 | Dec | 31 | 16.80 | Total | 1.2410 | 2.2798 | 14:03 |
| 2029 | Jun | 26 | 03.39 | Total | 1.8368 | 2.8301 | 00:35 |
| 2029 | Dec | 20 | 22.77 | Total | 1.1115 | 2.2062 | 19:43 |
| 2030 | Jun | 15 | 18.69 | Partial | 0.4966 | 1.4520 | 16:14 |
| 2030 | Dec | 09 | 22.68 | Penumbral | -0.1704 | 0.9455 | 20:08 |
| 2031 | May | 07 | 03.67 | Penumbral | -0.0948 | 0.8872 | 01:52 |
| 2031 | Jun | 05 | 11.98 | Penumbral | -0.8263 | 0.1327 | 10:56 |
| 2031 | Oct | 30 | 07.55 | Penumbral | -0.3237 | 0.7236 | 05:49 |

## DURING 21ST CENTURY

| U2 | P1 | P2 | MID | P3 | P4 | U3 | U4 |
|----|----|----|-----|----|----|----|----|
| ----- | ----- | ----- | 18:55 | ----- | ----- | ----- | 20:55 |
| ----- | ----- | ----- | 00:45 | ----- | ----- | ----- | 02:55 |
| 17:18 | 17:24 | ----- | 18:21 | ----- | 19:18 | 19:25 | 20:52 |
| 11:49 | 11:49 | 12:52 | 13:30 | 14:08 | 15:11 | 15:10 | 16:09 |
| 18:20 | 18:25 | 19:31 | 20:22 | 21:13 | 22:19 | 22:24 | 23:29 |
| 03:35 | 03:34 | 04:42 | 05:12 | 05:43 | 06:50 | 06:49 | 07:48 |
| 19:57 | 20:02 | ----- | 21:31 | ----- | 22:59 | 23:04 | 00:18 |
| ----- | ----- | ----- | 19:10 | ----- | ----- | ----- | 21:13 |
| ----- | ----- | ----- | 19:25 | ----- | ----- | ----- | 21:05 |
| ----- | ----- | ----- | 04:30 | ----- | ----- | ----- | 05:53 |
| ----- | ----- | ----- | 09:43 | ----- | ----- | ----- | 11:54 |
| 09:48 | 09:46 | 11:14 | 11:19 | 11:24 | 12:52 | 12:50 | 13:50 |
| 07:12 | 07:20 | ----- | 09:03 | ----- | 10:47 | 10:55 | 12:04 |
| 02:30 | 02:28 | 03:29 | 04:11 | 04:54 | 05:55 | 05:53 | 06:51 |
| 09:05 | 09:10 | 10:17 | 10:59 | 11:41 | 12:49 | 12:53 | 13:57 |
| ----- | ----- | ----- | 17:23 | ----- | ----- | ----- | 19:32 |
| 19:35 | 19:36 | ----- | 20:14 | ----- | 20:52 | 20:53 | 22:27 |
| ----- | ----- | ----- | 07:14 | ----- | ----- | ----- | 09:34 |
| 02:23 | 02:14 | ----- | 02:45 | ----- | 03:15 | 03:06 | 04:48 |
| 05:05 | 05:11 | 06:27 | 06:60 | 07:32 | 08:48 | 08:55 | 10:01 |
| 16:27 | 16:27 | 17:31 | 18:11 | 18:52 | 19:56 | 19:55 | 20:55 |
| 09:49 | 09:51 | 11:06 | 11:35 | 12:03 | 13:18 | 13:21 | 14:24 |
| 02:31 | 02:34 | ----- | 04:13 | ----- | 05:52 | 05:55 | 07:02 |
| ----- | ----- | ----- | 23:13 | ----- | ----- | ----- | 01:14 |
| ----- | ----- | ----- | 16:03 | ----- | ----- | ----- | 16:17 |
| ----- | ----- | ----- | 07:14 | ----- | ----- | ----- | 09:04 |
| 03:49 | 03:46 | ----- | 04:14 | ----- | 04:41 | 04:39 | 06:19 |
| 17:05 | 17:10 | ----- | 18:21 | ----- | 19:31 | 19:36 | 20:56 |
| 15:05 | 15:08 | 16:16 | 16:52 | 17:27 | 18:36 | 18:38 | 19:40 |
| 01:34 | 01:34 | 02:32 | 03:23 | 04:14 | 05:13 | 05:12 | 06:11 |
| 20:49 | 20:56 | 22:16 | 22:42 | 23:08 | 00:28 | 00:35 | 01:41 |
| 17:25 | 17:22 | ----- | 18:33 | ----- | 19:45 | 19:41 | 20:53 |
| ----- | ----- | ----- | 22:28 | ----- | ----- | ----- | 00:48 |
| ----- | ----- | ----- | 03:51 | ----- | ----- | ----- | 05:50 |
| ----- | ----- | ----- | 11:44 | ----- | ----- | ----- | 12:33 |
| ----- | ----- | ----- | 07:46 | ----- | ----- | ----- | 09:42 |

## CATALOGUE OF LUNAR ECLIPSES

| yyyy | mm | dd | Oppos | EclType | Magn(U) | Magn(P) | U1 |
|------|-----|-----|-------|-----------|---------|---------|-------|
| 2032 | Apr | 25 | 15.16 | Total | 1.1869 | 2.2256 | 12:22 |
| 2032 | Oct | 18 | 18.98 | Total | 1.0992 | 2.0897 | 16:25 |
| 2033 | Apr | 14 | 19.30 | Total | 1.0880 | 2.1760 | 16:12 |
| 2033 | Oct | 08 | 10.97 | Total | 1.3466 | 2.3126 | 08:19 |
| 2034 | Apr | 03 | 19.33 | Penumbral | -0.2350 | 0.8583 | 16:53 |
| 2034 | Sep | 28 | 02.94 | Partial | 0.0098 | 0.9967 | 00:41 |
| 2035 | Feb | 22 | 08.91 | Penumbral | -0.0573 | 0.9720 | 06:57 |
| 2035 | Aug | 19 | 01.00 | Partial | 0.0979 | 1.1559 | 22:46 |
| 2036 | Feb | 11 | 22.16 | Total | 1.2975 | 2.2834 | 19:34 |
| 2036 | Aug | 07 | 02.82 | Total | 1.4485 | 2.5320 | 23:45 |
| 2037 | Jan | 31 | 14.07 | Total | 1.2018 | 2.1850 | 11:25 |
| 2037 | Jul | 27 | 04.26 | Partial | 0.8046 | 1.8645 | 01:18 |
| 2038 | Jan | 21 | 04.00 | Penumbral | -0.1198 | 0.9044 | 01:46 |
| 2038 | Jun | 17 | 02.51 | Penumbral | -0.5331 | 0.4466 | 01:15 |
| 2038 | Jul | 16 | 11.80 | Penumbral | -0.5005 | 0.5050 | 09:58 |
| 2038 | Dec | 11 | 17.51 | Penumbral | -0.2949 | 0.8105 | 15:34 |
| 2039 | Jun | 06 | 18.80 | Partial | 0.8806 | 1.8330 | 16:25 |
| 2039 | Nov | 30 | 16.82 | Partial | 0.9372 | 2.0478 | 13:55 |
| 2040 | May | 26 | 11.79 | Total | 1.5304 | 2.4995 | 09:05 |
| 2040 | Nov | 18 | 19.10 | Total | 1.3925 | 2.4587 | 16:06 |
| 2041 | May | 16 | 00.88 | Partial | 0.0597 | 1.0806 | 22:27 |
| 2041 | Nov | 08 | 04.72 | Partial | 0.1662 | 1.1727 | 02:19 |
| 2042 | Apr | 05 | 14.28 | Penumbral | -0.2224 | 0.8746 | 12:15 |
| 2042 | Sep | 29 | 10.57 | Penumbral | -0.0094 | 0.9565 | 08:45 |
| 2043 | Mar | 25 | 14.43 | Total | 1.1089 | 2.1961 | 11:31 |
| 2043 | Sep | 19 | 01.79 | Total | 1.2515 | 2.2496 | 23:08 |
| 2044 | Mar | 13 | 19.69 | Total | 1.1978 | 2.2358 | 16:48 |
| 2044 | Sep | 07 | 11.41 | Total | 1.0395 | 2.0907 | 08:27 |
| 2045 | Mar | 03 | 07.88 | Penumbral | -0.0249 | 0.9645 | 05:40 |
| 2045 | Aug | 27 | 14.13 | Penumbral | -0.3987 | 0.6869 | 11:53 |
| 2046 | Jan | 22 | 12.86 | Partial | 0.0501 | 1.0420 | 10:56 |
| 2046 | Jul | 18 | 00.91 | Partial | 0.2408 | 1.2863 | 22:35 |
| 2047 | Jan | 12 | 01.37 | Total | 1.2310 | 2.2726 | 22:37 |
| 2047 | Jul | 07 | 10.56 | Total | 1.7484 | 2.7383 | 07:47 |
| 2048 | Jan | 01 | 06.95 | Total | 1.1217 | 2.2192 | 03:53 |
| 2048 | Jun | 26 | 02.14 | Partial | 0.6329 | 1.5865 | 23:38 |

## DURING 21ST CENTURY

| U2 | P1 | P2 | MID | P3 | P4 | U3 | U4 |
|----|----|----|-----|----|----|----|----|
| 13:26 | 13:29 | 14:41 | 15:14 | 15:46 | 16:59 | 17:02 | 18:05 |
| 17:26 | 17:25 | 18:40 | 19:03 | 19:26 | 20:41 | 20:40 | 21:41 |
| 17:20 | 17:26 | 18:49 | 19:13 | 19:37 | 21:00 | 21:06 | 22:14 |
| 09:16 | 09:14 | 10:16 | 10:55 | 11:34 | 12:36 | 12:34 | 13:32 |
| ----- | ----- | ----- | 19:06 | ----- | ----- | ----- | 21:20 |
| ----- | 02:35 | ----- | 02:46 | ----- | 02:57 | ----- | 04:51 |
| ----- | ----- | ----- | 09:06 | ----- | ----- | ----- | 11:14 |
| 00:24 | 00:34 | ----- | 01:11 | ----- | 01:48 | 01:58 | 03:36 |
| 20:33 | 20:32 | 21:35 | 22:12 | 22:49 | 23:53 | 23:52 | 00:51 |
| 00:50 | 00:56 | 02:04 | 02:51 | 03:39 | 04:47 | 04:52 | 05:58 |
| 12:23 | 12:22 | 13:29 | 14:01 | 14:32 | 15:39 | 15:38 | 16:37 |
| 02:29 | 02:33 | ----- | 04:09 | ----- | 05:45 | 05:49 | 06:60 |
| ----- | ----- | ----- | 03:50 | ----- | ----- | ----- | 05:53 |
| ----- | ----- | ----- | 02:44 | ----- | ----- | ----- | 04:13 |
| ----- | ----- | ----- | 11:35 | ----- | ----- | ----- | 13:11 |
| ----- | ----- | ----- | 17:44 | ----- | ----- | ----- | 19:54 |
| 17:27 | 17:24 | ----- | 18:54 | ----- | 20:23 | 20:20 | 21:22 |
| 15:04 | 15:12 | ----- | 16:55 | ----- | 18:38 | 18:46 | 19:55 |
| 10:02 | 10:01 | 10:60 | 11:46 | 12:32 | 13:31 | 13:29 | 14:27 |
| 17:09 | 17:13 | 18:20 | 19:03 | 19:47 | 20:53 | 20:57 | 22:00 |
| 00:10 | 00:14 | ----- | 00:42 | ----- | 01:10 | 01:15 | 02:57 |
| 03:48 | 03:49 | ----- | 04:33 | ----- | 05:18 | 05:19 | 06:47 |
| ----- | ----- | ----- | 14:30 | ----- | ----- | ----- | 16:45 |
| ----- | ----- | ----- | 10:45 | ----- | ----- | ----- | 12:44 |
| 12:38 | 12:44 | 14:05 | 14:31 | 14:57 | 16:18 | 16:24 | 17:31 |
| 00:08 | 00:08 | 01:15 | 01:51 | 02:26 | 03:33 | 03:33 | 04:34 |
| 17:51 | 17:53 | 19:05 | 19:37 | 20:10 | 21:21 | 21:24 | 22:27 |
| 09:33 | 09:37 | 11:04 | 11:20 | 11:35 | 13:02 | 13:06 | 14:12 |
| ----- | ----- | ----- | 07:42 | ----- | ----- | ----- | 09:45 |
| ----- | ----- | ----- | 13:54 | ----- | ----- | ----- | 15:55 |
| 12:40 | 12:37 | ----- | 13:02 | ----- | 13:26 | 13:24 | 15:07 |
| 00:02 | 00:08 | ----- | 01:04 | ----- | 02:01 | 02:06 | 03:34 |
| 23:39 | 23:42 | 00:51 | 01:26 | 02:00 | 03:10 | 03:12 | 04:15 |
| 08:46 | 08:45 | 09:44 | 10:34 | 11:24 | 12:23 | 12:23 | 13:21 |
| 04:59 | 05:06 | 06:26 | 06:53 | 07:20 | 08:40 | 08:46 | 09:53 |
| 00:46 | 00:42 | ----- | 02:01 | ----- | 03:21 | 03:17 | 04:25 |

## CATALOGUE OF LUNAR ECLIPSES

| yyyy | mm | dd | Oppos | EclType | Magn(U) | Magn(P) | U1 |
|------|-----|-----|-------|-----------|---------|---------|-------|
| 2048 | Dec | 20 | 06.66 | Penumbral | -0.1516 | 0.9653 | 04:06 |
| 2049 | May | 17 | 11.24 | Penumbral | -0.2116 | 0.7709 | 09:33 |
| 2049 | Jun | 15 | 19.45 | Penumbral | -0.7058 | 0.2537 | 18:07 |
| 2049 | Nov | 09 | 15.63 | Penumbral | -0.3596 | 0.6874 | 13:57 |
| 2050 | May | 06 | 22.45 | Total | 1.0741 | 2.1134 | 19:41 |
| 2050 | Oct | 30 | 03.26 | Total | 1.0494 | 2.0404 | 00:43 |
| 2051 | Apr | 26 | 02.32 | Total | 1.1954 | 2.2818 | 23:13 |
| 2051 | Oct | 19 | 19.22 | Total | 1.4086 | 2.3776 | 16:33 |
| 2052 | Apr | 14 | 02.49 | Penumbral | -0.1381 | 0.9504 | 23:59 |
| 2052 | Oct | 08 | 10.90 | Partial | 0.0776 | 1.0700 | 08:35 |
| 2053 | Mar | 04 | 17.17 | Penumbral | -0.0846 | 0.9391 | 15:15 |
| 2053 | Aug | 29 | 07.89 | Penumbral | -0.0378 | 1.0254 | 05:46 |
| 2054 | Feb | 22 | 06.78 | Total | 1.2749 | 2.2573 | 04:12 |
| 2054 | Aug | 18 | 09.36 | Total | 1.3001 | 2.3856 | 06:20 |
| 2055 | Feb | 11 | 22.81 | Total | 1.2189 | 2.2015 | 20:08 |
| 2055 | Aug | 07 | 10.95 | Partial | 0.9548 | 2.0133 | 07:58 |
| 2056 | Feb | 01 | 12.59 | Penumbral | -0.1140 | 0.9119 | 10:21 |
| 2056 | Jun | 27 | 09.80 | Penumbral | -0.6565 | 0.3199 | 08:46 |
| 2056 | Jul | 26 | 18.91 | Penumbral | -0.3551 | 0.6477 | 16:55 |
| 2056 | Dec | 22 | 01.57 | Penumbral | -0.3159 | 0.7922 | 23:39 |
| 2057 | Jun | 17 | 02.31 | Partial | 0.7504 | 1.7014 | 23:59 |
| 2057 | Dec | 11 | 00.77 | Partial | 0.9133 | 2.0246 | 21:52 |
| 2058 | Jun | 06 | 19.26 | Total | 1.6575 | 2.6274 | 16:32 |
| 2058 | Nov | 30 | 03.28 | Total | 1.4214 | 2.4868 | 00:18 |
| 2059 | May | 27 | 08.06 | Partial | 0.1784 | 1.2006 | 05:33 |
| 2059 | Nov | 19 | 13.16 | Partial | 0.2031 | 1.2093 | 10:44 |
| 2060 | Apr | 15 | 21.38 | Penumbral | -0.3202 | 0.7742 | 19:28 |
| 2060 | Oct | 09 | 18.68 | Penumbral | -0.0870 | 0.8826 | 16:56 |
| 2060 | Nov | 08 | 04.29 | Penumbral | -0.9398 | 0.0345 | 03:37 |
| 2061 | Apr | 04 | 21.81 | Total | 1.0310 | 2.1126 | 18:56 |
| 2061 | Sep | 29 | 09.53 | Total | 1.1570 | 2.1610 | 06:53 |
| 2062 | Mar | 25 | 03.61 | Total | 1.2633 | 2.2950 | 00:43 |
| 2062 | Sep | 18 | 18.60 | Total | 1.1445 | 2.2018 | 15:37 |
| 2063 | Mar | 14 | 16.25 | Partial | 0.0259 | 1.0108 | 14:00 |
| 2063 | Sep | 07 | 20.88 | Penumbral | -0.2738 | 0.8153 | 18:29 |
| 2064 | Feb | 02 | 21.62 | Partial | 0.0343 | 1.0266 | 19:42 |

## DURING 21ST CENTURY

| U2 | P1 | P2 | MID | P3 | P4 | U3 | U4 |
|---|---|---|---|---|---|---|---|
| ----- | ----- | ----- | 06:27 | ----- | ----- | ----- | 08:48 |
| ----- | ----- | ----- | 11:26 | ----- | ----- | ----- | 13:19 |
| ----- | ----- | ----- | 19:13 | ----- | ----- | ----- | 20:20 |
| ----- | ----- | ----- | 15:50 | ----- | ----- | ----- | 17:44 |
| 20:46 | 20:49 | 22:10 | 22:32 | 22:53 | 00:14 | 00:17 | 01:22 |
| 01:45 | 01:44 | 03:04 | 03:20 | 03:37 | 04:56 | 04:56 | 05:57 |
| 00:19 | 00:25 | 01:41 | 02:15 | 02:50 | 04:05 | 04:11 | 05:18 |
| 17:30 | 17:28 | 18:29 | 19:10 | 19:52 | 20:52 | 20:51 | 21:48 |
| ----- | ----- | ----- | 02:17 | ----- | ----- | ----- | 04:35 |
| 10:15 | 10:13 | ----- | 10:44 | ----- | 11:15 | 11:13 | 12:53 |
| ----- | ----- | ----- | 17:21 | ----- | ----- | ----- | 19:27 |
| 07:45 | ----- | ----- | 08:05 | ----- | ----- | 08:24 | 10:24 |
| 05:11 | 05:10 | 06:14 | 06:50 | 07:26 | 08:30 | 08:29 | 09:28 |
| 07:26 | 07:32 | 08:44 | 09:25 | 10:06 | 11:18 | 11:23 | 12:30 |
| 21:07 | 21:06 | 22:12 | 22:45 | 23:17 | 00:24 | 00:23 | 01:22 |
| 09:06 | 09:10 | ----- | 10:52 | ----- | 12:33 | 12:37 | 13:45 |
| ----- | ----- | ----- | 12:25 | ----- | ----- | ----- | 14:29 |
| ----- | ----- | ----- | 10:02 | ----- | ----- | ----- | 11:18 |
| ----- | ----- | ----- | 18:42 | ----- | ----- | ----- | 20:30 |
| ----- | ----- | ----- | 01:48 | ----- | ----- | ----- | 03:57 |
| 01:04 | 01:00 | ----- | 02:25 | ----- | 03:49 | 03:46 | 04:50 |
| 23:02 | 23:11 | ----- | 00:52 | ----- | 02:34 | 02:42 | 03:52 |
| 17:30 | 17:28 | 18:26 | 19:14 | 20:03 | 21:01 | 20:59 | 21:56 |
| 01:20 | 01:25 | 02:30 | 03:15 | 03:59 | 05:05 | 05:09 | 06:11 |
| 07:03 | 07:06 | ----- | 07:54 | ----- | 08:42 | 08:45 | 10:15 |
| 12:10 | 12:11 | ----- | 13:00 | ----- | 13:49 | 13:50 | 15:16 |
| ----- | ----- | ----- | 21:36 | ----- | ----- | ----- | 23:45 |
| ----- | ----- | ----- | 18:52 | ----- | ----- | ----- | 20:48 |
| ----- | ----- | ----- | 04:02 | ----- | ----- | ----- | 04:27 |
| 20:03 | 20:09 | 21:39 | 21:53 | 22:08 | 23:38 | 23:44 | 00:51 |
| 07:55 | 07:55 | 09:07 | 09:36 | 10:05 | 11:17 | 11:17 | 12:19 |
| 01:46 | 01:48 | 02:56 | 03:33 | 04:10 | 05:18 | 05:20 | 06:22 |
| 16:42 | 16:46 | 18:03 | 18:32 | 19:01 | 20:18 | 20:22 | 21:27 |
| 15:53 | 15:47 | ----- | 16:05 | ----- | 16:22 | 16:16 | 18:09 |
| ----- | ----- | ----- | 20:40 | ----- | ----- | ----- | 22:50 |
| 21:29 | 21:27 | ----- | 21:47 | ----- | 22:07 | 22:05 | 23:52 |

## CATALOGUE OF LUNAR ECLIPSES

| yyyy | mm | dd | Oppos | EclType | Magn(U) | Magn(P) | U1 |
|------|----|----|-------|---------|---------|---------|-----|
| 2064 | Jul | 28 | 07.68 | Partial | 0.1004 | 1.1436 | 05:29 |
| 2065 | Jan | 22 | 09.89 | Total | 1.2184 | 2.2623 | 07:08 |
| 2065 | Jul | 17 | 17.76 | Total | 1.6098 | 2.5968 | 15:01 |
| 2066 | Jan | 11 | 15.12 | Total | 1.1318 | 2.2314 | 12:02 |
| 2066 | Jul | 07 | 09.58 | Partial | 0.7694 | 1.7219 | 07:02 |
| 2066 | Dec | 31 | 14.68 | Penumbral | -0.1355 | 0.9814 | 12:06 |
| 2067 | May | 28 | 18.69 | Penumbral | -0.3381 | 0.6453 | 17:09 |
| 2067 | Jun | 27 | 02.87 | Penumbral | -0.5817 | 0.3789 | 01:19 |
| 2067 | Nov | 20 | 23.83 | Penumbral | -0.3849 | 0.6615 | 22:11 |
| 2068 | May | 17 | 05.58 | Partial | 0.9496 | 1.9898 | 02:52 |
| 2068 | Nov | 09 | 11.67 | Total | 1.0106 | 2.0021 | 09:09 |
| 2069 | May | 06 | 09.20 | Total | 1.3160 | 2.4008 | 06:04 |
| 2069 | Oct | 30 | 03.58 | Total | 1.4587 | 2.4307 | 00:55 |
| 2070 | Apr | 25 | 09.52 | Penumbral | -0.0282 | 1.0554 | 06:56 |
| 2070 | Oct | 19 | 18.98 | Partial | 0.1339 | 1.1318 | 16:37 |
| 2071 | Mar | 16 | 01.31 | Penumbral | -0.1220 | 0.8958 | 23:27 |
| 2071 | Sep | 09 | 14.85 | Penumbral | -0.1641 | 0.9045 | 12:50 |
| 2072 | Mar | 04 | 15.30 | Total | 1.2428 | 2.2215 | 12:45 |
| 2072 | Aug | 28 | 15.99 | Total | 1.1608 | 2.2486 | 13:00 |
| 2073 | Feb | 22 | 07.45 | Total | 1.2435 | 2.2252 | 04:46 |
| 2073 | Aug | 17 | 17.74 | Total | 1.0974 | 2.1549 | 14:44 |
| 2074 | Feb | 11 | 21.10 | Penumbral | -0.1034 | 0.9236 | 18:50 |
| 2074 | Jul | 08 | 17.09 | Penumbral | -0.7815 | 0.1920 | 16:21 |
| 2074 | Aug | 07 | 02.09 | Penumbral | -0.2152 | 0.7855 | 23:58 |
| 2075 | Jan | 02 | 09.66 | Penumbral | -0.3334 | 0.7767 | 07:45 |
| 2075 | Jun | 28 | 09.78 | Partial | 0.6177 | 1.5679 | 07:32 |
| 2075 | Dec | 22 | 08.80 | Partial | 0.8961 | 2.0072 | 05:54 |
| 2076 | Jun | 17 | 02.64 | Total | 1.7902 | 2.7614 | 23:55 |
| 2076 | Dec | 10 | 11.57 | Total | 1.4422 | 2.5062 | 08:36 |
| 2077 | Jun | 06 | 15.13 | Partial | 0.3062 | 1.3302 | 12:32 |
| 2077 | Nov | 29 | 21.71 | Partial | 0.2314 | 1.2372 | 19:17 |
| 2078 | Apr | 27 | 04.33 | Penumbral | -0.4302 | 0.6614 | 02:34 |
| 2078 | Oct | 21 | 02.91 | Penumbral | -0.1531 | 0.8204 | 01:13 |
| 2078 | Nov | 19 | 12.88 | Penumbral | -0.9076 | 0.0686 | 12:03 |
| 2079 | Apr | 16 | 05.05 | Partial | 0.9407 | 2.0167 | 02:13 |
| 2079 | Oct | 10 | 17.39 | Total | 1.0740 | 2.0840 | 14:46 |

## DURING 21ST CENTURY

| U2 | P1 | P2 | MID | P3 | P4 | U3 | U4 |
|----|----|----|-----|----|----|----|----|
| 07:07 | 07:15 | ----- | 07:52 | ----- | 08:29 | 08:36 | 10:14 |
| 08:10 | 08:13 | 09:23 | 09:57 | 10:31 | 11:41 | 11:44 | 12:47 |
| 15:60 | 15:59 | 16:59 | 17:47 | 18:35 | 19:35 | 19:34 | 20:33 |
| 13:09 | 13:16 | 14:35 | 15:03 | 15:31 | 16:50 | 16:57 | 18:04 |
| 08:07 | 08:03 | ----- | 09:29 | ----- | 10:54 | 10:51 | 11:55 |
| ----- | ----- | ----- | 14:28 | ----- | ----- | ----- | 16:50 |
| ----- | ----- | ----- | 18:54 | ----- | ----- | ----- | 20:38 |
| ----- | ----- | ----- | 02:39 | ----- | ----- | ----- | 03:60 |
| ----- | ----- | ----- | 00:03 | ----- | ----- | ----- | 01:54 |
| 03:58 | 04:01 | ----- | 05:40 | ----- | 07:20 | 07:22 | 08:29 |
| 10:11 | 10:10 | 11:37 | 11:45 | 11:52 | 13:20 | 13:19 | 14:21 |
| 07:10 | 07:16 | 08:27 | 09:08 | 09:50 | 11:01 | 11:07 | 12:13 |
| 01:52 | 01:50 | 02:50 | 03:33 | 04:16 | 05:15 | 05:14 | 06:11 |
| 08:50 | ----- | ----- | 09:20 | ----- | ----- | 09:49 | 11:43 |
| 18:09 | 18:09 | ----- | 18:49 | ----- | 19:29 | 19:29 | 21:01 |
| ----- | ----- | ----- | 01:30 | ----- | ----- | ----- | 03:33 |
| ----- | ----- | ----- | 15:04 | ----- | ----- | ----- | 17:17 |
| 13:43 | 13:42 | 14:47 | 15:21 | 15:56 | 17:01 | 16:60 | 17:58 |
| 14:08 | 14:14 | 15:32 | 16:04 | 16:35 | 17:53 | 17:59 | 19:07 |
| 05:45 | 05:44 | 06:49 | 07:23 | 07:57 | 09:03 | 09:02 | 10:01 |
| 15:51 | 15:55 | 17:15 | 17:40 | 18:05 | 19:25 | 19:29 | 20:36 |
| ----- | ----- | ----- | 20:55 | ----- | ----- | ----- | 22:60 |
| ----- | ----- | ----- | 17:20 | ----- | ----- | ----- | 18:19 |
| ----- | ----- | ----- | 01:54 | ----- | ----- | ----- | 03:50 |
| ----- | ----- | ----- | 09:53 | ----- | ----- | ----- | 12:01 |
| 08:39 | 08:36 | ----- | 09:54 | ----- | 11:12 | 11:08 | 12:16 |
| 07:05 | 07:13 | ----- | 08:54 | ----- | 10:35 | 10:43 | 11:53 |
| 00:53 | 00:51 | 01:48 | 02:38 | 03:28 | 04:25 | 04:24 | 05:21 |
| 09:38 | 09:42 | 10:47 | 11:32 | 12:17 | 13:22 | 13:26 | 14:28 |
| 13:54 | 13:57 | ----- | 14:59 | ----- | 16:00 | 16:03 | 17:26 |
| 20:41 | 20:41 | ----- | 21:33 | ----- | 22:25 | 22:26 | 23:49 |
| ----- | ----- | ----- | 04:34 | ----- | ----- | ----- | 06:34 |
| ----- | ----- | ----- | 03:06 | ----- | ----- | ----- | 04:59 |
| ----- | ----- | ----- | 12:38 | ----- | ----- | ----- | 13:12 |
| 03:22 | 03:27 | ----- | 05:09 | ----- | 06:50 | 06:55 | 08:04 |
| 15:48 | 15:49 | 17:08 | 17:28 | 17:49 | 19:07 | 19:08 | 20:10 |

## CATALOGUE OF LUNAR ECLIPSES

| yyyy | mm | dd | Oppos | EclType | Magn(U) | Magn(P) | U1 |
|------|-----|-----|-------|-----------|---------|---------|-------|
| 2080 | Apr | 04 | 11.41 | Total     | 1.3409  | 2.3663  | 08:32 |
| 2080 | Sep | 29 | 01.90 | Total     | 1.2384  | 2.3019  | 22:53 |
| 2081 | Mar | 25 | 00.50 | Partial   | 0.0879  | 1.0680  | 22:14 |
| 2081 | Sep | 18 | 03.75 | Penumbral | -0.1591 | 0.9337  | 01:14 |
| 2082 | Feb | 13 | 06.29 | Partial   | 0.0116  | 1.0041  | 04:24 |
| 2082 | Aug | 08 | 14.54 | Penumbral | -0.0344 | 1.0069  | 12:29 |
| 2083 | Feb | 02 | 18.35 | Total     | 1.2020  | 2.2476  | 15:35 |
| 2083 | Jul | 29 | 01.00 | Total     | 1.4739  | 2.4588  | 22:18 |
| 2084 | Jan | 22 | 23.26 | Total     | 1.1445  | 2.2454  | 20:10 |
| 2084 | Jul | 17 | 17.03 | Partial   | 0.9066  | 1.8586  | 14:27 |
| 2085 | Jan | 10 | 22.71 | Penumbral | -0.1197 | 0.9965  | 20:07 |
| 2085 | Jun | 08 | 02.05 | Penumbral | -0.4715 | 0.5133  | 00:41 |
| 2085 | Jul | 07 | 10.25 | Penumbral | -0.4550 | 0.5074  | 08:30 |
| 2085 | Dec | 01 | 08.16 | Penumbral | -0.3999 | 0.6454  | 06:33 |
| 2086 | May | 28 | 12.59 | Partial   | 0.8149  | 1.8563  | 09:55 |
| 2086 | Nov | 20 | 20.20 | Partial   | 0.9821  | 1.9739  | 17:42 |
| 2087 | May | 17 | 15.93 | Total     | 1.4482  | 2.5316  | 12:48 |
| 2087 | Nov | 10 | 12.08 | Total     | 1.4981  | 2.4731  | 09:24 |
| 2088 | May | 05 | 16.43 | Partial   | 0.0939  | 1.1727  | 13:45 |
| 2088 | Oct | 30 | 03.16 | Partial   | 0.1788  | 1.1822  | 00:45 |
| 2089 | Mar | 26 | 09.35 | Penumbral | -0.1707 | 0.8412  | 07:33 |
| 2089 | Sep | 19 | 21.92 | Penumbral | -0.2795 | 0.7947  | 20:01 |
| 2090 | Mar | 15 | 23.71 | Total     | 1.2001  | 2.1750  | 21:10 |
| 2090 | Sep | 08 | 22.74 | Total     | 1.0318  | 2.1221  | 19:48 |
| 2091 | Mar | 05 | 15.98 | Total     | 1.2774  | 2.2581  | 13:18 |
| 2091 | Aug | 29 | 00.65 | Total     | 1.2305  | 2.2874  | 21:38 |
| 2092 | Feb | 23 | 05.49 | Penumbral | -0.0840 | 0.9438  | 03:12 |
| 2092 | Jul | 19 | 00.40 | Penumbral | -0.9047 | 0.0666  | 00:04 |
| 2092 | Aug | 17 | 09.37 | Penumbral | -0.0812 | 0.9179  | 07:07 |
| 2093 | Jan | 12 | 17.73 | Penumbral | -0.3499 | 0.7613  | 15:51 |
| 2093 | Jul | 08 | 17.24 | Partial   | 0.4827  | 1.4328  | 15:04 |
| 2094 | Jan | 01 | 16.86 | Partial   | 0.8830  | 1.9933  | 13:59 |
| 2094 | Jun | 28 | 09.97 | Total     | 1.8186  | 2.7917  | 07:15 |
| 2094 | Dec | 21 | 19.94 | Total     | 1.4567  | 2.5188  | 16:58 |
| 2095 | Jun | 17 | 22.10 | Partial   | 0.4405  | 1.4669  | 19:25 |
| 2095 | Dec | 11 | 06.35 | Partial   | 0.2514  | 1.2563  | 03:55 |

## DURING 21ST CENTURY

| U2 | P1 | P2 | MID | P3 | P4 | U3 | U4 |
|---|---|---|---|---|---|---|---|
| 09:33 | 09:35 | 10:41 | 11:21 | 12:02 | 13:08 | 13:09 | 14:11 |
| 23:58 | 00:02 | 01:14 | 01:51 | 02:27 | 03:39 | 03:43 | 04:48 |
| 23:52 | 23:48 | ----- | 00:20 | ----- | 00:52 | 00:48 | 02:26 |
| ----- | ----- | ----- | 03:32 | ----- | ----- | ----- | 05:51 |
| 06:21 | 06:16 | ----- | 06:28 | ----- | 06:40 | 06:35 | 08:32 |
| 14:34 | ----- | ----- | 14:44 | ----- | ----- | 14:54 | 16:59 |
| 16:38 | 16:41 | 17:52 | 18:25 | 18:58 | 20:09 | 20:12 | 21:15 |
| 23:17 | 23:16 | 00:18 | 01:03 | 01:48 | 02:49 | 02:48 | 03:47 |
| 21:16 | 21:23 | 22:42 | 23:11 | 23:41 | 00:59 | 01:06 | 02:12 |
| 15:29 | 15:26 | ----- | 16:56 | ----- | 18:26 | 18:23 | 19:25 |
| ----- | ----- | ----- | 22:30 | ----- | ----- | ----- | 00:53 |
| ----- | ----- | ----- | 02:16 | ----- | ----- | ----- | 03:51 |
| ----- | ----- | ----- | 10:02 | ----- | ----- | ----- | 11:34 |
| ----- | ----- | ----- | 08:23 | ----- | ----- | ----- | 10:13 |
| 11:04 | 11:07 | ----- | 12:41 | ----- | 14:16 | 14:19 | 15:28 |
| 18:44 | 18:43 | ----- | 20:17 | ----- | 21:51 | 21:50 | 22:52 |
| 13:53 | 13:58 | 15:06 | 15:53 | 16:41 | 17:48 | 17:54 | 18:59 |
| 10:21 | 10:19 | 11:18 | 12:02 | 12:47 | 13:45 | 13:44 | 14:41 |
| 15:24 | 15:38 | ----- | 16:15 | ----- | 16:52 | 17:06 | 18:44 |
| 02:13 | 02:14 | ----- | 03:00 | ----- | 03:46 | 03:47 | 05:15 |
| ----- | ----- | ----- | 09:32 | ----- | ----- | ----- | 11:32 |
| ----- | ----- | ----- | 22:08 | ----- | ----- | ----- | 00:15 |
| 22:09 | 22:08 | 23:15 | 23:46 | 00:18 | 01:25 | 01:23 | 02:22 |
| 20:57 | 21:03 | 22:35 | 22:49 | 23:04 | 00:35 | 00:42 | 01:51 |
| 14:16 | 14:15 | 15:19 | 15:55 | 16:31 | 17:36 | 17:35 | 18:33 |
| 22:43 | 22:47 | 23:59 | 00:35 | 01:11 | 02:24 | 02:28 | 03:32 |
| ----- | ----- | ----- | 05:19 | ----- | ----- | ----- | 07:25 |
| ----- | ----- | ----- | 00:39 | ----- | ----- | ----- | 01:15 |
| ----- | ----- | ----- | 09:11 | ----- | ----- | ----- | 11:15 |
| ----- | ----- | ----- | 17:58 | ----- | ----- | ----- | 20:05 |
| 16:15 | 16:11 | ----- | 17:22 | ----- | 18:32 | 18:28 | 19:40 |
| 15:09 | 15:18 | ----- | 16:58 | ----- | 18:38 | 18:46 | 19:57 |
| 08:13 | 08:11 | 09:09 | 09:59 | 10:49 | 11:46 | 11:45 | 12:42 |
| 18:00 | 18:04 | 19:09 | 19:54 | 20:39 | 21:44 | 21:48 | 22:50 |
| 20:42 | 20:45 | ----- | 21:58 | ----- | 23:10 | 23:13 | 00:30 |
| 05:18 | 05:18 | ----- | 06:12 | ----- | 07:06 | 07:07 | 08:29 |

## CATALOGUE OF LUNAR ECLIPSES

| yyyy | mm | dd | Oppos | EclType | Magn(U) | Magn(P) | U1 |
|------|-----|----|-------|-----------|---------|---------|-------|
| 2096 | May | 07 | 11.13 | Penumbral | -0.5516 | 0.5375 | 09:33 |
| 2096 | Jun | 06 | 02.99 | Penumbral | -1.0660 | 0.0082 | 02:27 |
| 2096 | Oct | 31 | 11.27 | Penumbral | -0.2084 | 0.7690 | 09:37 |
| 2096 | Nov | 29 | 21.57 | Penumbral | -0.8851 | 0.0929 | 20:39 |
| 2097 | Apr | 26 | 12.17 | Partial | 0.8385 | 1.9089 | 09:24 |
| 2097 | Oct | 21 | 01.37 | Total | 1.0029 | 2.0189 | 22:45 |
| 2098 | Apr | 15 | 19.09 | Total | 1.4304 | 2.4494 | 16:13 |
| 2098 | Oct | 10 | 09.32 | Total | 1.3205 | 2.3900 | 06:17 |
| 2099 | Apr | 05 | 08.62 | Partial | 0.1614 | 1.1369 | 06:19 |
| 2099 | Sep | 29 | 10.75 | Penumbral | -0.0561 | 1.0405 | 08:08 |
| 2100 | Feb | 24 | 14.87 | Penumbral | -0.0199 | 0.9724 | 12:60 |
| 2100 | Aug | 19 | 21.49 | Penumbral | -0.1616 | 0.8783 | 19:34 |

## DURING 21ST CENTURY

| U2 | P1 | P2 | MID | P3 | P4 | U3 | U4 |
|-----|-----|-----|-------|-----|-------|-------|-------|
| ----- | ----- | ----- | 11:23 | ----- | ----- | ----- | 13:12 |
| ----- | ----- | ----- | 02:41 | ----- | ----- | ----- | 02:55 |
| ----- | ----- | ----- | 11:27 | ----- | ----- | ----- | 13:17 |
| ----- | ----- | ----- | 21:19 | ----- | ----- | ----- | 21:60 |
| 10:34 | 10:39 | ----- | 12:16 | ----- | 13:54 | 13:59 | 15:09 |
| 23:49 | 23:50 | 01:23 | 01:27 | 01:31 | 03:04 | 03:05 | 04:09 |
| 17:14 | 17:15 | 18:19 | 19:03 | 19:47 | 20:51 | 20:52 | 21:52 |
| 07:22 | 07:26 | 08:35 | 09:16 | 09:57 | 11:06 | 11:11 | 12:15 |
| 07:48 | 07:45 | ----- | 08:28 | ----- | 09:11 | 09:08 | 10:37 |
| 10:08 | ----- | ----- | 10:33 | ----- | ----- | 10:58 | 12:58 |
| ----- | ----- | ----- | 15:02 | ----- | ----- | ----- | 17:05 |
| ----- | ----- | ----- | 21:42 | ----- | ----- | ----- | 23:49 |

Abstract of Lunar Eclipses from the year 1901 to 2099
Total Elipses     : 164
Partial Elipses   : 124
Penumbral Elipses : 169
All Elipses       : 457

CATALOGUE

OF

SOLAR

ECLIPSES

DURING

21$^{ST}$ CENTURY

## LIST OF SOLAR ECLIPSES DURING 21ST CENTURY

| YYYY | MM | DD | Conj | SE_Type | Gamma | GE Position | | Magn |
|------|----|----|------|---------|-------|------|------|------|
| 2001 | Jun | 21 | 12:05 | Total | 0.5700 | 11.28S | 2.30E | 1.0498 |
| 2001 | Dec | 14 | 20:53 | Annular | 0.4088 | 0.63N | 131.05W | 0.9683 |
| 2002 | Jun | 10 | 23:46 | Annular | 0.1998 | 34.70N | 179.08W | 0.9964 |
| 2002 | Dec | 04 | 07:32 | Total | 0.3018 | 39.58S | 59.22E | 1.0246 |
| 2003 | May | 31 | 04:10 | Annular | 0.9960 | 68.84N | 21.03W | 0.9392 |
| 2003 | Nov | 23 | 22:51 | Total | 0.9631 | 73.49S | 90.59E | 1.0383 |
| 2004 | Apr | 19 | 13:35 | Partial | 1.1338 | 62.18S | 44.00E | 0.7361 |
| 2004 | Oct | 14 | 03:00 | Partial | 1.0352 | 61.82N | 153.89W | 0.9271 |
| 2005 | Apr | 08 | 20:37 | Annular | 0.3473 | 10.60S | 119.39W | 1.0076 |
| 2005 | Oct | 03 | 10:33 | Annular | 0.3300 | 12.90N | 28.35E | 0.9578 |
| 2006 | Mar | 29 | 10:12 | Total | 0.3850 | 23.26N | 16.63E | 1.0517 |
| 2006 | Sep | 22 | 11:40 | Annular | 0.4060 | 20.70S | 9.05W | 0.9353 |
| 2007 | Mar | 19 | 02:32 | Partial | 1.0741 | 61.56N | 55.31E | 0.8726 |
| 2007 | Sep | 11 | 12:32 | Partial | 1.1258 | 61.54S | 90.38W | 0.7498 |
| 2008 | Feb | 07 | 03:55 | Annular | 0.9570 | 67.95S | 151.92W | 0.9652 |
| 2008 | Aug | 01 | 10:22 | Total | 0.8303 | 65.84N | 71.75E | 1.0396 |
| 2009 | Jan | 26 | 07:59 | Annular | 0.2818 | 34.17S | 70.17E | 0.9284 |
| 2009 | Jul | 22 | 02:35 | Total | 0.0696 | 24.30N | 144.10E | 1.0802 |
| 2010 | Jan | 15 | 07:07 | Annular | 0.4009 | 1.68N | 69.12E | 0.9192 |
| 2010 | Jul | 11 | 19:34 | Total | 0.6794 | 19.85S | 121.90W | 1.0582 |
| 2011 | Jan | 04 | 08:51 | Partial | 1.0635 | 65.23N | 20.73E | 0.8559 |
| 2011 | Jun | 01 | 21:16 | Partial | 1.2129 | 68.39N | 46.83E | 0.6010 |
| 2011 | Jul | 01 | 08:38 | Partial | 1.4922 | 65.75S | 28.75E | 0.0957 |
| 2011 | Nov | 25 | 06:20 | Partial | 1.0538 | 69.19S | 82.50W | 0.9042 |
| 2012 | May | 20 | 23:53 | Annular | 0.4818 | 49.19N | 176.19E | 0.9441 |
| 2012 | Nov | 13 | 22:12 | Total | 0.3725 | 40.12S | 161.39W | 1.0503 |
| 2013 | May | 10 | 00:26 | Annular | 0.2706 | 2.15N | 175.21E | 0.9546 |
| 2013 | Nov | 03 | 12:47 | Annular | 0.3272 | 3.51N | 11.76W | 1.0161 |
| 2014 | Apr | 29 | 06:04 | Annular | 1.0006 | 71.36S | 131.00E | 0.9842 |
| 2014 | Oct | 23 | 21:44 | Partial | 1.0914 | 71.90N | 97.25W | 0.8098 |
| 2015 | Mar | 20 | 09:46 | Total | 0.9442 | 64.36N | 5.75W | 1.0448 |
| 2015 | Sep | 13 | 06:55 | Partial | 1.1004 | 72.84S | 2.39W | 0.7864 |
| 2016 | Mar | 09 | 01:58 | Total | 0.2598 | 10.09N | 148.73E | 1.0452 |
| 2016 | Sep | 01 | 09:08 | Annular | 0.3323 | 10.67S | 37.59E | 0.9738 |
| 2017 | Feb | 26 | 14:54 | Annular | 0.4582 | 34.80S | 31.31W | 0.9924 |
| 2017 | Aug | 21 | 18:26 | Total | 0.4372 | 37.10N | 87.73W | 1.0308 |
| 2018 | Feb | 15 | 20:52 | Partial | 1.2116 | 71.65S | 0.40E | 0.5989 |
| 2018 | Jul | 13 | 03:02 | Partial | 1.3542 | 68.54S | 127.32E | 0.3363 |
| 2018 | Aug | 11 | 09:47 | Partial | 1.1478 | 71.00N | 174.18E | 0.7361 |

## WITH GLOBAL TIMINGS IN 'UT'

| P1 | U1 | U2 | P2 | MID | P3 | U3 | U4 | P4 |
|---|---|---|---|---|---|---|---|---|
| 09:35 | 10:40 | 10:37 | ----- | 12:05 | ----- | 13:33 | 13:31 | 14:36 |
| 18:05 | 19:09 | 19:13 | 20:35 | 20:53 | 21:12 | 22:34 | 22:37 | 23:42 |
| 20:54 | 21:56 | 21:57 | 23:01 | 23:46 | 24:31 | 25:35 | 25:37 | 26:38 |
| 04:53 | 05:52 | 05:52 | 06:57 | 07:33 | 08:09 | 09:13 | 09:13 | 10:12 |
| 01:47 | 03:44 | ----- | ----- | 04:09 | ----- | ----- | 04:34 | 06:31 |
| 20:48 | 22:27 | 22:20 | ----- | 22:51 | ----- | 23:22 | 23:15 | 24:54 |
| 11:30 | ----- | ----- | ----- | 13:35 | ----- | ----- | ----- | 15:40 |
| 00:55 | ----- | ----- | ----- | 03:00 | ----- | ----- | ----- | 05:05 |
| 17:53 | 18:55 | 18:55 | 20:06 | 20:37 | 21:09 | 22:19 | 22:20 | 23:22 |
| 07:37 | 08:42 | 08:46 | 10:00 | 10:33 | 11:06 | 12:20 | 12:24 | 13:29 |
| 07:37 | 08:37 | 08:35 | 09:45 | 10:12 | 10:38 | 11:49 | 11:46 | 12:46 |
| 08:40 | 09:48 | 09:55 | 11:23 | 11:40 | 11:57 | 13:26 | 13:32 | 14:40 |
| 00:39 | ----- | ----- | ----- | 02:32 | ----- | ----- | ----- | 04:26 |
| 10:26 | ----- | ----- | ----- | 12:32 | ----- | ----- | ----- | 14:37 |
| 01:38 | 03:19 | 03:27 | ----- | 03:55 | ----- | 04:23 | 04:31 | 06:12 |
| 08:04 | 09:24 | 09:21 | ----- | 10:22 | ----- | 11:22 | 11:19 | 12:39 |
| 04:57 | 06:03 | 06:09 | 07:21 | 07:59 | 08:37 | 09:49 | 09:55 | 11:01 |
| 23:58 | 00:55 | 00:51 | 01:48 | 02:35 | 03:23 | 04:19 | 04:16 | 05:12 |
| 04:06 | 05:15 | 05:22 | 06:50 | 07:07 | 07:24 | 08:53 | 08:60 | 10:08 |
| 17:10 | 18:19 | 18:15 | ----- | 19:34 | ----- | 20:52 | 20:49 | 21:58 |
| 06:41 | ----- | ----- | ----- | 08:51 | ----- | ----- | ----- | 11:02 |
| 19:25 | ----- | ----- | ----- | 21:16 | ----- | ----- | ----- | 23:07 |
| 07:53 | ----- | ----- | ----- | 08:38 | ----- | ----- | ----- | 09:24 |
| 04:24 | ----- | ----- | ----- | 06:21 | ----- | ----- | ----- | 08:18 |
| 20:57 | 22:07 | 22:12 | ----- | 23:53 | ----- | 25:34 | 25:40 | 26:50 |
| 19:38 | 20:37 | 20:35 | 21:44 | 22:12 | 22:40 | 23:49 | 23:47 | 24:46 |
| 21:26 | 22:32 | 22:36 | 23:46 | 00:26 | 01:06 | 02:17 | 02:21 | 03:26 |
| 10:05 | 11:05 | 11:05 | 12:13 | 12:47 | 13:20 | 14:28 | 14:28 | 15:29 |
| 03:53 | 05:54 | ----- | ----- | 06:04 | ----- | ----- | 06:14 | 08:15 |
| 19:37 | ----- | ----- | ----- | 21:45 | ----- | ----- | ----- | 23:52 |
| 07:41 | 09:16 | 09:09 | ----- | 09:46 | ----- | 10:23 | 10:17 | 11:51 |
| 04:42 | ----- | ----- | ----- | 06:54 | ----- | ----- | ----- | 09:07 |
| 23:20 | 00:18 | 00:16 | 01:18 | 01:58 | 02:37 | 03:39 | 03:37 | 04:35 |
| 06:14 | 07:19 | 07:21 | 08:34 | 09:08 | 09:41 | 10:54 | 10:57 | 12:01 |
| 12:11 | 13:16 | 13:17 | ----- | 14:54 | ----- | 16:31 | 16:32 | 17:37 |
| 15:47 | 16:50 | 16:49 | 18:11 | 18:26 | 18:40 | 20:03 | 20:02 | 21:05 |
| 18:56 | ----- | ----- | ----- | 20:52 | ----- | ----- | ----- | 22:48 |
| 01:48 | ----- | ----- | ----- | 03:02 | ----- | ----- | ----- | 04:15 |
| 08:02 | ----- | ----- | ----- | 09:47 | ----- | ----- | ----- | 11:31 |

## LIST OF SOLAR ECLIPSES DURING 21ST CENTURY

| YYYY | MM | DD | Conj | SE_Type | Gamma | GE Position | | Magn |
|------|----|----|------|---------|-------|-------------|---|------|
| 2019 | Jan | 06 | 01:41 | Partial | 1.1420 | 68.04N | 153.56E | 0.7140 |
| 2019 | Jul | 02 | 19:23 | Total | 0.6468 | 17.45S | 109.01W | 1.0461 |
| 2019 | Dec | 26 | 05:18 | Annular | 0.4133 | 1.00N | 102.14E | 0.9703 |
| 2020 | Jun | 21 | 06:40 | Annular | 0.1209 | 30.63N | 79.62E | 0.9942 |
| 2020 | Dec | 14 | 16:14 | Total | 0.2939 | 40.48S | 68.03W | 1.0256 |
| 2021 | Jun | 10 | 10:43 | Annular | 0.9156 | 82.03N | 64.54W | 0.9437 |
| 2021 | Dec | 04 | 07:34 | Total | 0.9524 | 77.82S | 43.80W | 1.0371 |
| 2022 | Apr | 30 | 20:41 | Partial | 1.1909 | 62.73S | 71.41W | 0.6384 |
| 2022 | Oct | 25 | 11:00 | Partial | 1.0707 | 62.24N | 77.40E | 0.8606 |
| 2023 | Apr | 20 | 04:17 | Annular | 0.3953 | 9.64S | 125.66E | 1.0134 |
| 2023 | Oct | 14 | 17:59 | Annular | 0.3752 | 11.40N | 83.15W | 0.9522 |
| 2024 | Apr | 08 | 18:18 | Total | 0.3439 | 25.41N | 104.31W | 1.0568 |
| 2024 | Oct | 02 | 18:45 | Annular | 0.3508 | 22.02S | 114.55W | 0.9328 |
| 2025 | Mar | 29 | 10:49 | Partial | 1.0421 | 61.59N | 77.41W | 0.9340 |
| 2025 | Sep | 21 | 19:41 | Partial | 1.0647 | 61.41S | 153.55E | 0.8553 |
| 2026 | Feb | 17 | 12:13 | Annular | 0.9733 | 65.06S | 84.31E | 0.9633 |
| 2026 | Aug | 12 | 17:46 | Total | 0.8976 | 65.43N | 25.89W | 1.0388 |
| 2027 | Feb | 06 | 16:00 | Annular | 0.2948 | 31.38S | 48.56W | 0.9283 |
| 2027 | Aug | 02 | 10:07 | Total | 0.1417 | 25.57N | 33.13E | 1.0793 |
| 2028 | Jan | 26 | 15:08 | Annular | 0.3907 | 3.01N | 51.67W | 0.9209 |
| 2028 | Jul | 22 | 02:56 | Total | 0.6068 | 15.72S | 126.52E | 1.0562 |
| 2029 | Jan | 14 | 17:13 | Partial | 1.0556 | 64.29N | 114.13W | 0.8706 |
| 2029 | Jun | 12 | 04:06 | Partial | 1.2933 | 67.35N | 66.56W | 0.4592 |
| 2029 | Jul | 11 | 15:37 | Partial | 1.4207 | 64.86S | 85.79W | 0.2268 |
| 2029 | Dec | 05 | 15:02 | Partial | 1.0615 | 68.12S | 135.61E | 0.8899 |
| 2030 | Jun | 01 | 06:28 | Annular | 0.5619 | 56.67N | 80.04E | 0.9444 |
| 2030 | Nov | 25 | 06:51 | Total | 0.3870 | 43.78S | 71.13E | 1.0471 |
| 2031 | May | 21 | 07:15 | Annular | 0.1975 | 8.93N | 71.68E | 0.9591 |
| 2031 | Nov | 14 | 21:07 | Annular | 0.3082 | 0.61S | 137.76W | 1.0108 |
| 2032 | May | 09 | 13:25 | Annular | 0.9376 | 51.23S | 7.29W | 0.9958 |
| 2032 | Nov | 03 | 05:34 | Partial | 1.0655 | 71.14N | 132.31E | 0.8530 |
| 2033 | Mar | 30 | 18:02 | Total | 0.9769 | 71.45N | 152.87W | 1.0465 |
| 2033 | Sep | 23 | 13:53 | Partial | 1.1586 | 72.92S | 121.23W | 0.6877 |
| 2034 | Mar | 20 | 10:19 | Total | 0.2879 | 16.02N | 22.02E | 1.0461 |
| 2034 | Sep | 12 | 16:18 | Annular | 0.3936 | 18.30S | 72.55W | 0.9738 |
| 2035 | Mar | 09 | 23:05 | Annular | 0.4372 | 29.15S | 155.11W | 0.9921 |
| 2035 | Sep | 02 | 01:55 | Total | 0.3728 | 29.19N | 158.05E | 1.0322 |
| 2036 | Feb | 27 | 04:47 | Partial | 1.1946 | 72.30S | 131.75W | 0.6276 |
| 2036 | Jul | 23 | 10:31 | Partial | 1.4253 | 69.53S | 3.56E | 0.1981 |

## WITH GLOBAL TIMINGS IN 'UT'

| P1 | U1 | U2 | P2 | MID | P3 | U3 | U4 | P4 |
|---|---|---|---|---|---|---|---|---|
| 23:34 | ----- | ----- | ----- | 01:41 | ----- | ----- | ----- | 03:49 |
| 16:55 | 18:03 | 18:01 | ----- | 19:23 | ----- | 20:45 | 20:43 | 21:51 |
| 02:30 | 03:35 | 03:38 | 05:01 | 05:18 | 05:35 | 06:58 | 07:01 | 08:06 |
| 03:46 | 04:48 | 04:49 | 05:52 | 06:40 | 07:29 | 08:31 | 08:33 | 09:34 |
| 13:34 | 14:33 | 14:33 | 15:37 | 16:14 | 16:51 | 17:55 | 17:54 | 18:53 |
| 08:13 | 09:50 | 10:00 | ----- | 10:42 | ----- | 11:24 | 11:35 | 13:12 |
| 05:30 | 07:06 | 07:00 | ----- | 07:34 | ----- | 08:08 | 08:02 | 09:38 |
| 18:44 | ----- | ----- | ----- | 20:41 | ----- | ----- | ----- | 22:38 |
| 08:58 | ----- | ----- | ----- | 10:60 | ----- | ----- | ----- | 13:02 |
| 01:35 | 02:37 | 02:37 | 03:53 | 04:17 | 04:41 | 05:57 | 05:57 | 06:60 |
| 15:04 | 16:10 | 16:15 | 17:34 | 17:60 | 18:25 | 19:45 | 19:49 | 20:55 |
| 15:43 | 16:42 | 16:39 | 17:46 | 18:18 | 18:50 | 19:56 | 19:54 | 20:53 |
| 15:43 | 16:51 | 16:57 | 18:16 | 18:45 | 19:15 | 20:34 | 20:40 | 21:47 |
| 08:52 | ----- | ----- | ----- | 10:48 | ----- | ----- | ----- | 12:45 |
| 17:29 | ----- | ----- | ----- | 19:41 | ----- | ----- | ----- | 21:54 |
| 09:57 | 11:42 | 11:54 | ----- | 12:13 | ----- | 12:32 | 12:44 | 14:29 |
| 15:34 | 17:01 | 16:57 | ----- | 17:46 | ----- | 18:34 | 18:30 | 19:58 |
| 12:58 | 14:04 | 14:10 | 15:23 | 15:60 | 16:37 | 17:49 | 17:56 | 19:02 |
| 07:30 | 08:27 | 08:24 | 09:21 | 10:07 | 10:53 | 11:50 | 11:47 | 12:43 |
| 12:07 | 13:15 | 13:22 | 14:48 | 15:08 | 15:28 | 16:54 | 17:01 | 18:09 |
| 00:28 | 01:34 | 01:31 | ----- | 02:56 | ----- | 04:21 | 04:18 | 05:24 |
| 15:02 | ----- | ----- | ----- | 17:13 | ----- | ----- | ----- | 19:23 |
| 02:27 | ----- | ----- | ----- | 04:06 | ----- | ----- | ----- | 05:45 |
| 14:29 | ----- | ----- | ----- | 15:37 | ----- | ----- | ----- | 16:46 |
| 13:07 | ----- | ----- | ----- | 15:03 | ----- | ----- | ----- | 16:59 |
| 03:35 | 04:47 | 04:53 | ----- | 06:28 | ----- | 08:03 | 08:09 | 09:22 |
| 04:17 | 05:17 | 05:15 | 06:25 | 06:51 | 07:17 | 08:27 | 08:25 | 09:24 |
| 04:14 | 05:19 | 05:23 | 06:29 | 07:15 | 08:01 | 09:07 | 09:11 | 10:16 |
| 18:24 | 19:24 | 19:25 | 20:31 | 21:07 | 21:42 | 22:49 | 22:49 | 23:50 |
| 11:10 | 12:46 | 12:48 | ----- | 13:25 | ----- | 14:03 | 14:05 | 15:41 |
| 03:23 | ----- | ----- | ----- | 05:34 | ----- | ----- | ----- | 07:44 |
| 15:60 | 17:46 | 17:35 | ----- | 18:02 | ----- | 18:29 | 18:17 | 20:04 |
| 11:47 | ----- | ----- | ----- | 13:53 | ----- | ----- | ----- | 15:58 |
| 07:41 | 08:39 | 08:38 | 09:41 | 10:18 | 10:56 | 11:59 | 11:57 | 12:56 |
| 13:26 | 14:32 | 14:35 | 15:55 | 16:18 | 16:41 | 18:01 | 18:04 | 19:09 |
| 20:21 | 21:26 | 21:27 | 22:55 | 23:05 | 23:16 | 24:43 | 24:45 | 25:49 |
| 23:15 | 00:17 | 00:16 | 01:27 | 01:55 | 02:24 | 03:35 | 03:34 | 04:35 |
| 02:48 | ----- | ----- | ----- | 04:47 | ----- | ----- | ----- | 06:45 |
| 09:34 | ----- | ----- | ----- | 10:31 | ----- | ----- | ----- | 11:28 |

## LIST OF SOLAR ECLIPSES DURING 21ST CENTURY

| YYYY | MM | DD | Conj | SE_Type | Gamma | GE Position | | Magn |
|------|----|----|------|---------|-------|------|------|------|
| 2036 | Aug | 21 | 17:25 | Partial | 1.0823 | 71.75N | 46.87E | 0.8620 |
| 2037 | Jan | 16 | 09:48 | Partial | 1.1477 | 69.15N | 20.76E | 0.7047 |
| 2037 | Jul | 13 | 02:40 | Total | 0.7242 | 24.78S | 138.91E | 1.0415 |
| 2038 | Jan | 05 | 13:46 | Annular | 0.4165 | 2.08N | 25.59W | 0.9729 |
| 2038 | Jul | 02 | 13:32 | Annular | 0.0399 | 25.52N | 21.95W | 0.9914 |
| 2038 | Dec | 26 | 00:59 | Total | 0.2886 | 40.45S | 163.79E | 1.0270 |
| 2039 | Jun | 21 | 17:12 | Annular | 0.8317 | 79.67N | 101.72W | 0.9454 |
| 2039 | Dec | 15 | 16:23 | Total | 0.9454 | 82.48S | 176.21E | 1.0360 |
| 2040 | May | 11 | 03:42 | Partial | 1.2531 | 63.39S | 174.22E | 0.5305 |
| 2040 | Nov | 04 | 19:07 | Partial | 1.0999 | 62.82N | 53.40W | 0.8062 |
| 2041 | Apr | 30 | 11:52 | Total | 0.4491 | 9.65S | 11.94E | 1.0191 |
| 2041 | Oct | 25 | 01:35 | Annular | 0.4135 | 9.98N | 162.92E | 0.9468 |
| 2042 | Apr | 20 | 02:17 | Total | 0.2964 | 27.09N | 137.06E | 1.0617 |
| 2042 | Oct | 14 | 01:59 | Annular | 0.3030 | 23.82S | 137.83E | 0.9302 |
| 2043 | Apr | 09 | 18:56 | Total | 1.0038 | 61.78N | 151.88E | 1.0410 |
| 2043 | Oct | 03 | 03:01 | Annular | 1.0106 | 61.45S | 35.08E | 0.9435 |
| 2044 | Feb | 28 | 20:23 | Annular | 0.9950 | 62.78S | 30.08W | 0.9606 |
| 2044 | Aug | 23 | 01:16 | Total | 0.9609 | 64.58N | 121.95W | 1.0367 |
| 2045 | Feb | 16 | 23:55 | Annular | 0.3122 | 28.33S | 166.31W | 0.9286 |
| 2045 | Aug | 12 | 17:41 | Total | 0.2112 | 25.97N | 78.65W | 1.0776 |
| 2046 | Feb | 05 | 23:06 | Annular | 0.3775 | 4.86N | 171.67W | 0.9233 |
| 2046 | Aug | 02 | 10:20 | Total | 0.5355 | 12.81S | 15.22E | 1.0533 |
| 2047 | Jan | 26 | 01:33 | Partial | 1.0463 | 63.46N | 111.48E | 0.8881 |
| 2047 | Jun | 23 | 10:51 | Partial | 1.3763 | 66.32N | 178.28W | 0.3132 |
| 2047 | Jul | 22 | 22:35 | Partial | 1.3486 | 64.05S | 160.21E | 0.3580 |
| 2047 | Dec | 16 | 23:49 | Partial | 1.0661 | 67.02S | 6.83W | 0.8815 |
| 2048 | Jun | 11 | 12:58 | Annular | 0.6458 | 63.86N | 11.68W | 0.9443 |
| 2048 | Dec | 05 | 15:35 | Total | 0.3973 | 46.29S | 56.52W | 1.0442 |
| 2049 | May | 31 | 13:59 | Annular | 0.1199 | 15.29N | 30.07W | 0.9633 |
| 2049 | Nov | 25 | 05:32 | Annular | 0.2944 | 3.81S | 95.23E | 1.0059 |
| 2050 | May | 20 | 20:42 | Annular | 0.8696 | 40.21S | 123.99W | 1.0039 |
| 2050 | Nov | 14 | 13:29 | Partial | 1.0454 | 70.20N | 0.88E | 0.8858 |
| 2051 | Apr | 11 | 02:10 | Partial | 1.0160 | 72.30N | 32.10E | 0.9833 |
| 2051 | Oct | 04 | 21:01 | Partial | 1.2093 | 72.74S | 117.71E | 0.6018 |
| 2052 | Mar | 30 | 18:31 | Total | 0.3226 | 22.38N | 102.68W | 1.0469 |
| 2052 | Sep | 22 | 23:37 | Annular | 0.4480 | 25.76S | 175.03E | 0.9736 |
| 2053 | Mar | 20 | 07:08 | Annular | 0.4096 | 23.12S | 82.74E | 0.9920 |
| 2053 | Sep | 12 | 09:32 | Total | 0.3142 | 21.55N | 41.69E | 1.0331 |
| 2054 | Mar | 09 | 12:33 | Partial | 1.1715 | 72.73S | 97.76E | 0.6667 |

## WITH GLOBAL TIMINGS IN 'UT'

| P1 | U1 | U2 | P2 | MID | P3 | U3 | U4 | P4 |
|----|----|----|----|-----|----|----|----|----|
| 15:33 | ----- | ----- | ----- | 17:25 | ----- | ----- | ----- | 19:16 |
| 07:41 | ----- | ----- | ----- | 09:48 | ----- | ----- | ----- | 11:54 |
| 00:16 | 01:28 | 01:25 | ----- | 02:40 | ----- | 03:54 | 03:52 | 05:04 |
| 10:59 | 12:04 | 12:07 | 13:30 | 13:46 | 14:03 | 15:26 | 15:29 | 16:34 |
| 10:37 | 11:38 | 11:40 | 12:42 | 13:32 | 14:22 | 15:24 | 15:25 | 16:27 |
| 22:20 | 23:19 | 23:19 | 00:22 | 00:59 | 01:37 | 02:40 | 02:40 | 03:39 |
| 14:36 | 16:03 | 16:10 | ----- | 17:12 | ----- | 18:14 | 18:21 | 19:48 |
| 14:18 | 15:52 | 15:47 | ----- | 16:23 | ----- | 16:58 | 16:53 | 18:27 |
| 01:55 | ----- | ----- | ----- | 03:42 | ----- | ----- | ----- | 05:29 |
| 17:08 | ----- | ----- | ----- | 19:07 | ----- | ----- | ----- | 21:07 |
| 09:12 | 10:15 | 10:15 | 11:44 | 11:52 | 11:60 | 13:29 | 13:29 | 14:32 |
| 22:39 | 23:46 | 23:51 | 01:19 | 01:35 | 01:50 | 03:18 | 03:23 | 04:30 |
| 23:41 | 00:39 | 00:37 | 01:40 | 02:17 | 02:54 | 03:57 | 03:55 | 04:53 |
| 22:56 | 00:03 | 00:09 | 01:23 | 01:59 | 02:35 | 03:50 | 03:56 | 05:03 |
| 16:56 | ----- | 18:44 | ----- | 18:57 | ----- | 19:09 | ----- | 20:57 |
| 00:43 | 02:48 | ----- | ----- | 03:01 | ----- | ----- | 03:13 | 05:18 |
| 18:09 | 20:03 | ----- | ----- | 20:23 | ----- | ----- | 20:44 | 22:38 |
| 23:09 | 00:50 | 00:44 | ----- | 01:16 | ----- | 01:48 | 01:42 | 03:22 |
| 20:53 | 21:60 | 22:06 | 23:20 | 23:55 | 24:30 | 25:44 | 25:50 | 26:57 |
| 15:06 | 16:03 | 15:60 | 16:59 | 17:42 | 18:25 | 19:24 | 19:20 | 20:17 |
| 20:05 | 21:13 | 21:20 | 22:42 | 23:06 | 23:30 | 24:52 | 24:59 | 26:07 |
| 07:48 | 08:52 | 08:50 | ----- | 10:20 | ----- | 11:50 | 11:47 | 12:51 |
| 23:22 | ----- | ----- | ----- | 01:33 | ----- | ----- | ----- | 03:44 |
| 09:28 | ----- | ----- | ----- | 10:51 | ----- | ----- | ----- | 12:15 |
| 21:10 | ----- | ----- | ----- | 22:35 | ----- | ----- | ----- | 24:00 |
| 21:54 | ----- | ----- | ----- | 23:49 | ----- | ----- | ----- | 25:45 |
| 10:09 | 11:25 | 11:31 | ----- | 12:58 | ----- | 14:26 | 14:32 | 15:47 |
| 13:01 | 14:01 | 13:59 | 15:10 | 15:35 | 15:59 | 17:10 | 17:09 | 18:08 |
| 10:58 | 12:02 | 12:06 | 13:10 | 13:59 | 14:48 | 15:53 | 15:57 | 17:00 |
| 02:48 | 03:49 | 03:50 | 04:55 | 05:32 | 06:09 | 07:15 | 07:16 | 08:16 |
| 18:22 | 19:48 | 19:48 | ----- | 20:42 | ----- | 21:36 | 21:37 | 23:03 |
| 11:16 | ----- | ----- | ----- | 13:29 | ----- | ----- | ----- | 15:43 |
| 00:11 | ----- | ----- | ----- | 02:09 | ----- | ----- | ----- | 04:08 |
| 19:02 | ----- | ----- | ----- | 21:01 | ----- | ----- | ----- | 22:59 |
| 15:54 | 16:53 | 16:51 | 17:56 | 18:31 | 19:05 | 20:11 | 20:09 | 21:08 |
| 20:48 | 21:54 | 21:57 | ----- | 23:37 | ----- | 25:17 | 25:20 | 26:27 |
| 04:22 | 05:26 | 05:28 | 06:48 | 07:08 | 07:27 | 08:47 | 08:49 | 09:53 |
| 06:52 | 07:52 | 07:51 | 08:57 | 09:33 | 10:08 | 11:14 | 11:13 | 12:14 |
| 10:31 | ----- | ----- | ----- | 12:33 | ----- | ----- | ----- | 14:35 |

## LIST OF SOLAR ECLIPSES DURING 21ST CENTURY

| YYYY | MM | DD | Conj | SE_Type | Gamma | GE Position | | Magn |
|------|-----|-----|-------|---------|--------|--------|--------|--------|
| 2054 | Aug | 03 | 18:02 | Partial | 1.4946 | 70.46S | 121.23W | 0.0641 |
| 2054 | Sep | 02 | 01:08 | Partial | 1.0212 | 72.34N | 82.35W | 0.9771 |
| 2055 | Jan | 27 | 17:53 | Partial | 1.1548 | 70.21N | 112.31W | 0.6932 |
| 2055 | Jul | 24 | 09:56 | Total | 0.8010 | 33.32S | 25.79E | 1.0360 |
| 2056 | Jan | 16 | 22:15 | Annular | 0.4197 | 3.92N | 153.58W | 0.9761 |
| 2056 | Jul | 12 | 20:21 | Annular | 0.0421 | 19.54N | 123.87W | 0.9880 |
| 2057 | Jan | 05 | 09:47 | Total | 0.2845 | 39.40S | 35.05E | 1.0289 |
| 2057 | Jul | 01 | 23:39 | Annular | 0.7456 | 71.88N | 176.18W | 0.9465 |
| 2057 | Dec | 26 | 01:14 | Total | 0.9409 | 88.93S | 25.08E | 1.0358 |
| 2058 | May | 22 | 10:38 | Partial | 1.3197 | 64.16S | 60.93E | 0.4138 |
| 2058 | Jun | 21 | 00:18 | Partial | 1.4872 | 66.52N | 9.91E | 0.1251 |
| 2058 | Nov | 16 | 03:21 | Partial | 1.1231 | 63.52N | 174.12E | 0.7630 |
| 2059 | May | 11 | 19:21 | Total | 0.5083 | 10.78S | 100.50W | 1.0244 |
| 2059 | Nov | 05 | 09:17 | Annular | 0.4451 | 8.76N | 46.98E | 0.9418 |
| 2060 | Apr | 30 | 10:09 | Total | 0.2430 | 28.10N | 20.65E | 1.0662 |
| 2060 | Oct | 24 | 09:22 | Annular | 0.2624 | 25.87S | 28.17E | 0.9278 |
| 2061 | Apr | 20 | 02:56 | Total | 0.9593 | 64.86N | 59.30E | 1.0477 |
| 2061 | Oct | 13 | 10:30 | Annular | 0.9638 | 62.34S | 53.14W | 0.9471 |
| 2062 | Mar | 11 | 04:25 | Partial | 1.0230 | 61.45S | 147.33W | 0.9338 |
| 2062 | Sep | 03 | 08:52 | Partial | 1.0194 | 61.76N | 150.43E | 0.9736 |
| 2063 | Feb | 28 | 07:43 | Annular | 0.3352 | 25.26S | 77.43E | 0.9294 |
| 2063 | Aug | 24 | 01:20 | Total | 0.2770 | 25.63N | 168.38E | 1.0752 |
| 2064 | Feb | 17 | 06:59 | Annular | 0.3600 | 7.08N | 69.60E | 0.9264 |
| 2064 | Aug | 12 | 17:45 | Total | 0.4664 | 11.04S | 96.18W | 1.0497 |
| 2065 | Feb | 05 | 09:51 | Partial | 1.0342 | 62.75N | 22.02W | 0.9107 |
| 2065 | Jul | 03 | 17:32 | Partial | 1.4609 | 65.33N | 71.36E | 0.1653 |
| 2065 | Aug | 02 | 05:33 | Partial | 1.2771 | 63.32S | 46.46E | 0.4873 |
| 2065 | Dec | 27 | 08:38 | Partial | 1.0688 | 65.93S | 149.40W | 0.8769 |
| 2066 | Jun | 22 | 19:24 | Annular | 0.7323 | 70.41N | 96.59W | 0.9436 |
| 2066 | Dec | 17 | 00:22 | Total | 0.4043 | 47.53S | 175.75E | 1.0418 |
| 2067 | Jun | 11 | 20:40 | Annular | 0.0390 | 21.10N | 130.16W | 0.9672 |
| 2067 | Dec | 06 | 14:02 | Annular | 0.2850 | 6.04S | 32.51W | 1.0013 |
| 2068 | May | 31 | 03:55 | Total | 0.7974 | 31.09S | 123.13E | 1.0111 |
| 2068 | Nov | 24 | 21:31 | Partial | 1.0305 | 69.15N | 131.24W | 0.9096 |
| 2069 | Apr | 21 | 10:10 | Partial | 1.0615 | 71.70N | 101.36W | 0.9001 |
| 2069 | May | 20 | 17:51 | Partial | 1.4860 | 69.41S | 70.19W | 0.0862 |
| 2069 | Oct | 15 | 04:17 | Partial | 1.2524 | 72.31S | 5.35W | 0.5291 |
| 2070 | Apr | 11 | 02:35 | Total | 0.3641 | 29.08N | 134.90E | 1.0474 |
| 2070 | Oct | 04 | 07:06 | Annular | 0.4951 | 32.95S | 60.51E | 0.9732 |

## WITH GLOBAL TIMINGS IN 'UT'

| P1 | U1 | U2 | P2 | MID | P3 | U3 | U4 | P4 |
|---|---|---|---|---|---|---|---|---|
| 17:28 | ----- | ----- | ----- | 18:02 | ----- | ----- | ----- | 18:36 |
| 23:10 | ----- | ----- | ----- | 01:08 | ----- | ----- | ----- | 03:05 |
| 15:48 | ----- | ----- | ----- | 17:53 | ----- | ----- | ----- | 19:58 |
| 07:36 | 08:54 | 08:51 | ----- | 09:56 | ----- | 11:01 | 10:59 | 12:16 |
| 19:29 | 20:33 | 20:36 | 21:59 | 22:15 | 22:31 | 23:55 | 23:57 | 25:02 |
| 17:25 | 18:27 | 18:28 | 19:30 | 20:21 | 21:11 | 22:13 | 22:15 | 23:17 |
| 07:08 | 08:07 | 08:06 | 09:09 | 09:47 | 10:24 | 11:28 | 11:27 | 12:26 |
| 20:56 | 22:17 | 22:23 | ----- | 23:39 | ----- | 24:54 | 25:01 | 26:21 |
| 23:08 | 00:41 | 00:36 | ----- | 01:13 | ----- | 01:51 | 01:46 | 03:19 |
| 09:03 | ----- | ----- | ----- | 10:38 | ----- | ----- | ----- | 12:13 |
| 23:22 | ----- | ----- | ----- | 00:18 | ----- | ----- | ----- | 01:14 |
| 01:23 | ----- | ----- | ----- | 03:21 | ----- | ----- | ----- | 05:19 |
| 16:43 | 17:48 | 17:47 | ----- | 19:21 | ----- | 20:54 | 20:53 | 21:58 |
| 06:22 | 07:30 | 07:35 | ----- | 09:17 | ----- | 10:58 | 11:04 | 12:12 |
| 07:33 | 08:30 | 08:28 | 09:28 | 10:09 | 10:50 | 11:51 | 11:48 | 12:45 |
| 06:18 | 07:24 | 07:30 | 08:42 | 09:22 | 10:02 | 11:14 | 11:20 | 12:27 |
| 00:52 | 02:31 | 02:23 | ----- | 02:56 | ----- | 03:29 | 03:21 | 05:00 |
| 08:09 | 09:53 | 10:07 | ----- | 10:30 | ----- | 10:53 | 11:07 | 12:51 |
| 02:13 | ----- | ----- | ----- | 04:25 | ----- | ----- | ----- | 06:37 |
| 06:51 | ----- | ----- | ----- | 08:52 | ----- | ----- | ----- | 10:53 |
| 04:41 | 05:48 | 05:54 | 07:11 | 07:43 | 08:14 | 09:31 | 09:37 | 10:44 |
| 22:46 | 23:43 | 23:40 | 00:42 | 01:20 | 01:59 | 03:01 | 02:57 | 03:55 |
| 03:58 | 05:05 | 05:12 | 06:32 | 06:59 | 07:26 | 08:46 | 08:53 | 10:00 |
| 15:10 | 16:13 | 16:10 | ----- | 17:45 | ----- | 19:19 | 19:17 | 20:19 |
| 07:39 | ----- | ----- | ----- | 09:51 | ----- | ----- | ----- | 12:03 |
| 16:31 | ----- | ----- | ----- | 17:33 | ----- | ----- | ----- | 18:35 |
| 03:54 | ----- | ----- | ----- | 05:33 | ----- | ----- | ----- | 07:11 |
| 06:43 | ----- | ----- | ----- | 08:38 | ----- | ----- | ----- | 10:33 |
| 16:40 | 18:00 | 18:07 | ----- | 19:24 | ----- | 20:42 | 20:48 | 22:08 |
| 21:48 | 22:48 | 22:46 | 23:59 | 00:22 | 00:45 | 01:57 | 01:56 | 02:55 |
| 17:39 | 18:43 | 18:46 | 19:49 | 20:40 | 21:31 | 22:34 | 22:38 | 23:41 |
| 11:17 | 12:18 | 12:19 | 13:24 | 14:02 | 14:40 | 15:45 | 15:46 | 16:47 |
| 01:30 | 02:49 | 02:49 | ----- | 03:55 | ----- | 05:01 | 05:01 | 06:20 |
| 19:15 | ----- | ----- | ----- | 21:30 | ----- | ----- | ----- | 23:46 |
| 08:16 | ----- | ----- | ----- | 10:09 | ----- | ----- | ----- | 12:03 |
| 17:12 | ----- | ----- | ----- | 17:51 | ----- | ----- | ----- | 18:31 |
| 02:25 | ----- | ----- | ----- | 04:17 | ----- | ----- | ----- | 06:09 |
| 23:58 | 00:58 | 00:56 | 02:05 | 02:35 | 03:04 | 04:13 | 04:11 | 05:11 |
| 04:19 | 05:26 | 05:29 | ----- | 07:06 | ----- | 08:43 | 08:46 | 09:53 |

## LIST OF SOLAR ECLIPSES DURING 21ST CENTURY

| YYYY | MM | DD | Conj | SE_Type | Gamma | GE Position | | Magn |
|------|----|----|------|---------|-------|------|------|------|
| 2071 | Mar | 31 | 15:00 | Annular | 0.3750 | 16.81S | 37.32W | 0.9921 |
| 2071 | Sep | 23 | 17:18 | Total | 0.2619 | 14.27N | 76.68W | 1.0335 |
| 2072 | Mar | 19 | 20:10 | Partial | 1.1415 | 72.90S | 30.63W | 0.7177 |
| 2072 | Sep | 12 | 08:57 | Total | 0.9654 | 69.92N | 100.36E | 1.0560 |
| 2073 | Feb | 07 | 01:55 | Partial | 1.1646 | 71.16N | 114.74E | 0.6772 |
| 2073 | Aug | 03 | 17:13 | Total | 0.8763 | 43.27S | 89.32W | 1.0296 |
| 2074 | Jan | 27 | 06:43 | Annular | 0.4244 | 6.54N | 78.58E | 0.9799 |
| 2074 | Jul | 24 | 03:08 | Annular | 0.1238 | 12.85N | 133.61E | 0.9841 |
| 2075 | Jan | 16 | 18:34 | Total | 0.2803 | 37.32S | 94.15W | 1.0313 |
| 2075 | Jul | 13 | 06:04 | Annular | 0.6585 | 63.38N | 95.06E | 0.9468 |
| 2076 | Jan | 06 | 10:05 | Total | 0.9376 | 87.59S | 179.05W | 1.0345 |
| 2076 | Jun | 01 | 17:29 | Partial | 1.3895 | 65.00S | 51.59W | 0.2901 |
| 2076 | Jul | 01 | 06:50 | Partial | 1.4013 | 67.55N | 98.43W | 0.2730 |
| 2076 | Nov | 26 | 11:40 | Partial | 1.1411 | 64.35N | 40.12E | 0.7297 |
| 2077 | May | 22 | 02:44 | Total | 0.5721 | 13.13S | 148.01E | 1.0292 |
| 2077 | Nov | 15 | 17:05 | Annular | 0.4704 | 7.82N | 70.82W | 0.9372 |
| 2078 | May | 11 | 17:55 | Total | 0.1841 | 28.25N | 93.83W | 1.0704 |
| 2078 | Nov | 04 | 16:53 | Annular | 0.2290 | 27.95S | 83.41W | 0.9257 |
| 2079 | May | 01 | 10:48 | Total | 0.9087 | 66.46N | 45.89W | 1.0513 |
| 2079 | Oct | 24 | 18:09 | Annular | 0.9244 | 63.64S | 159.91W | 0.9485 |
| 2080 | Mar | 21 | 12:18 | Partial | 1.0577 | 61.44S | 85.93E | 0.8732 |
| 2080 | Sep | 13 | 16:36 | Partial | 1.0725 | 61.61N | 25.84E | 0.8739 |
| 2081 | Mar | 10 | 15:22 | Annular | 0.3647 | 22.43S | 36.98W | 0.9305 |
| 2081 | Sep | 03 | 09:04 | Total | 0.3384 | 24.73N | 53.78E | 1.0722 |
| 2082 | Feb | 27 | 14:46 | Annular | 0.3372 | 9.52N | 47.51W | 0.9299 |
| 2082 | Aug | 24 | 01:13 | Total | 0.4005 | 10.32S | 151.87E | 1.0454 |
| 2083 | Feb | 16 | 18:05 | Partial | 1.0182 | 62.18N | 154.37W | 0.9404 |
| 2083 | Jul | 14 | 24:12 | Partial | 1.5458 | 64.41N | 38.08W | 0.0177 |
| 2083 | Aug | 13 | 12:32 | Partial | 1.2073 | 62.69S | 67.47W | 0.6124 |
| 2084 | Jan | 07 | 17:28 | Partial | 1.0708 | 64.90S | 68.16E | 0.8736 |
| 2084 | Jul | 03 | 01:48 | Annular | 0.8200 | 75.43N | 169.85W | 0.9422 |
| 2084 | Dec | 27 | 09:11 | Total | 0.4092 | 47.47S | 47.67E | 1.0398 |
| 2085 | Jun | 22 | 03:19 | Annular | 0.0442 | 26.18N | 131.02E | 0.9706 |
| 2085 | Dec | 16 | 22:35 | Annular | 0.2790 | 7.27S | 160.85W | 0.9973 |
| 2086 | Jun | 11 | 11:05 | Total | 0.7219 | 23.29S | 12.39E | 1.0175 |
| 2086 | Dec | 06 | 05:36 | Partial | 1.0200 | 68.05N | 96.11E | 0.9259 |
| 2087 | May | 02 | 18:02 | Partial | 1.1130 | 70.93N | 127.51E | 0.8025 |
| 2087 | Jun | 01 | 01:25 | Partial | 1.4193 | 68.40S | 165.15E | 0.2130 |
| 2087 | Oct | 26 | 11:43 | Partial | 1.2881 | 71.67S | 130.33W | 0.4692 |

## WITH GLOBAL TIMINGS IN 'UT'

| P1 | U1 | U2 | P2 | MID | P3 | U3 | U4 | P4 |
|---|---|---|---|---|---|---|---|---|
| 12:13 | 13:17 | 13:18 | 14:33 | 15:00 | 15:27 | 16:42 | 16:44 | 17:47 |
| 14:36 | 15:36 | 15:35 | 16:38 | 17:18 | 17:58 | 19:01 | 19:00 | 19:60 |
| 18:04 | ----- | ----- | ----- | 20:09 | ----- | ----- | ----- | 22:15 |
| 06:55 | 08:36 | 08:25 | ----- | 08:57 | ----- | 09:29 | 09:18 | 10:59 |
| 23:51 | ----- | ----- | ----- | 01:55 | ----- | ----- | ----- | 03:58 |
| 14:57 | 16:23 | 16:20 | ----- | 17:13 | ----- | 18:06 | 18:03 | 19:29 |
| 03:57 | 05:01 | 05:04 | 06:28 | 06:43 | 06:57 | 08:22 | 08:24 | 09:28 |
| 00:12 | 01:15 | 01:17 | 02:20 | 03:09 | 03:57 | 05:00 | 05:02 | 06:05 |
| 15:55 | 16:54 | 16:53 | 17:56 | 18:34 | 19:12 | 20:15 | 20:14 | 21:13 |
| 03:16 | 04:32 | 04:38 | ----- | 06:04 | ----- | 07:30 | 07:36 | 08:52 |
| 07:60 | 09:32 | 09:27 | ----- | 10:05 | ----- | 10:43 | 10:39 | 12:11 |
| 16:09 | ----- | ----- | ----- | 17:29 | ----- | ----- | ----- | 18:50 |
| 05:29 | ----- | ----- | ----- | 06:49 | ----- | ----- | ----- | 08:10 |
| 09:43 | ----- | ----- | ----- | 11:40 | ----- | ----- | ----- | 13:36 |
| 00:11 | 01:17 | 01:16 | ----- | 02:45 | ----- | 04:13 | 04:12 | 05:19 |
| 14:10 | 15:19 | 15:25 | ----- | 17:05 | ----- | 18:46 | 18:51 | 20:00 |
| 15:18 | 16:15 | 16:12 | 17:11 | 17:55 | 18:39 | 19:38 | 19:35 | 20:32 |
| 13:48 | 14:54 | 15:01 | 16:11 | 16:54 | 17:36 | 18:46 | 18:53 | 19:59 |
| 08:40 | 10:08 | 10:02 | ----- | 10:48 | ----- | 11:34 | 11:28 | 12:56 |
| 15:44 | 17:21 | 17:31 | ----- | 18:09 | ----- | 18:48 | 18:58 | 20:34 |
| 10:09 | ----- | ----- | ----- | 12:18 | ----- | ----- | ----- | 14:27 |
| 14:40 | ----- | ----- | ----- | 16:36 | ----- | ----- | ----- | 18:31 |
| 12:21 | 13:29 | 13:35 | 14:55 | 15:22 | 15:49 | 17:09 | 17:15 | 18:23 |
| 06:31 | 07:29 | 07:26 | 08:31 | 09:04 | 09:38 | 10:43 | 10:39 | 11:38 |
| 11:44 | 12:51 | 12:58 | 14:14 | 14:46 | 15:17 | 16:34 | 16:40 | 17:47 |
| 22:36 | 23:37 | 23:35 | 00:49 | 01:13 | 01:37 | 02:51 | 02:49 | 03:50 |
| 15:52 | ----- | ----- | ----- | 18:05 | ----- | ----- | ----- | 20:18 |
| 23:49 | ----- | ----- | ----- | 24:12 | ----- | ----- | ----- | 24:35 |
| 10:42 | ----- | ----- | ----- | 12:32 | ----- | ----- | ----- | 14:22 |
| 15:34 | ----- | ----- | ----- | 17:28 | ----- | ----- | ----- | 19:23 |
| 23:10 | 00:36 | 00:44 | ----- | 01:48 | ----- | 02:52 | 03:00 | 04:26 |
| 06:37 | 07:37 | 07:36 | 08:49 | 09:11 | 09:33 | 10:46 | 10:45 | 11:45 |
| 00:19 | 01:23 | 01:26 | 02:29 | 03:19 | 04:10 | 05:13 | 05:16 | 06:19 |
| 19:49 | 20:50 | 20:51 | 21:57 | 22:35 | 23:13 | 24:19 | 24:20 | 25:21 |
| 08:36 | 09:50 | 09:49 | ----- | 11:05 | ----- | 12:20 | 12:20 | 13:33 |
| 03:19 | 05:33 | ----- | ----- | 05:36 | ----- | ----- | 05:40 | 07:54 |
| 16:14 | ----- | ----- | ----- | 18:02 | ----- | ----- | ----- | 19:51 |
| 00:25 | ----- | ----- | ----- | 01:25 | ----- | ----- | ----- | 02:25 |
| 09:57 | ----- | ----- | ----- | 11:43 | ----- | ----- | ----- | 13:30 |

## LIST OF SOLAR ECLIPSES DURING 21ST CENTURY

| YYYY | MM | DD | Conj | SE_Type | Gamma | GE Position | | Magn |
|------|-----|-----|-------|---------|--------|--------|---------|--------|
| 2088 | Apr | 21 | 10:30 | Total | 0.4122 | 36.03N | 14.89E | 1.0477 |
| 2088 | Oct | 14 | 14:45 | Annular | 0.5347 | 39.75S | 55.95W | 0.9729 |
| 2089 | Apr | 10 | 22:43 | Annular | 0.3331 | 10.30S | 155.08W | 0.9921 |
| 2089 | Oct | 04 | 01:12 | Total | 0.2163 | 7.43N | 162.92E | 1.0336 |
| 2090 | Mar | 31 | 03:37 | Partial | 1.1040 | 72.80S | 156.62W | 0.7814 |
| 2090 | Sep | 23 | 16:53 | Total | 0.9153 | 60.72N | 40.92W | 1.0563 |
| 2091 | Feb | 18 | 09:52 | Partial | 1.1782 | 71.95N | 17.76W | 0.6548 |
| 2091 | Aug | 15 | 00:32 | Total | 0.9488 | 55.48S | 150.78E | 1.0217 |
| 2092 | Feb | 07 | 15:08 | Annular | 0.4317 | 9.94N | 48.83W | 0.9842 |
| 2092 | Aug | 03 | 09:57 | Annular | 0.2042 | 5.62N | 30.20E | 0.9797 |
| 2093 | Jan | 27 | 03:20 | Total | 0.2747 | 34.29S | 136.30E | 1.0342 |
| 2093 | Jul | 23 | 12:29 | Annular | 0.5718 | 54.75N | 1.19E | 0.9465 |
| 2094 | Jan | 16 | 18:57 | Total | 0.9344 | 87.51S | 14.37W | 1.0343 |
| 2094 | Jun | 13 | 00:19 | Partial | 1.4617 | 65.91S | 163.75W | 0.1612 |
| 2094 | Jul | 12 | 13:22 | Partial | 1.3148 | 68.57N | 152.62E | 0.4225 |
| 2094 | Dec | 07 | 20:03 | Partial | 1.1547 | 65.27N | 95.24W | 0.7045 |
| 2095 | Jun | 02 | 10:05 | Total | 0.6396 | 16.76S | 37.01E | 1.0334 |
| 2095 | Nov | 27 | 01:00 | Annular | 0.4900 | 7.25N | 169.72E | 0.9331 |
| 2096 | May | 22 | 01:35 | Total | 0.1204 | 27.41N | 153.18E | 1.0740 |
| 2096 | Nov | 15 | 00:33 | Annular | 0.2023 | 29.85S | 163.22E | 0.9238 |
| 2097 | May | 11 | 18:32 | Total | 0.8526 | 67.75N | 149.55W | 1.0540 |
| 2097 | Nov | 04 | 01:58 | Annular | 0.8921 | 65.99S | 87.72E | 0.9495 |
| 2098 | Apr | 01 | 20:01 | Partial | 1.0996 | 61.59S | 38.39W | 0.7999 |
| 2098 | Sep | 25 | 00:27 | Partial | 1.1196 | 61.61N | 100.71W | 0.7849 |
| 2098 | Oct | 24 | 10:32 | Partial | 1.5395 | 62.18S | 95.21W | 0.0075 |
| 2099 | Mar | 21 | 22:52 | Annular | 0.4011 | 20.05S | 149.27W | 0.9319 |
| 2099 | Sep | 14 | 16:55 | Total | 0.3946 | 23.45N | 62.76W | 1.0687 |
| 2100 | Mar | 10 | 22:26 | Annular | 0.3084 | 12.04N | 162.69W | 0.9339 |
| 2100 | Sep | 04 | 08:46 | Total | 0.3388 | 10.53S | 39.01E | 1.0405 |

## WITH GLOBAL TIMINGS IN 'UT'

| P1 | U1 | U2 | P2 | MID | P3 | U3 | U4 | P4 |
|-------|-------|-------|-------|-------|-------|-------|-------|-------|
| 07:55 | 08:55 | 08:53 | 10:08 | 10:30 | 10:52 | 12:06 | 12:04 | 13:05 |
| 12:00 | 13:08 | 13:11 | ----- | 14:45 | ----- | 16:19 | 16:22 | 17:30 |
| 19:55 | 20:58 | 20:59 | 22:10 | 22:43 | 23:16 | 24:27 | 24:29 | 25:31 |
| 22:30 | 23:29 | 23:28 | 00:29 | 01:12 | 01:55 | 02:56 | 02:55 | 03:54 |
| 01:26 | ----- | ----- | ----- | 03:36 | ----- | ----- | ----- | 05:47 |
| 14:47 | 16:15 | 16:09 | ----- | 16:53 | ----- | 17:38 | 17:31 | 18:60 |
| 07:51 | ----- | ----- | ----- | 09:52 | ----- | ----- | ----- | 11:53 |
| 22:21 | 23:59 | 23:56 | ----- | 00:32 | ----- | 01:07 | 01:04 | 02:42 |
| 12:23 | 13:27 | 13:29 | 14:56 | 15:08 | 15:20 | 16:46 | 16:48 | 17:52 |
| 07:01 | 08:04 | 08:06 | 09:12 | 09:57 | 10:42 | 11:47 | 11:50 | 12:53 |
| 00:41 | 01:40 | 01:39 | 02:41 | 03:20 | 03:58 | 05:01 | 04:60 | 05:58 |
| 09:37 | 10:50 | 10:55 | ----- | 12:30 | ----- | 14:04 | 14:10 | 15:22 |
| 16:51 | 18:22 | 18:18 | ----- | 18:57 | ----- | 19:36 | 19:31 | 21:03 |
| 23:18 | ----- | ----- | ----- | 00:19 | ----- | ----- | ----- | 01:19 |
| 11:43 | ----- | ----- | ----- | 13:21 | ----- | ----- | ----- | 14:60 |
| 18:08 | ----- | ----- | ----- | 20:03 | ----- | ----- | ----- | 21:58 |
| 07:35 | 08:43 | 08:42 | ----- | 10:05 | ----- | 11:28 | 11:26 | 12:35 |
| 22:05 | 23:15 | 23:21 | ----- | 00:60 | ----- | 02:39 | 02:45 | 03:55 |
| 22:58 | 23:54 | 23:51 | 00:48 | 01:35 | 02:22 | 03:19 | 03:16 | 04:12 |
| 21:28 | 22:33 | 22:40 | 23:49 | 00:33 | 01:18 | 02:27 | 02:33 | 03:39 |
| 16:20 | 17:41 | 17:36 | ----- | 18:32 | ----- | 19:29 | 19:24 | 20:45 |
| 23:31 | 01:02 | 01:10 | ----- | 01:58 | ----- | 02:45 | 02:53 | 04:24 |
| 17:56 | ----- | ----- | ----- | 20:01 | ----- | ----- | ----- | 22:06 |
| 22:37 | ----- | ----- | ----- | 00:27 | ----- | ----- | ----- | 02:18 |
| 10:16 | ----- | ----- | ----- | 10:32 | ----- | ----- | ----- | 10:48 |
| 19:52 | 21:00 | 21:07 | 22:34 | 22:52 | 23:10 | 24:37 | 24:44 | 25:52 |
| 14:22 | 15:21 | 15:18 | 16:29 | 16:54 | 17:20 | 18:30 | 18:27 | 19:27 |
| 19:24 | 20:31 | 20:37 | 21:50 | 22:26 | 23:01 | 24:15 | 24:21 | 25:27 |
| 06:06 | 07:07 | 07:05 | 08:13 | 08:46 | 09:19 | 10:26 | 10:25 | 11:25 |

Abstract of Solar Eclipses from 2001 to 2100

```
Total Eclipses    :  68
Annular Eclipses  :  79
Partial Eclipses  :  77
All Eclipses      : 224
```

www.ingramcontent.com/pod-product-compliance
Lightning Source LLC
Chambersburg PA
CBHW051047050326
40690CB00006B/631